*Basque Politics and Nationalism
on the Eve of the Millennium*

Basque Studies Program
Occasional Papers Series, No. 6

EDITED BY WILLIAM A. DOUGLASS,

CARMELO URZA, LINDA WHITE,

AND JOSEBA ZULAIKA

Basque Politics and Nationalism on the Eve of the Millennium

Basque Studies Program
University of Nevada, Reno

Basque Studies Program

Occasional Papers Series, No. 6

Editor: William A. Douglass

Basque Studies Program

University of Nevada, Reno

The paper used in this book meets

the requirements of American

National Standard for Information

Sciences—Permanence of Paper

for Printed Library Materials,

ANSI Z 39.48-1984.

Binding materials were selected for

strength and durability

9 8 7 6 5 4 3 2 1

Library of Congress

Cataloging-in-Publication Data

Basque politics and nationalism on

the eve of the millennium /

edited by William A. Douglass

. . . [et al.].

p.   cm. — (Basque Studies

Program occasional papers series;

no. 6)

Includes bibliographical

references.

ISBN 1-877802-04-2 (hardcover :

alk. paper)

1. Nationalism—Spain—País

Vasco—Congresses.   2. País Vasco

(Spain)—Politics and government—

20th century—Congresses.

I. Douglass, William A.   II. Series.

DP302.B55 B28   1999

320.54'089'9992—dc21   99-051532

Contents

Acknowledgments

We wish to acknowledge the generous financial support of the Secretariat of External Affairs and the Ministry of Culture of Eusko Jaurlaritza (the Government of the Basque Autonomous Community), without which neither the academic conference "Basques in the Contemporary World: Migration, Identity, and Globalization" (Reno 1998) nor this publication of some of its results would have been possible. *Eskerrik asko!*

Queremos agradecer la generosa ayuda recibida de la Consejería de Cultura y el Secretariado de Asuntos Exteriores del Gobierno Vasco, sin la cual no habría sido posible la celebración del congreso "Vascos en el Mundo Contemporáneo: Emigración, Identidad, y Globalización" (Reno 1998), ni la publicación de algunos de sus resultados. *¡Eskerrik asko!*

Eusko Jaurlaritzaren Kultura Sailak eta Kanpo Harremanetarako Idazkaritzak eskeinitako diru laguntza eskuzabala eskertu nahi dugu, "Euskaldunak Gaurko Munduan: Emigrazioa, Identitatea, eta Globalizazioa" (Reno 1998) kongresua eta ondorengo zenbait emaitzen argitalpena posibilitatu duelako. Eskerrik asko!

vii

*Basque Politics and Nationalism
on the Eve of the Millennium*

Introduction

The articles in the present volume were originally given as shorter presentations at an international conference, "Basques in the Contemporary World: Migration, Identity, and Globalization," held in Reno, Nevada (July 6–9, 1998). Convened by the Basque Studies Program of the University of Nevada, Reno, and the University Studies Abroad Consortium, the Reno conference was attended by seventy-seven scholars from around the world.

Several interests coincided in the organization of the conference, and included the numerological. The organizers were not impervious to the ubiquitous millenarian fascination of our times. Indeed, the millennium is but the last key date in a recent series of significant "milestones" for those of us interested in the Basque Country and its emigrant diaspora(s).

First, there was the global (or at least occidental) fixation upon the quincentennial of Columbus's first voyage of discovery. For Basque scholars, this proved to be a watershed event in that it stimulated an enormous amount of academic interest and scholarly production regarding historical ties between Europe and the Americas. Indeed, this was so much the case that in the historiography of Basque involvement in both Spanish (and French) colonialism, and the more recent massive European transatlantic emigration, it is now realistic to speak in terms of the pre- and post-quincentennial scholarship. Concern with the Basque emigrant diaspora(s) worldwide consequently has always been a priority of the research agenda of the Basque Studies Program, and in light of so much new material, it seemed appropriate to review the state of affairs. Such thinking informed the initial planning of the Reno conference.

There were immediate complications and challenges, given that, during the 1990s, diasporic studies had become fashionable in their own right within the humanities and social sciences. However, focus

1

had shifted away from the assimilation (or lack thereof) of immigrant populations within First-World, Euro-settler societies (Denoon 1983) and the persistence of their contacts with a "Mother Country" (à la Handlin 1973, Hansen 1940, or Thomas and Znaniecki 1958). Instead diasporic studies were now intertwined inextricably within a "cultural studies" matrix that included investigations of gender, sexual preference, relations between the First World and the Third World/ Fourth World, the empowerment of literary criticism, and the implosion or deconstruction of anthropology (and, to a lesser degree, of the other social sciences) as part of the ascendancy of postcolonial, postnational, poststructural, and postmodern discourses. In short, anyone's diaspora is now less a meaningful, stand-alone object of study, but is rather one aspect of the problematics of identity formation and cultural hybridity within an increasingly transnational and globalized world.

In the Basque case, other recent (somewhat linked) commemorative dates include the centenary of the founding of the modern Basque nationalist movement by Sabino de Arana y Goiri in 1895, and that of the final demise of the Spanish empire in 1898 (with the loss of Cuba, Puerto Rico, and the Philippines as a result of the Spanish-American War). Both centenaries created considerable introspection and scholarly assessment, the former primarily within Basque circles and the latter within Hispanic ones (including countries of the former empire).

The issue of identity formation (and maintenance) is particularly acute within Basque society and culture. Sometimes touted as western Europe's oldest people and speaking a language that thus far remains the sole known representative of its own language family, Basques would seem to be living, indisputable representatives of their own ethnic and cultural reality. However, the absence of a Basque nation-state in a world politically defined in terms of such units, a centuries-old international boundary that partitions "northern" Basques into a French sphere of influence and "southern" Basques into a Spanish one, and a century-old Basque ethnonationalist movement (primarily within the Spanish state) that is western Europe's second-most virulent and violent (being surpassed only by that of Northern Ireland), conspire to pose and confound the issues of Basque authenticity and identity.

And then there was the migration factor. For at least five centuries, the entire Basque Country has been one of Europe's prime areas of emigration—its people moving to destinations within Spain and France, others to countries within the Spanish and French colonial frameworks, and still others to countries that lie beyond the Spanish and French spheres of influence (Douglass and Bilbao 1975). Consequently, every inhabited continent on the globe has received a Basque immigrant contingent. Some Basque "colonies" are centuries old (e.g., most Latin-American ones and that of the Philippines), while others are quite recent (the Basque presence in Australia dates from the early twentieth century and that of British Columbia postdates World War II). Some host societies experienced relatively steady Basque immigration over several generations (e.g., the western United States), while in others (e.g., Argentina, Venezuela, Mexico) Basques entered in successive waves highly conditioned by circumstances in both the sending and receiving areas.

Such a rich and diverse emigration/immigration history provides a plethora of fascinating variations on the theme of immigrant assimilation versus ethnicity maintenance within host societies, as well as on the theme of the structuring over time of relations between the Old-World Basque Country and its several emigrant diasporas.

While a seedbed of transatlantic emigrants, the Spanish Basque region itself has, for more than a century, been a recipient of massive immigration from other parts of Spain. During the latter half of the nineteenth century, Bizkaia and, to a lesser degree, Gipuzkoa together emerged as belonging to one of the Spanish state's two most-industrialized regions (Catalunya being the other). For several generations the relative prosperity of the Basque Country has attracted job seekers from throughout the Spanish state. The newcomers and their descendants now approximate the size of the "native" Basque population. There are obvious social, cultural, linguistic, economic, and political challenges inherent in such a massive (and relatively rapid) demographic shift. Indeed, the genesis of Basque nationalism is commonly interpreted as a reaction against this challenge to Basque cultural survival.

Contemporary Basque society within the Spanish state has been described as being socially and culturally polarized between the so-called two communities. The Basque political spectrum has a plethora of parties divided clearly into Spanish-nationalist and Basque-nationalist blocs (each with its own left-right continuum). For the quarter of a century since Franco's death, there has been political impasse reflective of the relatively equal balance of power between these contending forces. Governance of the Basque Autonomous Community, created under the new Spanish Constitution (1978), has therefore been a continuous exercise in coalition politics. However, in spring of 1999, and after ETA's truce the previous autumn, the governing coalition was constituted exclusively by Basque nationalist parties. This may be a change of historic importance.

As if such contention and confusion of identity were not enough, there is the additional dynamism provided by Spanish and French (and therefore also Basque) membership in the European Union. Basques within both the Spanish and French states, along with all of their fellow European Unionists, are now challenged to redefine and reconfigure their personal and collective identities in terms of a progressively integrated Europe without frontiers. The opportunities afforded to Basque separatists and even regionalists by circumventing Madrid and Paris are obvious; the inevitable new constraints stemming from Brussels are less so. The attraction of reframing identity in "Basque-European" terms seems evident at one level; the difficulties (and even the advisability) of doing so are less apparent.

In sum, our conference evolved from a (re)consideration of traditional Basque emigration and its diaspora(s) to a focus on a stateless people divided between two western European countries and among several host societies around the globe, a people challenged in its European homeland by severe internal social, cultural, and political divisions and externally by profound change in the wider nation-state and continental political and economic settings. Stated differently, our conference examined the structure and significance of "Basqueness" in Buenos Aires and Boise, Bilbao and Brussels, in an increasingly interconnected and globalized world on the eve of the new millennium.

Thanks to the generous support of the Basque Government it was possible to publish three volumes of Reno-Conference Proceedings in this Occasional Papers Series of the Basque Studies Program of the University of Nevada, Reno. One of the volumes regards Basque cultural studies, broadly defined. Another is dedicated to the Basque emigrant diaspora. The present volume contains articles on Basque politics, including ethnonationalism. The article by Manuel Castells was given as the keynote address of the Reno Conference. It situates Basque nationalism within the broader context of an increasingly globalized world in which the relevance and efficacy of the existing nation-states are eroding. By inference, the essay raises the question of the wisdom of ethnonationalist aspirations of the Basques for their own nation-state when political energies might be better spent in effecting international ties and obtaining greater participation in transnational and interregional political structures—particularly within the European Union. Above all, Castells believes that the first priority must be to resolve the "Basque problem"—that is, the political violence—a resolution that is unlikely to be achieved solely by police repression of ETA (the violent Basque separatist organization).

Xavier Rubert de Ventós considers the Basque nationalist claim to political sovereignty within the broader framework of similar such aspirations by other nations without states. He finds them to be as legitimate and rational as those of any of the world's existing (triumphant) nation-states. At the same time, he argues that in the contemporary world the "national" should be but one of the aspects informing the identities of free individuals. Configuring such a political reality, one based upon a mutual respect of one another's differences, is particularly critical to successful formation of a new Europe—given the continent's bloody history.

Gurutz Jáuregui Bereciartu concurs with both the Castells and the de Ventós theses, advocating that the real challenge for Basque ethnonationalists is not the creation of an (anachronistic) nation-state, but is rather the formation of Basque civil society in which mutual respect for political, linguistic, and socioeconomic differences is paramount. Without such tolerance, he foresees continuing gridlock for an indefinite period within a polarized Basque political process.

Alfonso Pérez-Agote echoes the call for greater consensual political integration of contemporary Basque society, while underscoring the importance of Basque identity as its focal point. Nor does he restrict identity construction to the Old-World Basque context, but rather he discusses aspects of identity formation within the Basque emigrant diaspora. He also analyzes the evolution of Basque nationalism in the post-Franco era, and then highlights its present circumstances in terms of the tendencies toward both fission and fusion within the rank and file.

Iñaki Zabaleta analyzes international news coverage, and particularly that in the *New York Times*, of Basque-related events and its capacity to influence the Basque image. He finds that ETA and the political violence framed as terrorism discourse predominate. The article then situates Basque news coverage within that of political violence in other parts of the world as a conditioner of how Basques are perceived in the international context.

Cameron Watson analyzes newspaper cartoons, press reports, and cinematic depictions of ETA activists, as well as ETA's own propaganda about itself, in order to discuss the ways in which the organization is depicted for strategic purposes. His analysis underscores the extent to which, the political violence and its victims notwithstanding, the conflict is as much about imposing imagery and labels as it is about instrumental warfare.

Begoña Aretxaga is also concerned with imagery, but more from a perspective that is internal to Basque society and its present political conflict. She finds amazing congruence in the victimology expressed by both the violent activists engaged in street violence, or *kale borroka*, and the Basque police, or *ertzainas*, sent to suppress it. Each questions the other's legitimacy, while both may find themselves at odds with the "Law" and subject to future judicial accountability as they deal with one another in the charged context of the violent street confrontations.

Jeremy MacClancy and James E. Jacob consider the unresolved issue within the Basque nationalist perspective of the ultimate territorial configuration of a future Basque nation-state. While irredentist Basque nationalism claims sovereignty over Navarra and Iparralde, or the French Basque area, in point of fact in neither region is there demonstrable significant electoral support for political union with the Basque Autonomous Community. Therefore, the present reality and future prospects of Basque nationalism, viewed from either Bayonne or Pamplona, differ markedly from the perspective of Vitoria-Gasteiz, Bilbao, or San Sebastián.

Ane Muñoz Varela approaches the many challenges and contradictions of Basque nationalism by detailing the efforts and involvement to date (and projected future ones) of the government of the Basque Autonomous Community that transcend the local context. Her article documents a rich array of past, present, and future initiatives to demonstrate that Basque political arrangements transcend local issues and/or a test of wills between Vitoria-Gasteiz and Madrid. Rather, Basque contemporary political reality already encompasses extensive regional alignments within the Spanish state, the Pyrenees, and southwestern Europe, as well as considerable involvement with various agencies and programs of the European Union.

William A. Douglass also focuses upon Eusko Jaurlaritza in terms of its attempts to energize and mobilize the Basque diaspora(s) both to ensure persistence of Basque cultural identity in the recipient societies of former Basque immigration and to strengthen the ties of diasporic Basques with the mother country. Also at issue are the ways in which this ostensibly cultural mission assumes political overtones, providing the Basque Government with channels through which to pursue its own "foreign policy" despite the fact that foreign affairs are reserved for the central government under the Spanish Constitution.

William A. Douglass
Carmelo Urza
Linda White
Joseba Zulaika

Bibliography

Douglass, William A., and Jon Bilbao. *Amerikanuak: Basques in the New World.* Reno: University of Nevada Press, 1975.

Denoon, Donald. *Settler Capitalism: The Dynamics of Dependent Development in the Southern Hemisphere.* Oxford: Clarendon Press, 1983.

Handlin, Oscar. *The Uprooted.* 2d ed. Boston: Little, Brown, 1973.

Hansen, Marcus Lee. *The Atlantic Migration, 1607–1860; A History of the Continuing Settlement of the United States.* Cambridge: Harvard Univeristy Press, 1940.

Thomas, William I., and Florian Znaniecki. *The Polish Peasant in Europe and America.* New York: Dover Publications, 1958.

Introducción

Los artículos del presente volumen fueron presentados originalmente, en versiones más reducidas, en la conferencia internacional "Vascos en el Mundo Contemporáneo: Emigración, Identidad y Globalización" que tuvo lugar en Reno, Nevada (6–9 de julio de 1998). Organizado por el Programa de Estudios Vascos de la Universidad de Nevada, Reno, y el Consorcio de Estudios Universitarios en el Extranjero, el congreso de Reno fue atendido por setenta y siete investigadores de todo el mundo.

Varios intereses coincidieron en la organización del congreso, incluyendo el hecho de ser final del siglo. Los organizadores eran conscientes de la fascinación milenarista de los tiempos presentes. El milenio supone efectivamente una fecha clave más en la serie reciente de hitos significativos para los interesados en el País Vasco y sus diásporas.

Primero tuvo lugar la celebración a escala mundial (o por lo menos del mundo occidental) del quinto centenario del primer viaje de Colón a América. Para los investigadores vascos esto resultó ser una oportunidad decisiva para estimular el interés académico sobre los lazos históricos existentes entre Europa y las Américas. Hasta tal grado fue esto así que hoy en día cabe hablar de una historiografía anterior y posterior al quinto centenario en lo que concierne a la participación vasca en los colonialismos tanto español como francés, así como de la más reciente masiva emigración europea transatlántica. Por tanto, el empeño en estudiar las diásporas vascas a través del mundo ha sido siempre un asunto prioritario en el Programa de Estudios Vascos, y a la luz de tanto material nuevo, parecía apropiado revisar el estado de la cuestión. Así se fraguó la planificación inicial del congreso de Reno.

En seguida tuvimos que enfrentarnos con complicaciones y retos nuevos, dado el hecho de que, durante la década de 1990, los estudios diaspóricos se habían puesto de moda dentro de las humanidades y de las ciencias sociales. Sin embargo, el terreno propio de estos estudios había cambiado. Del interés previo en la asimilación, o falta de asimilación, de las poblaciones emigrantes dentro del Primer Mundo y de las sociedades de pobladores europeos (Denoon 1983), así como de la persistencia de sus contactos con la "Madre Patria" (à la Handlin 1973, Hansen 1940 o Thomas y Znaniecki 1958), el énfasis de los estudios de diáspora se situaba ahora dentro del campo de los "estudios culturales" que abarcaba todo: estudios de género, preferencia sexual, relaciones entre el Primer Mundo y el Tercer o Cuarto Mundo, la relevancia de la crítica literaria y la deconstrucción de la antropología (y en menor grado de las otras ciencias sociales), todo ello como parte del resurgimiento de los discursos postcoloniales, postnacionales, postestructurales y postmodernos. En resumen, la diáspora de cualquiera es ahora menos un objeto de estudio significativo en sí que un aspecto de la problemática de la formación de identidad y mestizaje cultural dentro de un mundo cada día más globalizado y transnacional.

En el caso específico vasco, otras fechas conmemorativas relacionadas de alguna forma son el centenario de la fundación del movimiento nacionalista vasco moderno por Sabino de Arana y Goiri en 1895, y el hundimiento final del Imperio Español en 1898 (con la pérdida de Cuba, Puerto Rico y las Filipinas como resultado de la Guerra Hispano-Americana).

El tema de la formación y mantenimiento de la identidad es particularmente relevante dentro de la sociedad y cultura vascas. Representado a veces como el pueblo más antiguo de Europa y hablando un idioma que hasta ahora se mantiene como el único de su familia linguística, podría parecer que los vascos son muestras vivas indisputables de su propia realidad étnica y cultural. Sin embargo, la ausencia de un estado-nación vasco en un mundo definido políticamente en tales términos, una frontera internacional multisecular que posiciona a los vascos del "Norte" en la esfera de influencia francesa y a los vascos del "Sur" en la española y un siglo del movimiento nacionalista vasco (principalmente dentro del estado español) que se ha mostrado como el segundo más virulento y violento de la Europa del Oeste (después de Irlanda del Norte) conspiran para plantear y confundir los temas de la autenticidad e identidad vascas.

Y después se dio el elemento de la emigración. Durante al menos cinco siglos, el País Vasco ha sido uno de los primeros lugares de emigración—enviando emigrantes a destinos dentro de España y Francia, a países comprendidos entre las colonias españolas y francesas y a otros territorios más allá de las esferas de influencia española y francesa (Douglass y Bilbao 1975).

En consecuencia, no hay continente habitado que no haya recibido contingentes de emigración vasca. Algunas "colonias" vascas tienen cientos de años (e.g., la mayoría de las latino-americanas y la de Filipinas), mientras que otras son muy recientes (la presencia vasca en Australia data del principio del siglo veinte y la de British Columbia se formó tras la Segunda Guerra mundial). Algunas de las sociedades huéspedes experimentaron una inmigración relativamente continua durante varias generaciones (e.g., el oeste de Estados Unidos), mientras que en otras (e.g., Argentina, Venezuela, México) los vascos entraron en olas sucesivas muy condicionados por las circunstancias tanto de las áreas que los enviaban como de las que los recibían.

Semejante riqueza y diversidad en la historia de la emigración/inmigración vasca proporciona una plétora de variaciones fascinantes en el tema del inmigrante-asimilación-versus-mantenimiento-etnicidad-dentro-sociedades-huéspedes, así como de la estructuración a través del tiempo de las relaciones entre el País Vasco del Viejo Mundo y sus varias diásporas de emigrantes.

A la vez que semillero de emigrantes transatlánticos, la región vasco-española ha sido también, por más de un siglo, receptora de inmigración masiva de otras partes de España. Durante la segunda mitad del siglo diecinueve, Vizcaya y, en menor medida, Guipúzcoa se erigieron como una de las dos regiones españolas más industrializadas (siendo Cataluña la otra región). Durante varias generaciones la prosperidad relativa del País Vasco ha atraído a emigrantes en busca de trabajo de otras partes del estado español. El número de los recién llegados y sus descendientes se aproxima ahora al número de la población "nativa" vasca. Semejante cambio demográfico masivo y relativamente rápido presenta obvios retos sociales, culturales, lingüísticos, económicos y políticos. De hecho, la génesis del nacionalismo vasco se interpreta conmúnmente como una reacción ante esta amenaza contra la sobrevivencia cultural vasca.

La sociedad vasca contemporánea dentro del estado español ha sido descrita como polarizada social y culturalmente entre las así llamadas "dos comunidades." El espectro político vasco tiene una plétora de partidos políticos divididos entre los dos bloques del nacionalismo español y del nacionalismo vasco (cada uno con su polaridad derecha/izquierda). Durante el cuarto de siglo desde la muerte de Franco se ha dado un impasse político invencible que es reflejo de la igualdad relativa en la balanza de poder entre estas fuerzas en disputa. El gobierno de la Comunidad Autónoma Vasca, creada bajo la Constitución española de 1978, ha sido por tanto un ejercicio continuo de la política de coaliciones. En este sentido, la nueva coalición gubernamental formada en la primavera de 1999 con partidos exclusivamente nacionalistas, tras la tregua indefinida de Euskadi ta Askatasuna (ETA), parece ser un cambio histórico.

Como si semejante confusión y conflictividad no fueran suficientes, existe también el dinamismo añadido de la participación española y francesa (y por tanto también vasca) en la Unión Europea. Junto con los demás europeos, también los vascos dentro de los estados español y francés están abocados a redefinir y reconfigurar sus identidades colectivas y personales en relación a una Europa progresivamente integrada y sin fronteras. Las oportunidades que esto presenta a los separatistas e incluso a los regionalistas vascos para saltar los controles de Madrid o Paris son obvias, aunque lo son menos las de saltarse las normativas que provengan de Bruselas. Hasta cierto punto, el atractivo de enmarcar la identidad en términos "vasco-europeos" es evidente, aunque las dificultades (e incluso la conveniencia) de hacerlo así son menos obvias.

En suma, el congreso evolucionó de reconsiderar la emigración tradicional vasca y sus diásporas a concentrarse en un pueblo sin estado dividido entre dos naciones europeas y entre varias sociedades huéspedes alrededor del globo, un pueblo con el reto interno en su patria europea de grandes divisiones tanto sociales como políticas y culturales, y el reto externo de enormes transformaciones en el estado-nación así como en la política europea y en los mercados económicos. Dicho de otra forma, el congreso examinó la estructura y el

significado de la "vasquidad" en Buenos Aires y Boise, Bilbao y Bruselas, en un mundo cada vez más interconectado y globalizado a las
puertas del nuevo milenio.

Gracias a una ayuda generosa del Gobierno Vasco ha sido posible
la publicación en tres volúmenes de las ponencias del congreso de
Reno en esta "Occasional Papers Series" del Programa de Estudios
Vascos de la Universidad de Nevada, Reno. Uno de ellos está dedi-
cado a las diásporas de emigrantes vascos; otro con el campo de los
estudios culturales vascos. Este volumen recoge los artículos sobre los
temas de la política y nacionalismo vascos.

El artículo de Manuel Castells fue la ponencia central del congreso.
Sitúa el nacionalismo vasco dentro del contexto más amplio de un
mundo cada vez más globalizado en el que los estados-nación actuales están perdiendo relevancia y eficacia. Por consiguiente, el ensayo
se pregunta si las aspiraciones etnonacionalistas por tener su propio
estado-nación son acertadas cuando las energías políticas podrían
estar mejor empleadas en establecer relaciones internacionales y en
obtener una participación mayor en las estructuras políticas transna-
cionales e interregionales, dentro de la Unión Europea en particular.
Por encima de todo, Castells cree que la prioridad primera debe con-
sistir en resolver el "problema vasco," es decir, la violencia política,
una resolución que difícilmente puede ser obtenida sólo con la repre-
sión policial de ETA.

Xavier Rubert de Ventós considera las demandas vascas de soberanía política dentro de un marco más amplio de reclamaciones por
otras nacionalidades sin estado propio. Considera que estas demandas son tan legítimas y racionales como las de los estados-nación existentes en el mundo. Al mismo tiempo argumenta que en el mundo
contemporáneo lo "nacional" no debería ser sino un aspecto más de
las identidades de los individuos libres. Configurar semejante realidad política, basada sobre el respeto mutuo hacia las diferencias de
cada uno, es particularmente crucial para lograr con éxito la creación
de una nueva Europa, dada la historia sangrienta del continente.

Gurutz Jáuregui Bereciartu coincide con las tesis de Castells y de
Ventós, abogando que el reto verdadero para el etnonacionalismo
vasco no es la creación (anacrónica) de un estado-nación, sino más
bien la formación de una sociedad civil vasca en la que el respeto
mutuo por las diferencias políticas, lingüísticas, y socioeconómicas

fuera primordial. Sin semejante tolerancia él prevé un estancamiento indefinido en un proceso político vasco polarizado.

Alfonso Pérez-Agote se hace eco de la necesidad de una mayor integración política de la sociedad vasca contemporánea, a la vez que subraya la importancia de la identidad vasca como su enfoque central. No restringe la construcción de identidad al contexto vasco europeo, sino que se plantea aspectos de formación de identidad dentro de la diáspora de la emigración vasca. Analiza también la evolución del nacionalismo vasco en la época post-franquista y hace hincapié en las situaciones actuales en base a señalar las tendencias tanto hacia la fisión como hacia la fusión dentro de las bases sociales.

Iñaki Zabaleta analiza las noticias internacionales, y en particular el *New York Times,* referentes a temas vascos y su capacidad para influenciar la imagen vasca. Se encuentra con que predominan las noticias sobre ETA y sobre acciones violentas enmarcadas dentro del discurso del terrorismo. El artículo compara las noticias sobre los vascos con las noticias de violencia política en otras partes del mundo como condicionante de cómo son percibidos los vascos en el contexto internacional.

Cameron Watson examina las tiras cómicas de los periódicos, los reportajes de prensa y las descripciones fílmicas de los activistas de ETA, así como la propaganda de ETA sobre sí misma, para conocer cómo se representa a la organización por razones estratégicas. Su análisis subraya hasta qué punto, dejando de lado la violencia política y sus víctimas, tanto como de una guerra en el sentido instrumental el conflicto consiste en imponer imágenes y etiquetas.

Begoña Aretxaga trata también de imágenes, pero desde una perspectiva que es interna a la sociedad vasca y a su conflicto político. Halla una congruencia sorprendente entre la victimología tanto de los activistas violentos envueltos en la *kale borroka,* como de la policía vasca, o *ertzainas,* encargados de impedir la misma. Cada uno cuestiona la legitimidad del otro, a la vez que ambos pueden encontrarse con problemas con la "Ley" y sujetos a futuros juicios mientras se enfrentan uno al otro en el contexto cargado de las confrontaciones callejeras violentas.

Jeremy MacClancy y James E. Jacob consideran el tema no resuelto dentro de la perspectiva nacionalista de la configuración territorial última de un futuro nación-estado vasco. Mientras que un nacionalismo vasco irredento exige soberanía sobre Navarra e Iparralde, de hecho en ninguna de las dos regiones se da un apoyo electoral significativo para la unión política con la Comunidad Autónoma Vasca. Comparadas con las de Vitoria, Bilbao o San Sebastián, la realidad actual y las perspectivas futuras del nacionalismo vasco son, por tanto, marcadamente diferentes desde Bayona o Pamplona.

Ane Muñoz de Varela estudia los muchos retos y contradicciones del nacionalismo vasco a base de detallar los esfuerzos y los compromisos hasta el presente (así como los proyectos para el futuro) que trascienden el contexto local del Gobierno de la Comunidad Autónoma Vasca. Su artículo despliega una variada lista de iniciativas pasadas, presentes y futuras para probar que los planes políticos vascos trascienden asuntos locales y/o suponen algo más que una prueba de fuerza entre Vitoria-Gasteiz y Madrid. La realidad política vasca contemporánea incluye ya, más bien, amplias colaboraciones regionales con el estado español, los Pirineos y la Europa del sudeste, así como una participación considerable con varias agencias y programas de la Unión Europea.

William A. Douglass también se centra en los esfuerzos del Gobierno Vasco para dar vida y movilizar las diásporas vascas tanto para asegurar la permanencia de la identidad cultural vasca en las sociedades receptoras de la inmigración vasca de antaño como para reforzar los lazos de los vascos diaspóricos con la tierra madre. También se examinan las formas en que esta misión en apariencia cultural asume tonos políticos, proporcionando al Gobierno Vasco canales para llevar a cabo su propia "política exterior" a pesar del hecho de que los asuntos exteriores son jurisdicción exclusiva del gobierno central de acuerdo con la Constitución española.

William A. Douglass
Carmelo Urza
Linda White
Joseba Zulaika

Hitzaurrea

Saiakera hauek Renon aurkeztu eta irakurri ziren 1998ko uztailaren 6tik 9ra "Euskaldunak Gaurko Munduan: Emigrazioa, Identitatea eta Globalizazioa" izeneko jardunaldietan. Nevada Unibertsitateko Renoko Euskal Mintegiak eta "University Studies Abroad Consortium"ak deitu zituen jardunaldiok. Gainerakoan, mundu denetik etorritako 77 ikerlarik partu hartu zuten bertan. Interes desberdinek egin zuten bilkura hau beharrezko. Milurtearen akabera izatea izan zen arrazoietako bat. Izan ere, milurtea data esanguratsu bat gehiago da Euskal Herriaren eta honen migrazio-diasporen azterketan arduraturik ari diren begiraleentzat. Hasteko, Colonen lehen bidaiaren aurkikuntzaren bostehunurrena izan zen. Horrek berealdiko arreta sortu zuen. Euskal ikerlarientzat gertakizun erabakigarria izan zen urteurrena, zeren Europaren eta Amerikaren arteko harreman historikoei buruzko interes akademiko handia piztu baitzuen eta, ondorioz, baita ikerketa-lan ugari eragin ere. Are gehiago, egun, bostehunurrenaren aurreko eta ondorengo ikerketa-egoeraz mintza gintezke, hala Espainiako eta Frantziako kolonialismoetan nola europar jatorriko emigrazio trasatlantikoan euskaldunek izan duten parte hartzeari dagokionez. Eta jakina da munduan zeharreko euskal migratzaileen diasporak prioritate bat izan direna beti Renoko Euskal Mintegiaren ikerketen gai-zerrendan. Beraz, hainbat langai berriren aurrean, ikerketen egoera aztertzea bidezko zirudien. Asmo hori gogoan pentsatu zen, hasieran, Renoko jardunaldiak eratzea.

1990eko hamarkadan diasporarko ikerketak modan jarri zirela kontutan harturik, laster sortu ziren nahasketa eta erronkak. Ikerketa hauen eremua, hala ere, aldatu egin zen: Lehen Munduko populazio migratzaileen asimilazioaz edo asimilazio ezaz arduratzen zen lehenengo, edo eta europarrek kolonizatutako gizarteez (Denoon 1983) eta "Ama Lurra"rekin zituzten harremanen iraupenaz (Handlin 1973,

15

Hansen 1940, edo Thomas and Znaniecki-ren erara 1958). Harrezkero, ostera, ikerketa diasporikoak "azterketa kulturalak" sailaren barruan ezarri zituzten, non edozerk baitzuen sarrera: genero eta preferentzia sexualen gaineko ikerketak, Hirugarren Mundu/Lehen Munduen arteko harremanak, kritika literarioaren ahalmenak, antropologiaren dekonstrukzioa (eta, maila apalagoan, baita beste giza-zientziena ere) . . . e.a. Eta, hau guztiau, diskurtso postkolonial, postnazional, postestruktural eta postmodernoen garapenaren adierazpen gisa. Labur beharrez, edonoren diasporak ez du gaur esanahi hain konkreturik. Egun, identitate-formazioaren eta gero eta mundu globalizatuagoko mestizaia kulturalaren problematikaren alderdi bat besterik ez da diaspora.

Euskal kasuan, beste zenbait data ere baziren, oroitzeko modukoak. Esaterako, euskal nazionalismoaren sorreraren ehunurteurrena, (1895ean Sabino Arana eta Goirik sortua), eta inperio espainiarraren akabera 1898ean (Gerra Espainiar-Amerikarraren ondorioz Kuba, Puerto Rico eta Filipinas galdu ondoren).

Ez dago esan beharrik identitatearen moldatze eta iraupena arazo larria dela euskal gizartearen eta kulturaren baitan. Mendebaldeko Europako herririk zaharrena dela esan izan da inoiz; beste inorekin harremanik ez duen hizkuntza bat mintzatzen duela; ondorioz, euskaldunak beren errealitate etniko eta kulturalaren ordezkari bizi eta ukaezinak direla esan daiteke. Hala ere, euskal benetakotasunaren eta nortasunaren arazoak nahasiagoak gertatzen dira, kontutan hartzen badugu euskaldunek ez dutela beren estatu-naziorik, eta, berez, estatu-nazioak direla gaur egungo mundu politikoa definitzen dutenak. Kontuan hartu behar da, gainera, mendeetan zehar nazioarteko muga dutela euskaldunek, beren buruak Frantziaren eraginaren esparruan jartzen dituena Iparraldean, eta Espainiarenean Hegoaldean. Gogoan hartzekoa ere da, azken mendean mugimendu etnonazionalista bat dutela (estatu espainiarraren baitan batik bat), Mendebaldeko Europan denik eta mugimendurik gogorren eta konponbiderik zailekoena, Ipar Irlandakoaren ondoan.

Hori gutxi eta, horra migrazioaren faktorea ere. Bostehun urtean zehar gutxienez, Euskal Herri osoak migratzaileak bidali ditu, Espainia eta Frantzia aldera batzuetan, edo herrialde horien kolonietara beste batzuetan. Zenbaitetan, berriz, baita bi herri horien eraginesparruetatik at zeuden lurraldeetara ere (Douglass and Bilbao 1975).

Ondorioz, biztanlerik duen edozein kontinentek izan ditu euskal migratzaileak. Euskal "kolonia" batzuek mendeetan eta mendeetan iraun dute; Hegoameriketakoek, adibidez, edo Filipinakoek. Beste zenbait oso berriak dira (Australian den euskal presentzia mende honetakoa da, eta British Columbiakoa bera, Bigarren Mundu-Gerra ondorengoa). Gizarte hartzaile batzuek belaunaldietan zehar jaso zituzten euskal migrazioaren uhinak, Mendebaldeko Estatu Batuetan adibidez; beste batzuetan, aldiz, gizarte hartzaileen eta bidaltzaileen egoerak bultzatuta sartu ziren euskaldunak (Argentina, Venezuela, Mexiko).

Halako emigrazio/inmigrazio historia aberats eta pluralak aldaera ugari eskaintzen ditu migratzaile asimilatu versus gizarte hartzailean etnizitate iraupenaren gaian. Mundu zaharreko Euskal Herriaren eta migratzaileen diasporen arteko harremanen egituratzea ere ez da badaezpadako gaia.

Migrazio transatlantikoaren hazitegia izan bada ere, Hego Euskal Herria bera Espainiako beste lurraldeetatik etorritako inmigrazio masiboaren hartzaile izan da mende batez baino gehiagoan, hemeretzigarren mendearen bigarren zatian Bizkaia, eta neurri txikiagoan Gipuzkoa, Espainiako bi lurralderik industrializatuenetakoak izan baitziren (Katalunia izan zen hurren). Zenbait belaunalditan zehar Euskal Herriaren aberastasun erlatiboak erakarri zituen lan bila zebiltzan Espainiar horiek. Etorri berriak eta hauen ondorengoak, gutxi gora-behera, euskal jatorrikoak hainbat izatera heldu ziren. Aldaketa demografiko masibo eta azkarrak eragin zituen erronka sozial, kultural, linguistiko, ekonomiko eta politikoak begibistakoak dira. Izan ere, euskal nazionalismoaren sorrera euskal kultura bizirik irauteko erronkari aurre egiteko erreakzio izan zela interpretatu izan ohi da.

Estatu espainiarraren barruan dagoen gaurko Euskal Herria "bi komunitate"-ren artean, sozialki eta kulturalki polarizaturik, dagoen gizartea dela uste izan da. Euskal espektru politikoa bloke nazionalista espainiarraren eta bloke nazionalista euskaldunaren artean zatiturik dago, bakoitzak bere ezker/eskuin alde eta guzti. Francoren heriotzaren ondoko mende laurdenean nagusitu den impasse politikoak, bestalde, agerian utzi du bi indar-bloke hauen artean dagoen berdintasun erlatiboa. Ondorioz, Espainiako Konstituzio berriarekin sortu zen Euskal Autonomia Erkidegoaren gobernatzea koaliziopolitikaren ariketa amaigabe bat izan da.

Zentzu honean, ETAren suetenaren ondoren 1999ko udaberrian euskal indar nazionalistek osatutako gobernu-akordioak aldaketa historikoa dakar.

Nahasmendu hauek aski ez eta Frantziak eta Espainiak Europako Batasunean parte hartzetik datozenak erantsi behar dira, euskaldunak ere Batasun horren parte egiten baititu. Gainerako europarrak bezala, euskaldunak ere beren talde eta norbanakoaren identitateak berdefinitzera eta berregituratzera beharturik daude gero eta batuagoa eta mugarik gabekoagoa izango den Europan. Madril edo Paris saihesteko aukerak ageriak izango dira euskal separatista edo euskalzaleentzat, baina Bruselatik etorriko diren muga eta limitazio berriak ere ez dira amaituko. Euskal identitatea "Eusko-Europar" moldeetan eratzeko lilura ulergarria da maila batean; hain liluragarria ere ez, hala ere, horrek dakartzan zailtasun eta komenentziak.

Labur esateko, Renoko biltzarrak hasieran euskal migrazio tradizionala eta honen diaspora gogoan izan arren, azkenean estaturik gabeko eta bi nazio europarren artean dagoen herri zatikatua aztertzera lerratu zen. Herri bat, munduan zehar gizarte hartzaile askoren artean bizi dena, Europan bertan ere zatiketa sozial, kultural eta politiko zorrotzen desafioak jasotzen dituena barnetik, eta kanpotik, berriz, estatu-nazioaren baitan eta kontinenteko egoera politiko eta ekonomikoetan gertatzen ari diren aldaketa sakonak nozitzen dituena. Beste modu batera esateko, gure biltzarrak euskalduntasunaren egitura eta esanahia aztertu zituen, dela Buenos Airesen edo Boisen, dela Bilbon edo Bruselan, milurte berriaren atarian gero eta elkarlotuago eta globalizatuago dagoen mundu batean, alegia.

Eusko Jaurlaritzaren laguntza zabalari esker izan da posible Renoko biltzarrari buruzko hiru aleak argitaratzea Nevadako Unibertsitateko, Renoko Euskal Mintegiaren liburu sail honetan. Ale bat Euskal Herriari buruzko Kultur Azterketetan kokatzen diran saiakerak biltzen dituzte (hizkuntza, literatura, zinema, kirolak, identitatea). Besteak euskal migratzaileen diasporari buruzkoak. Ale honetako saiakerek euskal politikarekin zerikusia duten gaiak lantzen dituzte, nazionalismoa barne delarik.

Manuel Castells-en lana Renoko jardunaldietako oinarrizko hitzaldia izan zen. Gero eta globalizatuagoa den mundu zabalaren baitan kokatzen du euskal nazionalismoa gaur eguneko estatu-nazioen garrantzia eta eraginkortasuna galtzen ari dela arguadiatuz. Ondorioz, saiakerak euskal nazionalismoak duen estatu-nazio propio baten nahiaren egokitasuna zalantzan jartzen du, indar politikoak agian hobe gasta zitezkeenean harreman internazionalak finkatzen eta egitura politiko transnazional eta interregionaletan partehartze handiagoa lortzen –batik bat European Batasunaren baitan-. Castells-en ustez, gauza guztien gainetik lehentasuna "Euskal arazoa," hau da, biolentzia politikoa, konpontzeari eman behar zaio, ETA polizialki erasotuz bakarrik lortzea ezinezko dirudien konponketa.

Euskal nazionalismoak duen burujabetasun politikorako nahia Xavier Rubert de Ventósek antzeko beste estatugabeko nazioen asmoen egitura zabalagoan jartzen du. Nahi hauek gaur egungo estatu-nazioek dituztenak bezain zilegi eta arrazoizko aurkitzen ditu berak. Bestalde, gaur egungo munduan norbanako askeen identitateen alderdi bat "nazionala" izan behar duela defendatzen du. Horrelako errealitate politiko bat gauzatzea, non batak bestearen diferentziengana errespetua azalduko duen, bereziki beharrezkoa da Europa berri bat eratu nahi bada, kontutan harturik kontinentearen historia odoltsua.

Gurutz Jáuregui Bereciartu bat dator Castells eta de Ventósen tesiekin, euskal etnonazionalismoarentzat benetako erronka ez dela estatu-nazio anakroniko bat sortzea argudiatuz, baizik eta euskal gizarte zibil bat eratzea, non berezitasun politiko, hizkuntzazko eta sozioekonomikoenganako elkarren arteko errespetua oinarrizko izan behar duen. Horrelako tolerantziarik gabe irteerarik ez duen polarizazio amaiezinekoa ikusten du berak euskal prozesu politikoan.

Alfonso Pérez-Agotek ere adostasun politiko bateratuago baten beharra ikusten du, honen ardatz bezala euskal identitatearen garrantzia azpimarratuz. Nortasunaren politika hau ez du mugatzen Euskal Herriko testuingurura bakarrik, baizik eta euskal migrazio diasporatara ere zabaltzen du identitate eraikuntza. Franco ondorengo nazionalismo euskaldunaren bilakabidea ere aztertzen du, gaur egungo egoeran taldeen fisio eta fusiorako joerak azpimarratuz.

Iñaki Zabaletak komunikabide internazionalen jokabidea aztertzen du, *New York Times*-ena bereziki, euskal berriak eman eta Euskal Herriaren irudia moldatzeko orduan. ETAren inguruko berriak, terrorismoren diskurtsuaren baitan emanak, dira nagusiki. Euskal berrien erreportaiak munduko beste alderdietako indarkeria egoerek baldintzaturik ikusten du beraren idatziak; euskaldunen oharmena testuinguru internazional honetan kokatzen du.

Cameron Watson-ek egunkarietako komiki-zerrendetan, erreportaietan eta zinema irudietan ETAko ekintzaileak nola agertzen diren aztertzen du, eta bide batez ETAk bere buruaz egiten duen propaganda ere bai, arrazoi estrategikoengatik erakundea nola ikusia den jakiteko. Indarkeria politikoa eta honen biktimak kontutan harturik ere, burruka instrumentala bezainbat iruditeria bat eta etiketa batzuk inposatzeko ahalegina dela gatazka azpimarratzen du.

Begoña Aretxaga ere iruditeriaz arduratzen da, baina euskal gizartearen eta bere oraingo burruka politikoaren barnekoarekin. Antzekotasun handia aurkitzen du kale borrokan parte hartzen duten gazte eta hauei aurre egitera bidalitako ertzainen arteko biktimologietan. Bakoitzak bestearen zilegitasuna auzitan jartzen du, bi taldeek "Lege"arekin arazoak izan ditzaketelarik eta kaleko egoera bortitzean elkaren kontra burrukatzen duten bitartean.

Jeremy MacClancy eta James E. Jacobek euskal nazionalismoaren ikuspegian oraindik konpongabea den geroko euskal estatu-nazioaren azken lurralde antolakuntza dute gai. Azkeneraino joan nahi duen euskal nazionalismoak Nafarroa eta Iparraldeaz ere burujabetasuna eskatzen duen bitartean, egiatan bi lurralde hauetan ez dago Euskal Autonomi Erkidegoarekin batasun politikoa osatzeko sostengu esangaratsurik hauteskundeetan. Ondorioz, euskal nazionalismoaren gaur egungo errealitate eta gerorako ikuspegiak oso desberdin dira Baiona edo Iruñetik begiratu ala Gasteiz, Bilbo edo Donostiatik.

Ane Muñoz Varelak euskal nazionalismoaren erronka eta kontraesan ugari arakatzen ditu gaur arte eta aurrera begira Eusko Jaurlaritzak izan dituen ahalegin eta konpromezuak aztertuz. Bere idatziak iraganeko, gaurko eta aurrerako ekimen ugari dokumentatzen ditu, euskal antolamendu politikoak tokian tokiko arazoak gainditzen dituela defendatzen du edota edo Gasteiz eta Madrilen artekoa sokatira bat baino zerbait gehiago direla. Euskal egoera politiko gaurkoak baditu dagoeneko eskualde harreman-sare zabalak estatu espainiarrarekin, Pirineo eta Europa hegomendebalekoarekin, Europako Batasuneko zenbait agentzia eta programekin neurri handiko partaidetza duen bezala.

William A. Douglass-ek ere Eusko Jaurlaritzaren ahaleginak aztertzen ditu euskal diasporak suspertu eta mugiarazteko. Euskal migrazioa jaso duten gizarteetan euskal identitate kulturalaren iraupena segurtatzea eta diasporako euskaldunen ama aberriarenganako loturak indartzea dute ahalegin hauek helburu. Baita ere aztergai diren itxuraz eginkizun kultural hutsak diren harreman hauen esanahi politikoak, Eusko Jaurlaritzari "kanpo-arazo"etako bideak lantzeko bideak ematen baitizkio, nahiz eta kanpo-arazoak gobernu zentralaren esparrukoak izan konstituzio espainiarraren arabera.

William A. Douglass
Carmelo Urza
Linda White
Joseba Zulaika

Manuel Castells

Globalization, Identity, and the Basque Question

In this lecture I will concentrate on issues related to the interaction among globalization, cultural identity, and transformation of states, followed by consideration of their application to the Basque Country.[1] I shall examine how theory, debate, and qualitative analysis may or may not be useful in understanding the so-called Basque question, which I will also try to define in more specific terms.

First, let me try to clarify what we mean by globalization, because when we proceed to the analysis of the current trends in globalization, identity, and transformation of state, the whole understanding of the "Basque question" could be seen in a different light. Globalization is the process by which, in a given dimension of society—the economy, for instance—its core activities acquire the technological and organizational potential to work as a unit, in real time, on a planetary scale. Globalization is not the same as internationalization. A global economy is not a world economy. A world economy in the Western hemisphere has existed at least since the sixteenth century. Peru and Spain were connected to the world economy in that century. Yet, with one Spanish galleon arriving in Lima once a year, I would suggest that it was not exactly the same kind of international interaction that we have today. What is new is that now there exists a technological infrastructure in terms of information systems, telecommunications, and rapid transportation systems both for people and for goods and services that allows this economy to work as a unit in real time.

By core activities I mean, for instance, capital, which is not a small matter in a capitalist economy. Global financial markets are both the unit of investment and the allocators of capital. The significant figure we all cite is that every day, in 1998, 1.5 trillion dollars were exchanged in the world currency market. This is the equivalent, more or less, of the entire French GNP, which is the fourth highest in the world, exchanged daily.

World capital is interconnected. That doesn't mean that all financial resources are saved and invested worldwide. It means that, through the connection that exists, what happens to your savings and mine, to your pension funds and mine, is being decided daily in these exchanges. So your pension funds are on the move, but don't even try to determine where they are, because it doesn't matter. In the next five minutes they will be somewhere else. Some time ago, I was in the Tokyo stock exchange and I asked someone to introduce to me the broker in Numura securities. I asked him, "Are you exchanging securities constantly?"

"Absolutely."

"So do you invest by the second?"

"Our programs tell us what to do every second."

"And do you invest over the long term?"

"Oh yes, certainly."

"Meaning what?"

"Oh, I may be holding onto the same security for fifteen minutes!" That was long-term investment.

We also use the information gleaned from a core of international trade activities—accounting, financial consulting, and even entertainment services—to understand our world better, and this in turn contributes to the globalization process. Our entire lives are communicated to each other by these international trade services. I'm sure that those of you who have never been in Reno before nevertheless feel very familiar with these surroundings, because you have seen them many times, whether in Reno or Las Vegas, in films, and so on.

International foreign direct investment has multiplied by a factor of ten in the last five years. Foreign direct investment, more than international trade, is the central element of the internationalization of production at unprecedented levels. Production systems, again both in goods and services, are now fully internationalized at their core. Multinational corporations are a part of this. In terms of employment, they account for little more than 75 million workers. It seems a lot, but it is not really, not in terms of the total labor force worldwide. However, in output these 75 million people produce more than one-third of all internationally destined goods and services. The ancillary companies and services that relate to multinational corporations, as either suppliers or customers, constitute the key production systems in the economy. So while it is true that multinational corporations are but a small proportion of the world economy, at the same time they are its decisive core.

Information and management are also globalized. Management on-line, information networks, information about technology, information about labor, science and technology itself—all are currently globalized.

Labor is a little bit more complicated. Highly skilled labor, meaning, for example, financial researchers, software engineers, or market traders, is global in terms of its specialty. But in spite of unprecedented migration over the last six years, most labor in general tends to be local. And that is precisely the contradiction. Capital is globalized at its core, most labor continues to be local, and this division between space and time of capital and labor is one of the major issues of our age.

Globalization, however, has other dimensions. It cannot be limited strictly to economics. The media are today both globalized and localized. They are globalized in their control. There are both capital and media businesses owned by extraordinarily powerful conglomerates—Murdoch's Star Channel, for instance. But this doesn't mean that we see the same thing in the media everywhere. Markets are customized. Audiences are localized. A most exciting example was when Catalan Television obtained the *exclusive* rights to a popular American television program in Spain. So if you wanted to watch *Dallas* in Spain, you had to watch it in Catalan. For a more sophisticated example, Murdoch's Star Channel distributed the BBC's World News in China until chastised by the Chinese government for its liberal views. Star canceled the BBC news service at that point. But in Hong Kong, Star produces and distributes soap operas in Cantonese based on traditional Chinese history. Subsequently, they are translated into Mandarin and then broadcast to the rest of China. So it's this relationship between global control and customization of local culture that characterizes the phenomenon of media globalization. It's CNN and local news at the same time, and this is the critical point that we need to understand. Science, technology, and higher education are also global at their very core. Sports, some of the most significant human activities, are strongly globalized. Players from around the world are imported to play on local teams. As you know, in Barcelona we have the best football team. No one can beat us. But most of our players are Dutch and Brazilian. Also, people follow other countries' sports, such as the NBA, which is now popular in Spain. So sports are at the same time local and global.

Religion is globalized. By the way, the Catholic church was always a multinational organization, from its very beginning. Nowadays we have the global expansion of religions all over the world, so there are no local ones any longer. Religion is increasingly a part of global activity.

And more sinister matters are globalized as well. Crime is globalized, and that's a new reality. Crime as such is certainly a very old activity for humankind. It started with illegal traffic in apples, but since then has been transformed into the relationship between the local identity of criminal networks and the globalization of their capital and business activities. Russia's network, Colombia's network, the Chechen network, the Sicilian network—all these are rooted in history, in identity, in local relationships, in face-to-face interactions, and are then globalized. How globalized are they? According to some United Nations sources, it could be that as much as one trillion dollars a year is being laundered in international systems after originating in criminal activity. Again, one trillion dollars at this time is about the amount of the GNP of Italy, the fifth largest in the world. So various forms of global crime and their connections have created a planetary web of activity which is one of the most important dimensions of our existence today. Global crime matters, in terms of financial markets, in terms of politics, and in terms of relationships between government and society, and the players are not just the traditional ones— Colombians, or Russians, or the South Italians. Mexico, for example, is at this juncture a society and a state permeated from top to bottom with criminal networks. Many other regions and countries could be mentioned as well.

Not everything is globalized. As a matter of fact, the lives of an overwhelming proportion of people on this planet are not globalized at all, whether in terms of the way people meet, the way they relate to one another, the way they build their lives, the way they live with their families, or the way they do their jobs. What happens is that although most people are not globalized at home, they accept into their lives the core system of activities in the various dimensions which are indeed global. Moreover, globalization is an extremely uneven system, because of technological sensibilities and the deregulation of institutions and law that we have witnessed recently. It is also a system that can link together that which is considered valuable by an interested party while excluding or switching off that which the activating agent wishes to ignore. And this is a ceaseless activity. There is extraordinary power and flexibility in this global organization built on networks that allow unity of what matters and fragmentation of that which does not.

Globalization ideology proposes that we are living in a fishbowl in which we are all citizens of the world, but we are not. We are actually living in a world in which everything that matters—that is, everything that is controlled by dominant interests—is globalized and linked, whereas everything that the world's dominant interests ignore is not.

Given this process of globalization, a number of alternative values and alternative logics have developed over the last decade. If there is one truth in human activity, just one that could be characterized as a permanent law in social organization, it is that wherever there is domination, there develops resistance to it. There is no historical society in which this has not happened. However, the forms of resistance to domination by these global networks are extremely complicated and quite unacceptable today. Why? Well, how do you control it? How do you oppose the logic of the network, a network that has no problem disconnecting you if you become too much trouble? It is always possible to find some other element that could be functionally equivalent to you and pose fewer problems—be it capital, labor, nations, state government, the judiciary, or the media. So, over the last ten to fifteen years, instead of the traditional forms of resistance to the system based on social movements developed from within it—for example, labor *vis à vis* capital, the citizen *vis à vis* the state—we have witnessed, on the one hand, entrenchment of the system, and on the other, the creation of autonomy outside its logic by people rooting themselves in identity.

Why is identity important? Because if everything can be co-opted or switched off, only the most basic bastions can ultimately resist the power of a closed-network society. You cannot buy my God, and if my values derive from my God they are superior. If I have my nation, or if I have my ethnic group or my gender identity, if I am gay, if I am a part of a spiritual group, this is what clearly matters for me. This is much more valuable. So I don't care if I am switched off by you because you are switched off by me—by my core value system. So it is this opposition, external to the logic of the system, that is the last challenge to it. It is the only and ultimate defense against the extraordinarily pervasive, overwhelmingly inclusivist logic that permeates the global network. This opposition is found in the various movements based on identities such as the labor movement, the environmental movement, the feminist movement, movements of sexual identity, and movements based on human rights. But the most important movement in the world, the most entrenched in terms of its ability to resist, is fundamentalism, which can occur as a regional movement, a national movement, or an ethnic movement and, moreover, in the guise of various religions, some of which are fundamentalist and some of which are not. That is one important thing that I want to tell you. All of these identity-based movements are organized around what I call communalism.

One little note: I am using the terms fundamentalism and communalism analytically and without positive or negative weighting. Communalism simply means that I first close off my cultural identity, and its expression of meaning, in order to protect my personal values, and from there we can negotiate. Communalism can also define a movement, like the American militia movement, which is quite communal and patriotic, or there are the Zapatistas in Mexico, who defend their Indian identity. Both are communalist and both are movements countering globalization. Those familiar with the American militia movement know that its explicit values are very similar to those of the much more *simpático* Zapatista movement. Both are explicitly opposing the destruction of their identity and their livelihood by the processes of globalization emanating from the multinationals and governments.

Religious fundamentalism, as distinguished from a particular religious movement, is probably the most important force in the world today. In my opinion Christian fundamentalism is the most significant social movement in the contemporary United States—whether in terms of the number of people affected, the size of its audience, or its capacity to influence specific events. There are other groups in the country who feel threatened by globalization, but, for the moment, the Christian coalition, with about 1.5 million paying members and a direct appeal that reaches about 5 million people, is the most politically significant. I would say that, on a global scale, nationalism is predominant.

One of the great surprises for what I would call the European rationalist intellectuals was that, when finally the cold war was over and a new adventure was possible, when it seemed people were going to love each other, suddenly it looks more like they want to defend their particular national identity. Why? How can people be so "irrational"? Maybe human beings are "irrational" by definition. However, I do not find nationalism as process to be irrational, but rather cultural, because in fact the construction of the "nation" is as ideological as the cultural construction of the "citizen." There is no such thing as a citizen in nature. The concept is as much a social, political, and historical construction as is a nation. So identity-based movements are the main entities that confront globalization by denying the superior value of the market and production per se. They do so by positing networks rooted in cultural and historical identity.

In between the processes of globalization and what I call identification, we have a crisis of the nation-state. It stems from the incapacity of the nation-state to control the global flows of everything that matters. In the case of the European Union, the nation-state is increasingly unable to control capital flows, economic policy, budgetary matters, national production networks, and defense. Months ago I said to a friend, who is still speaking in terms of French sovereignty and French nationality, that every time France has a problem it calls upon NATO. So much even for European sovereignty. So global flows of everything are at this point completely at odds with the traditional powers of nation-states. The issue of the growing crisis in the identification of nation-states, or, for that matter, in that of all societies, also undermines the legitimacy and the effectiveness of the nation-state.

Why? The legitimacy of the nation-state is built on the state, rather than on the nation. That's how Europe was built. Remember, for instance, that in Italy, at the moment of unification, less than five percent of the populace used Italian as their vernacular. Most of the processes of political legitimization in Europe were based on the notion of the state unifying the nations, not the other way around. It was not the nations becoming the state, but rather the successful state declaring which were going to be its particular recognized component nations. So, in fact, the principle of cultural legitimacy differs from that of citizenship legitimacy.

This is even clearer in the case of religious identity. The Islamic countries may be very strong as authoritarian states, but they are not based on state legitimacy. What is the principle of legitimacy in Islamic states? The community of believers. The unit of residency, the "öuma," is the community of believers and, therefore, the Arab national states are instruments or reflections of this "öuma." France is an exception, because it is the only European nation formed on the basis of the tradition of citizen identity. But it required the liquidation of various cultures by the armies of the revolution and the schools of the Third Republic.

So, on both sides, the nation-state has come increasingly under attack. But nation-states in Europe are rooted in society. They are social actors. They react, they maneuver, and they *out*maneuver. And in Europe, as in the rest of the world, they have tried to solve twin crises: the crisis of effectiveness and the crisis of legitimacy, which are the two main historical premises of a nation-state. If states cannot control global flows, they try to band together to be able to at least manage some of them, to have greater power, greater ability to negotiate together, and to intervene together within these global flows. That's what the European states are doing. They constructed in Europe what I call "the Brussels Cartel," because it is certainly not based on a European identity, project, or concept. It's a defensive alliance against the Japanese and the Americans, and against the loss of control *vis à vis* global capital flows, information technology, and so on. This defensive alliance will then try to see if it can manage the New World with coordinated action in a European Central Bank, to defend the Euro better than its components defended the franc, the peseta, and the mark.

So the ability to bring together a number of institutions means shared sovereignty. States lose individual sovereignty and share in a supernational institution. The same is true of other institutions, and not just those in the European Union. NATO is an example, as are a number of United Nations agencies designed to intervene in problems that are increasingly global in nature. Take environmentalism, for instance. It is not possible to control the ozone layer from the European Union, so there must be environmental organizations to handle this process at a different level. It is not a matter simply of what states can or cannot do, but rather of how much citizens will tolerate from their states. States have to come up with something to tell people: "We are doing what we can. And if we cannot do it individually, we will do so collectively." Through supranational communal efforts the traditional role of nation-states is modified.

I don't think that the nation-state is going to disappear, but we are already seeing a different form of it: a state made of supranational and co-national institutions, a state connected at all levels of civil society, including NGOs, or what I call Neo Governmental Organizations.

All this taken together, all these relationships form the actual structure and practice in the exercise of power. This is what I call *the network state*. It is a state, it has power, it has delegation of power, it has some level of representation, but everything is shared, negotiated, contradicted, and sometimes opposed in this network of interaction. And this is the real world of political personnel, political leaders, and political institutions.

So what about the Basque question? I hope the foregoing helps us to understand some of the processes involved in approaching it. Basque national identity has been constructed and maintained for centuries—consciously so for at least one century. For proof of how important and how much of a defining principle this Basque national identity is beyond class and religious beliefs, consider the Spanish Civil War. There was no hesitation on the part of the Basque bourgeoisie to align themselves with forces that were engaged in what, to some extent, was a class war *against* the Spanish State. The Basque bourgeoisie was on the side of the Republic because it embodied the most important defining principle of Basqueness. The Spanish Catholic Church was an active actor in the Civil War on the Fascist side. However, the Basque church clearly sided with the Republic. Basque national identity also endures in the Basque diaspora. By the way, the Catalan and Galician diasporas are also very important. I don't know much about the existence of an actual "Spanish diaspora," one that transcends the Asturian diaspora or the Andalusian diaspora. There is, however, a key issue in Basque national identity: the linguistic question. The lack of the use of the Basque language in the Basque Country has been an obstacle to self-recognition, a critical matter for future development of Basque identity.

In the new global system that is emerging, in which strong identity is the fundamental antidote against disappearing into the uncontrolled global flows, there is a strong Basque identity. One of the fundamental means of expressing any cultural identity today is through the Internet-based community. It is growing and will require further development of Basque language communication strategies.

So, the first Basque question concerns, of course, the language. The second question concerns the complex relationship between the indisputable Basque national identity and the Basque State. The relationship between cultural identity and the state in the Basque case regards the lack of a Basque nation-state.

Remember, the Spanish State was never a nation-state; it was an imperial state, which is very different. It was not founded on the revolutionary model, or even on sovereignty delegated to the state by the nation. In the pre-democratic period, Spain was a unity of destiny in the universal realm, according to its intellectuals. It was formed by systematically exterminating the multinational character of the state. To be sure, there were efforts to form a modern nation-state based on concession by the citizenry of sovereignty to the central state. There were two serious attempts to accomplish this in the twentieth century. The first, from 1931 to 1936, was a federalist initiative to destroy the multinational character of the state, which ended in civil war. The second attempt was from 1977 to 1978, when the new Spanish Constitution was created. In this particular instance, the Spanish State was also built upon a very complicated political architecture. Article Two of the Spanish Constitution says that Spain is an indivisible

nation, made up of nationalities and regions. Article Two also states
that even though Spain is indivisible, its peoples have the right to self-
determination. Any logician would say there is inherent contradiction, and that's what is so interesting. The writers of the Spanish Constitution found themselves in an ambiguous situation that could not
be resolved by a decree that would declare Spain to be either a federalist state or a centralized one. This was not feasible and the reality
was changing too quickly. So it was decided to write a modifiable
constitution. Article Two can be reinterpreted, extended one way or
the other, depending on the future social and political transformations that Spain endures.

Here is an example of political intelligence, the ability to live within
the mobile constitution of Spain. In practice, today the Spanish State
is no longer a sovereign one. It is a link, a link in a network, a link in
a chain that connects the European Union, NATO, the Spanish State,
Euskadi, local governments, and many other types of institutions.
There has been a transfer of power and resources to the Basque
government and other autonomous regions. There is a fundamental
problem with regard to the transfer of powers, particularly exempli-
fied in the continued presence of the Guardia Civil and the Spanish
police, a very dramatic issue in the Basque Country. There are still
some other important matters to settle, too, such as the existence of a
Basque soccer team. But, seriously, the Basque state that exists today
is effectively constructing Basque identity.

So what is the problem? What is the real Basque question? Well, it
is symbolism. And symbolism is real. Millions of people have died
for, and because of, symbolism. It has to be taken seriously. But let's
start from the opposite position, one that says it's symbolic and therefore it doesn't matter. In real-life cooperational terms, once we get rid
of the Guardia Civil in the Basque Country, the drastic need for this
symbolism is greatly reduced.

Last, I don't want to avoid the problem that conditions the development of the Basque Country and Basque identity at this point. I
refer to the civil war going on in the Basque Country in terms of the
militant wing of ETA. I am absolutely against what ETA is doing in
the Basque Country, and totally against terrorist activities. I think
they are senseless and useless in a democratic system, and I believe
they are counterproductive. They block the extraordinary develop-

mental potential of both cultural and economic resources, and they waste energies that could be used to concentrate on the development of Basque identity and to build a new kind of state within the framework of the European Union. We have to understand, however, that all this stems from the dynamics of forty years of struggle against Franco's dictatorship. It comes from open wounds that have not yet healed. It comes from indignation and from suffering. It comes from the adversarial history caused by decades of oppression and feelings of helplessness. And it will not just go away. Also it is an absolute illusion to think that there can be a police solution to the violence. A recent survey asked people in Euskadi and the rest of the Spanish State for their opinion on a number of issues related to the Basque Country, but particularly regarding this question: Do you think a police solution to ETA is possible? In Euskadi, 70% of the respondents said no and in Spain, 65% said no. The people know it and the politicians know it. Franco tried everything. Suarez tried everything. The socialists tried, the Basque Nationalist Party tried. The violence simply cannot be terminated through police action. Something else has to be attempted. Northern Ireland is an example of the very complicated political process that may or may not work for the Basque Country.

In conclusion, if terrorism ceases, if the civil war that is still going on in the Basque Country concludes, if the new Basque State adapts to the new form of the network state, I see extraordinary possibilities of economic development, cultural identity, and social creativity for Euskadi within the new global economy. And, in this sense, I think Basque leaders need to engage themselves in the most important political issue of the day—the management of ambiguity. If they can accomplish this, then maybe we can also effect the endless construction and reconstruction of identity in Euskadi, to the benefit of all.

Note

1. This lecture was delivered in July 1998, before ETA's truce and the process of negotiation in Euskadi. The text has been edited stylistically, but remains true to the original substance.

Xavier Rubert de Ventós

The Rationality of National Passions

There are unconscious nationalisms (often exclusivist, and much more dangerous if they possess a state apparatus) and conscious ones, potentially more inclusive. Nevertheless, we cannot say of either that they are mere atavistic phenomena. For, above all, they are rational responses—in the sense that they are "functional" or "adaptive"—to the problems of their environment. This is what I shall attempt to demonstrate.

The proliferation of fundamentalisms and nationalisms is often considered to be a throwback to political "prehistory." But is it just a return of the prophets and magicians, or also a reaction to the sorcerer's apprentices who tried to replace them with an enlightened bureaucracy? Is it all a new obscurantism or simply the return of the identities at whose expense Leviathan was constructed? In short, who is the "bad guy," responsible for the fact that these identities tend to affirm themselves against the state instead of being legitimated by it? Is their return a new evil or the symptom of an old illness?

It is undeniable that many of these identities tend to reappear in forms that we could consider pathological: hysterical and exclusivist, messianic and terrorist. But if that which is repressed returns as a symptom it is precisely because, not being able to express itself verbally or rationally, it appears as a phobia, as a compulsive tic, as paranoia, or as persecutional mania—all of which are resources that states themselves try to manipulate for their own purposes.

The new tribalisms and religious fundamentalisms provide a renewed identity to members of societies that are artificially divided. The recuperation of mythical origins seems to provide these nations with the identity and dignity that they lost when they were incorporated into nation-states whose "modernization" consisted in the establishment of the official party line and whose "vertebration" was

34

the army. The opposite reaction is the similarly fundamentalist attempt to assimilate to the point of disappearance.

Addiction to dependency is one of the features that any student of human behavior has to reckon with. It is known that the offspring of predators take longer to grow than do those of their prey. And of the predators, it is the offspring of the human species who take the longest time to mature and become competent and independent. It is foreseeable, then, that this long period of dependency should develop in humans a marked sense of belonging. This is neither good nor bad, it's simply the way it is. No doubt, this addiction to dependency can become dangerous, and the most dangerous of such human passions, as has been explained from La Boétie to Tolstoy and from Céline to Canetti, is when they combine (as Fichte suggested) territorial (Roman) expansionism with spiritual (Christian) universalism. The mixture of the two universalisms, like that of sulfur and carbon, produces this explosive political powder keg called the modern state, bent on the double "mission" of *homogenizing* all that is internal to it (language, education, history, the calendar, and so on) while *segmenting* instrumentally the peoples or countries that fall without (Berlin, Yalta, and Versailles are well-known examples).

It is worth looking at the genealogy of these two universalisms that spring from the Procrustean bed of Rome and Christianity. The Greek synthesis of genealogy and politics, the tribal and the local, in Rome undergoes a radical transformation of scale, a shifting sequence from aristocratic *time* to democratic *space* to imperial *number*. The polis—something that can be "seen" with one's eyes—gives way to the empire—something that can only be narrated or imagined. Citizenship is no longer a topological concept but is instead a legal one (although not yet ideological, or doctrinal either—it has no pretense of being a spiritual unity, as Christianity would do later). Romans lose their collective memory of the institutions and the art that they have merely copied from Greece, but whatever they relinquish in artistic authenticity and religious cult they gain in territorial extension and tolerance. The gods of the conquered countries are "domesticated" and become part of the official Olympus. Indifferent to origins or beliefs, the territorial organization is eclectic, syncretic, and cosmopolitan.

Conversely, the triumph of Christianity represents the other pole:

the genealogical or tribal taken to the spiritual limits. A jealously affirmed and universalist local God replaces the peaceful coexistence of foreign deities in the Roman pantheon. The Christian God becomes the model for all the absolutist ideologies and all the "new men" of the future. The new state finds a spiritual rationale, rather than merely a spatial one, for its expansion. Thus, as we have territorial expansion without ideological or spiritual unity in Rome, in the Middle Ages we have spiritual expansion without territorial unity. The European drama is the lack of synchrony between the two processes. If the Roman empire achieved territorial expansion prior to the consolidation of Christian spiritual identity, with the Middle Ages there emerge the "Christian States" in which ideological *universalism* becomes allied with national particularism, thereby constituting the endless battlefield that has been Europe.

Both Procrustean beds—the Roman and Christian derivations that unilaterally radicalize the territorial and the spiritual poles—both principles become the sulfur and carbon that, when juxtaposed and then commingled with the earth's salt, will turn into the gunpowder that will inevitably create the explosion. The modern national conflict is thus served. These modernized tribes we call the states will no longer fight for territory per se; rather, the conflict becomes a homeostatic process of maintaining mutual balance, at least until the "total wars" of this century.

This is the kind of nation-state that has kept Europe in a permanent state of civil war. It has been no less explosive where it has carved up the periphery, dividing peoples and creating "buffer" and "client" states as means of maintaining what is called the balance of power. It is in the name of this balance, for example, that the existence of what did not exist was blithely decreed (Yugoslavia), as well as the non-existence of what *did* exist (Kurdistan); that which had once been one was divided ("I like Germany so much that I want two of them," as Mauriac said cynically), or what was plural became united (the USSR).

And why should we be surprised now (when the cold war has ended and the world has defrosted) that people want to recover their own profile, often confronting and rejecting the tragic, sinister caricatures that powers that be had "designed" for them? How dare we say that the revindicators constitute the great danger of our times?

It is a commonplace to argue that we are witnessing the resurgence of fundamentalisms of all kinds, that a sense of belonging is more important than a doctrine, that identity has substituted for ideological debate. However, such fundamentalism (the utopia of a particular identity) is filling a void in the wake of another, that of the modern utopias (the fundamentalism of universal progress). So the true symptom of our times is that all are today fundamentalists. And we are even more so to the degree that we accuse others of defending an identity that we do not deem to be "fundamental," always assuming that it is the other who is the irredentist.

Some fundamentalisms promote the illusion that they act in the name of universal interests, whereas others are self-aware that they vindicate but one particular way of existence. However, it is very cynical or very naïve to maintain that the "impressionism" of Palestinian or Armenian, Catalan or Corsican nationalism is more destabilizing than the traditional "expressionism" of the French, Russian, or Spanish counterparts. And one needs to have a very particular notion of modernity to assume that the former are the products of fanaticism and the latter—those that designed the world in terms of the very genocide or massive repression of the former—of rationality.

And what of the states that were designed by the international conferences of 1815, 1919, and 1945? Aren't they too large to confront local issues and too small to confront the global ones? The autonomy and diversity that peoples, and even cities, now vindicate seem somehow to be the translation or cultural version of the ecological variety that we are destroying so as to bring us to the brink of global environmental disaster. When biologists defend "necessary variety" (Ashby), the "profusion of the small" (Margalef), or a "baroque minimum" in nature (Wagensberg), the defense of analogous diversity in political culture is anything but irrational.

Such "small" nationalisms can even be taken as a paradigm of the very idea of identity or belonging for various reasons. First, they are the most resistant not only to state formations but also to international ones. Thus Basque nationalism does not appear to be soluble within the Spanish state, just as French and British nationalisms seem insoluble within the European Union, as is U.S. nationalism within the United Nations. Second, nationalism has been the most popular ideology of the century, and has therefore been the inspiration behind all revolutions from the American to the Russian one. Third, nationalism is adaptable in that it tends to incorporate several of the other forms of belonging (ethnic, cultural, geographic) and can thereby configure identity such as the religious in Iran, the cultural in Catalonia, the ethnic in Euskadi, the "continental" in France, or the "peninsular" in Spain. Fourth, nationalism is the most ambiguous and conflictive phenomenon, one that is easily capable of pitting liberationist movements and dominant states against one another (which can quickly replace cosmopolitan rhetorics with nationalist poetics).

And if such nationalist movements must be considered merely sentimental impulses, archaic instincts, and prehistoric reflexes, then let us welcome the return to prehistory—to language, to ethnicity, to religion—to the time before the belief in progress had turned history into Myth and reason into the Absolute State. Let us welcome also the return of geography asserting its rights against the abstractions of national geometries. Instead of debating which is the primary contradiction and which the secondary, we should be forced to learn of Macedonia and Bohemia, and to assess the importance of Estonian Lutheranism, Lithuanian Catholicism, and Bulgarian Orthodoxy. Let us welcome too the return to primary sentiments—charity, honesty, piety—that emanate today from people such as Havel, Michnik, and Mandela.

Let us welcome even German nationalism—so that we know what are we dealing with—in contradiction of those who pretended that a nation can be maintained in a permanent state of guilt. Or against those who thought, like Habermas, that this emphatic "we," which is present in all nationalisms, in Germany could be dissolved into a "sober postnational identity" or into a "constitutional patriotism based on the abstract idea of the universalization of democracy and human rights." What is disappearing today is the dogmatic world designed in Vienna in 1815, following the principles of dynastic legitimacy and a balance of powers, complemented later in Versailles and Yalta by debating the dogmas of the working-class struggle and anticommunism, and frozen, until yesterday, into the standoff of nuclear deterrence and the cold war. Understanding all *that* required perhaps the help of large theoretical geometries. But in order to react to a more sensory and plastic image of the new world that is dawning, what is needed is a politics that, like art, is less avant-garde and a little more figurative.

It is well known that the avant-garde tried to capture the aesthetic essences by ridding art of representational appearances and anecdotes. The pure Message of Redemption was austerity itself, departure from the traditional canons, the rhetorical figures, the natural forms, and the melodic rules. True art had to capture pure architectural "functionality," musical "sonority," plastic "structure," literary "textuality," and so on. Such artistic fundamentalism went hand in hand with a political one that aimed at creating a new world order by, say, the *entente cordiale* of France and Great Britain in 1904 whereby Africa could be partitioned with a rule and compass as if it were some Mondrian painting. And this is how decolonization produced today's unlikely African states.

But certain facts are stubborn and everywhere we are now witnessing "the return of the repressed." At present only truly figurative politics can obviate that such return becomes a mere hangover or assumes hysterical forms, possibly even catastrophic ones given the distribution of nuclear power. We need a figurative politics that will take into account the unity of nature as well as the diversity of peoples and cultures, that will provide support to the diversity of identities, as well as to the new ecological responsibilities that were once in God's hands but now are only in our own. In short, after so many years of avant-garde and doctrinary politics, we need to return to politics that are simply figurative and credible.

But if the nationalistic sentiment is basically rational, the analysis we apply to it must be equally so. For it is just as simplistic for the state to assail all other nationalisms as xenophobic or exclusivist as it is for the revindicators to claim that there exist large, evil, aggressive nationalisms and small, good, defensive ones. There are, no doubt, examples of both, but to understand the strategy followed by either, we must place them in context where the variables that enter into their formation/construction can be pondered—and analyzed.

This is what I tried to do in my book *Nationalisms*, by using four variables (cultural complexity, territorial cohesion, socioeconomic modernization, and political consolidation) with which I drew, for the diverse nationalisms, a profile of their relative degree or level of "fundamentalism." The integration of the four variables, by a particular movement, as I said in the text, favors the "normal modernization of peoples" and minimizes the temptations of "return to immaculate origins" or the "fundamentalist backlash." In effect:

a) The less pristine a culture is and the more it is made up of elements from different derivations, the more it is able 1) to assimilate what comes from without; 2) not to dissolve upon minimal contact with the outside (as was the case of the Latin American empires of the sun when faced with a handful of "divine" Europeans); and 3) not to attempt to recover identity through an appeal to a return to the original, pristine, good, sacred times of yore.

b) The greater the territorial cohesion of a country, the greater the "overlap" in its language, law, and geographical incarnation, and the more able it is to "progress" and not "regress" pathologically. There is a minimum of equilibrium among land, law, Lord, legacy, and language upon which future political structure shall be based and without which it becomes a straitjacket. In this same sense, I have suggested that the effect that territory has upon law is to dedramatize and secularize. Hence, a people without land, like the Jews, tended toward the mythification of the law, which they have turned into a "transportable country." The "communitarian" basis of the very nature of pluralism and liberalism ought to be studied in such terms. As Rawls has finally recognized in *Political Liberalism,* it is on just such a cultural basis that a consensus can be reached regarding what is "right" without claiming for it that which is "good."

c) *Socioeconomic modernization,* in the sense that Weber gave to the term (cities, monetary economy, division of labor, communications systems, mobility, secularization), used to refer to the *political consolidation* of territories. But it was not always so. And wherever some of the Weberian factors have emerged without the others, nationalist tensions naturally arise. Today, this is especially true among the economically rich (and politically poor) regions of Europe. Such is the case of the Basque country, for example, where socioeconomic modernization (factor *c*), while appearing earlier than in the rest of Spain, failed to "mutate the state" (factor d), but rather "found itself in the state," that is to say, nurtured and structured by outsiders. This could explain, for example, the apparent paradox of the success of a "vernacular" program such as Sabino de Arana's, with its fundamentalist flavor (Catholicism, genealogy), within a modern and dynamic civil society. Yet Basque society must provide this program with the "complexity" required to develop a discourse that transcends ETA's fundamentalism—a fundamentalism which has something of the "españolismo" it denounces (the one that exported to the world words like *guerrillero, paseíllo, desesperado,* and *desaparecido*). We hope that the new dangers of "social dualization" won't reinforce this fundamentalism, so pathetically Spanish, and that we will be able to overcome both the radical and naïve "spirit of independence" which, according to Angel Ganivet, characterized "the peninsular soul," and which María Zambrano described as "the absolutism of individual existence as reply and complement to the absolutism of the state."

It is not a question of preaching a return to supposedly natural or basic communities, but one of seeking a certain correspondence between what we used to call the infrastructure and the superstructure; between the real system of interests and dependencies, on the one hand, and the political or administrative organization that must transform them on the other.

It is a fact, for example, that for many years there was a tacit pact between Madrid and the Catalan bourgeoisie whereby the latter agreed to forego political power in exchange for economic protectionism and the law and order offered by the central government. Not without reason did Unamuno speak about the "clamoring of these merchants of the Levant" (Machado) who "are always ready to sell their souls for a tariff." Maybe it was so. But today neither the import duty, nor the value of the currency, nor the rate of inflation depend solely on Madrid, but rather on a conglomerate in which the IMF, Brussels, NATO, the Bundesbank, and so on, all converge. And if we think, as I do, that the only viable political and territorial formations are those that translate reasonably (or, at the very least, that do not betray) the real fabric of interests and dependencies, it is clear that we must seek political formulae that will give our countries, nations, and cities the degree of shared sovereignty that corresponds to their real situation. Hence, rather than simply vindicating *sovereignty* (which is nothing more than the concentric, and now mythic, integration of all political, economic, and military powers into one univocal state, and of all the services—health, transportation, education, and so on—under a sole administration), we must propagate functional nuclei of interdependency that will organize their *state as an occasional conglomerate of fluxes and functions,* an important one of which—but only one of which—is national culture understood as the sediment and "mise en scène" of a *collective memory without pretensions to truth or universality of any kind.*

What this means, obviously, is that the European omelet cannot be made, as De Gaulle wished, from the hard-boiled eggs that are today's so-called sovereign states, but rather must emerge among areas and regions, cities, leagues, and nationalities that group together occasionally and sectorially according to criteria of efficiency. (You may perhaps be wondering, "And what ideology or mythology will 'act as the soul' of these political groupings?" And I would respond, "Thank God, politics is ceasing to be the religion of the twentieth century and is abandoning the state in order to rise into the pantheon of the traditional religions or, conversely, to come down to earth to reside among people and their many afflictions.")

We have defined the new state to which we aspire as a sporadic conglomerate of functions that may not only be eventually separated but that also lacks any Manifest Destiny. Reference is to a complex, uncentered, and non-pyramidal formation that takes its stability from the very richness and cross-pollination of its components. The "models" we have for them are: 1) *zoological,* in the centerless system of ants; 2) *vernacular,* in the organization of many peoples (the Navajos, for example, for whom there exists no authority beyond one unifying the *traditional* heads of the lineage, the *charismatic* heads of the age groups, or the *rational* heads of the groups formed for war); 3) a contemporary image in the functionings of *unzoned* cities; 4) a *precedent* in what at some point (out of weakness if not out of determination) was the Austro-Hungarian empire: a *place* where one could be from a nation, a citizenry, a language, and a culture that were not exactly coterminous (for example, Muslim by culture, Croat by language, Hungarian by nationality, and an Austrian citizen).

The psychological correlate of this form of political grouping is one defined by Musil in *The Man without Qualities*. A man, Musil said, has a bunch of distinct characters or identities: "one as a citizen, one from the state, one conscious and another unconscious, one sexual and another professional, etc., and yet one more, that of his fantasy, that allows him all but one thing: to take too seriously the previous ones."

Thus the occasional and functional groupings of the new European states ought to find their correspondence in the multiple groupings that configure the free individuals who live in them. Individuals who are not free by virtue of any universal vocation, but rather by belonging to independent and quite diverse groups: a religious faith, a political preference, a political system, a national conscience, a sporting club, and so on, without there necessarily being precise connections among them.

Gurutz Jáuregui Bereciartu

Basque Nationalism at a Crossroads

The constitutional design of the State of Autonomies (Estado de las Autonomías), approved in Spain in 1978, has had a doubly positive effect. First, it has favored the depoliticization of many historical problems that have plagued the relationship between the Basque Country and Spain. Second, it has facilitated the reframing of some of these conflicts in new terms. At the same time, certain problems that resulted from the antagonism between the Spanish state and the Basque Country have been kept alive in the latter as a source of internal conflict. Basque nationalism has traditionally manifested a clear tendency to assign to external agents the responsibility for problems that, in reality, were endogenous to its own people. Now, autonomy has both permitted and forced Basque society to face itself.

Among the negative aspects, it is necessary to point out that the State of Autonomies has not been able to solve, in definitive fashion, the so-called Basque problem. Evidence of this lies in the continuing distrust, and even the rejection, of the autonomy model by an important sector of Basque society.

I will examine some of the residual difficulties, distinguishing between internal ones—those endogenous to Basque society itself—and external problems that derive from the relationship between Basques and the Spanish state.

Internal Problems

The Basque Country is still far from attaining an acceptable level of homogeneity and social integration. Basque society is, at present, very conflictive and convulsed, an internally divided entity. This division reflects not only the existence of a strongly polarized society but, above all, the absence of a basic and common substratum, that is, a set of values subscribed to by all political and social sectors of the Basque Country.

For the first time in the last two centuries, the Basque Country has its own political power. However, after almost twenty years, Basque society continues to be profoundly divided and unstructured. It is undergoing a serious identity crisis that, in turn, poses problems for the present fragile situation as well as its future development.

For this reason, it seems logical to ask if the Statute of Autonomy actually constitutes a useful and valid instrument and, if so, what has prevented it from acting as a factor in the greater consolidation of Basque society? In my opinion, the answer is that the Statute is intrinsically valid, yet is insufficient for resolving the problems definitively.

It is important to clarify that I use here the word "insufficient" in neither a quantitative sense, that is, of a greater or lesser degree of political power, nor a qualitative one, meaning a better or worse design for relations between the Basque Autonomous Community and the Spanish state. Rather, I am referring to another kind of insufficiency, one that is extrinsic to the Statute itself. Let me elaborate.

The good performance of any democratic system demands the existence of a minimal, double-faceted consensus among its citizenry. First, there is the need for some procedures and common basic institutions; second, there must be a common social consensus, expressed in a positive attitude and loyalty toward those institutions. Such loyalty still allows citizens to be in radical disagreement, through democratic methods, with the institutions and procedures themselves. The Statute provides the institutional consensus; the social one is manifest in a feeling that I would define as "Basqueness."

Traditionally, the political institutionalization of any society tends to be the culmination of a previous process of social and cultural integration and sedimentation. I think that in the Basque case, however, such institutionalization transpired long before the construction of a corresponding Basque civil society. In the Basque Country today, the Statute serves as its political-institutional vertebral column. However, it lacks the marrow that confers that most essential element: vitality. This lack has thus far spelled the failure of all attempts at structuring a modern Basque society. What are the reasons for this futility?

It is obvious that nationalism has played a primary role in Basque history for the last hundred years. Clearly, though, its influence throughout this period has been ambivalent. Nationalism presents some positive aspects, among them its effective contribution to the development of a Basque consciousness, but there are also some negative aspects. One of these was the strict identification between Basqueness and Basque nationalism. Basque nationalism tended to be projected as a collective movement endeavoring to respond to Basqueness as a whole, thus claiming for itself the role of the only legitimate representative of the community. Furthermore, this collective program was planned exclusively for the Basque ethnic community, which was confused with the nationalist community, so that any non-nationalist was considered to be non-Basque.

I think that it is precisely in such reductionism that we can discern the fundamental cause of the current situation. Upon narrowly defining Basqueness with this exclusionary concept of nationalism, the Basque nationalist movement displaced, and still does today, the essential marrow—the Basque people themselves—as a broad category within which the nationalist and non-nationalist both fit and can coexist.

I am not attempting to establish guilt, but simply to discuss a reality. We must not forget that the historical option of the PNV for an excluding nationalism was provoked not only by its ideological convictions but also its rejection of the Socialist Party, as well as its oligarchic claim on both nationalism and Basqueness. As a consequence, both nationalist and non-nationalist forces have been unable to formulate a basic message or program for the whole of Basque society. How can this impasse be overcome?

In the nation-building process it is necessary to distinguish between two phenomena that frequently appear conflated, but which are not exactly the same. One is the building of a nation, per se; the other, which is different, is nationalism. Nation-building refers to the development of the identity of a people or nation. Nationalism deals with the specific activities, instruments, methods, ideologies, or programs employed in nation-building.

Both processes have been expressed in a simultaneous and complementary way throughout history. This does not mean, however, that both must work together. Nation-building is a process of creation of a country or nation. Nationalism is the force, or sometimes one of the forces, at play in that creation. There can be only one force, or there can be several working simultaneously. In Euskadi, Basque nationalism has failed in its attempt to establish a nationalist nation-building process. As is well known, an important sector of the Basque population rejects nationalism or, at least, does not share its values and objectives. What is the reason for this failure?

The existence of several concepts or models of nation-building does not constitute in itself an especially serious problem. The most important difficulty stems from the lack of a common vision of the Basque Country shared by the various social and political forces. Creation of a common agenda, or at least a minimal substratum of agreement, would seem to be the necessary priority for the nationalist and non-nationalist sectors of Basque society if there is to be any possibility of building the Basque nation. Both forces must find common ground regarding a more basic concept, that which I have termed "Basqueness." Thus constituted, Basqueness would be the glue holding together the common effort. It would be perfectly compatible with the different visions or models of nation-building—all of which are legitimate—as outlined by nationalist and non-nationalist groups alike.

Like most occurrences of nationalism, the Basque version has traditionally sustained its activity in the idea of *aberrigintza,* or patriotism, and the achievement of the necessary political power that is normally structured through an independent state. In this manner, the political power and the institutions would be able to achieve the necessary cultural, social, and territorial integration. The experience of recent years has demonstrated that the existence of autonomous political institutions constitutes a necessary, but insufficient, condition for achieving such objectives.

Consequently, it seems necessary to substitute for *aberrigintza* a broader process of *herrigintza,* or country-building. While *aberrigintza* is limited to acts in the political arena, *herrigintza* affects other areas: social, economic, cultural, and so forth. The latter is more encompassing and more open than *aberrigintza,* since it is premised on the widest possible definition of Basqueness. It would purport to allow nationalist and non-nationalist political forces to meet and work together. *Herrigintza* constitutes the only possible means of transforming the old Euskal Herria into a modern Euskadi that can be projected to the world. In contrast, *aberrigintza* runs the risk of depriving the Basque nation-building project of both its internal and external legitimacy. Basqueness must fulfill two indispensable requirements: a capacity to maintain an open and democratic system, and an ability to formulate a common agenda and to pursue it efficaciously. The configuration of such a common project must be effected:

1. Territorially, through attainment of an adequate balance in the integration of the various territories into a common framework while respecting pluralism and the autonomy of each component.

2. Socially, through the promotion of social integration while recognizing Basque social pluralism.

3. Culturally, through the maintenance and development of a common, but plural, collective identity, based on the existence of two, or even three, languages.

4. Economically, through the achievement of the international competitiveness that is compatible with territorial autonomy. This presupposes the participation in, and support of, economic, technological, and social projects that incorporate and accommodate Basque society within the wider world.

5. Politically, through the establishment of a structure capable of guaranteeing the identity of the Basque people, while commanding loyalty for the defense of that common institutional framework.

These elements constitute factors internal to Basque society itself. In this regard, the primary challenges are the social integration of Basque society and its modernization. The political structure, however, transcends in several important ways the territorial confines of the Basque Country. From this external perspective, the fundamental problem lies in defining the relationships—institutional, political, and so forth—to maintain with Spain (and France).

External Problems

Certain external problems can be specified: those that are derived from the daily application in the Basque Country of Spanish constitutional and statutory norms; and those flowing from the absence of a political model that facilitates smooth collaboration between the Basque Autonomous Community and the Spanish state.

From a nationalist perspective, the principal political problem arises from the lack of the state's recognition of the right to self-determination of the Basque Country. The Spanish Constitution does not permit territorial separation. This is a fundamental and delicate problem for which the Spanish state has not managed to find an adequate solution.

The content of the right of self-determination is not unequivocal. Theoretically, it supposes the decision-making capacity of a people to choose freely among an enormous range of options, including autonomy, federation, confederation, secession from a constituted state, and creation of an independent one. In the Basque case, this right traditionally has been identified with the claim to an independent nation-state.

However, I believe that this problem could lose a large part of its virulence and relevance through the possible solutions afforded by the European Union (EU). For that reason, it is crucial to have an adequate response from both the Spanish state and the EU in order to solve this matter (as well as other similar ones throughout western Europe).

The intensification of trade, the mobility of people as a consequence of economic well-being and the easing of travel restrictions, the progressive similarity of cultures resulting from the ever-increasing exchange of goods, ideas, and communications—in a word the "transnationalization" of all aspects of life—is rapidly putting an end to the classical concept of frontier, understood as a line of separation, and substituting for it greater development of international cooperation, thereby shattering as well the age-old notion of sovereignty.

The practice of international relations is no longer exclusive to states, but includes many other institutions and organizations. Among them we can distinguish the regional ones that are acquiring great significance within the newly emerging Europe. In accord with this set of new realities, it becomes necessary to seriously reconsider the form and the content of the right to self-determination. On the eve of the new millennium, for Basques to aspire to self-determination and the attainment of an independent nation-state is tantamount, in my opinion, to bucking the tide of contemporary world history. I favor an approach in which the idea of creating a Basque sovereign state is relegated to a claim for a significant protagonism and participation, along with other nationalities and regions, in the configuration of future European institutions.

In the Basque case, this new strategy seems positive and necessary for two reasons: (1) as I indicated before, it is the direction in which the world as a whole is evolving; and (2) the new approach would not be divisive for Basque society, but rather could serve as its rallying point. At present, the claim of the right to secession does not favor the social, economic, cultural, and political strengthening of Euskadi. To the contrary, it implies yet another huge crack in an already weakened Basque social edifice. However, a policy directed at making the institutionalized presence of Euskadi felt within the EU could become the banner for Basque nationalists and non-nationalists alike.

In short, I believe that the definitive solution to the "Basque problem" will be intimately tied to the evolution of the institutional development of the EU. In such development it seems necessary to grant major significance to the nationalities and regions. The importance of establishing adequate formulations that accommodate them meaningfully within the emerging structure cannot be overemphasized. Adequate Basque participation in the configuration of the European Union could lessen some of the most serious conflict within Basque society itself.

Some European states, such as Germany, Austria, and Belgium, among others, have been capable of solving similar problems through formulations adapted to their own circumstances. In Germany, with its perfectly symmetrical and homogeneous federalism, there are multilateral relations among the Federal Government and the Länder. In Belgium, where two de facto nations exist, there are bilateral relationships among Belgium, Wallonie, and Flanders.

In my opinion, an intermediate hybrid system that allows the establishment of multilateral or bilateral relations could be constructed in Spain. One must take into account that the origin of the Statute of Autonomies is rooted in the existence of two different, but confluent, causes: peripheral nationalism and regionalism.

Regionalism represents an organizational criterion based on territory. The fundamental reason for nationalism is the existence of a people who share common cultural elements and an intense feeling of belonging to that collectivity. Regionalism and nationalism are therefore grounded in different principles. The former obeys a logic of organizational efficiency; the latter emphasizes the logic of difference. Each demands its own distinct constitutional guarantees. To ensure the guarantee of efficiency, it is indispensable to establish multilateral relationships; to secure the guarantee of difference, bilateral relations are critical.

On the threshold of the new century it becomes necessary to desanctify the concepts of nation and nationalism. Given its social reality, the nation is a contingent phenomenon and is therefore subject to multiple factors, events, and historical vagaries. The construction of nations often explores paths unforeseen by their proponents and takes on a life of its own as people adapt to the vagaries of specific historical moments.

And what of nation-building in the Basque case? I believe that, contrary to what has transpired thus far, the current winds blow in the direction of greater social integration. Traditionally, nationalism in general and Basque nationalism in particular have been overtly committed to the idea that the construction of a nation necessarily implies the creation of an independent state. Indeed, in the Modern Age the measure of any successful nationalism has been such culmination.

However, Europe currently constitutes a very complex reality expressed at three political levels: (1) the nation-states, which are affected by a serious crisis; (2) certain supra-state organisms, as yet weak, but which will necessarily become inexorably strong within a short time; and (3) certain ethnic formations, revindicated or in some cases consolidated, which are proclaiming their own political power. The present national problem in Europe has little to do with the creation of new states, but rather with the disappearance, or at least transformation, of the existing ones.

Euskadi has two choices. One of them, the classic and traditional option, would be to aspire to independent statehood. The second path would be to seek sufficient political power within the framework of the EU to be able to safeguard its own identity (Basqueness). Thus far Basque nationalism has pursued the goal of independence for a unified Euskal Herria (that is, unification of Iparralde, Euskadi, and Navarra). Such an objective collides with several formidable obstacles. The French state refuses to even entertain such a possibility. Even the federalist-tinged Spanish Constitution of 1978 rules it out, since it specifically guarantees cultural diversity and regional political autonomy but only within a unified Spain. Then there is the clear refusal of the Navarrese to form part of the Basque Autonomous Community. It is also doubtful that a majority of Euskadi's citizens would vote for independence in a plebiscite. In short, Basque nationalism is practically nonexistent in Iparralde, weak in Navarra, and lacks significant majority support in the Basque Autonomous Community. Therefore, what is the best choice, even in strictly utilitarian terms? The nationalist *aberrigintza* posture, which demands an independent state? Or advocacy of *herrigintza*, which is focused upon the search for economic, social, and cultural integration and unity of the various territories of Euskal Herria while, nevertheless, respecting their individual political characters?

At the moment Euskal Herria is divided into several political entities. I consider it unrealistic, and even unjust, to call for unification based on a presumed and ubiquitously diffuse "Basque" ethnos. The perfectly legitimate aspiration to the territorial integration desired by nationalist forces can never be based on ethnos, given the demographic realities and clear cultural differences in the Basque Country. Rather, if it is to have legitimacy and staying power, it must be the result of the freely expressed will of the citizenry.

In practical terms, the policy that demands that Iparralde and Navarra join Euskadi has been rejected by the Navarrese and the French Basques and produces further divisiveness. It is much more appropriate to create, from a basis of mutual respect and autonomy, instruments of collaboration that address the resolution of our common problems (economic, cultural, technological, and so forth). ·

I think that, thus far, excessive emphasis has been placed on consolidating the political-institutional structure of Euskadi to the neglect of other important social, economic, or simply human aspects. The existence of a country does not depend solely upon the attainment of political power within a sovereign structure. A previous social, cultural, and economic substratum is also necessary—one that does not yet exist in either the whole of Euskal Herria or in the Basque Autonomous Community itself.

Which is more positive— to demand secession and the creation of an independent Basque state, or to establish increasingly close, fixed, and stable institutionalized connections among the Basques and neighboring regions such as the Aquitaine, the High Pyrenees, and others? Given the present dismantling of borders in Europe, should we be emphasizing the creation of new ones (namely, the confines of a newly independent Basque state)? Is it not more rational and productive to increase and improve relations among border territories, while seeking an expanded Basque presence within the real centers of European power? Which is more rational: to inform our national vision with the past or with the future?

Alfonso Pérez-Agote

The Future of Basque Identity

There are two Enlightenment expectations that have not been fulfilled, to date at least. The first is that when science comes in through the door, religion leaves through the window. Today, the question of the meaning of life, and of the universe in general, continues to be the elusive object of the human quest and a social construction. The second expectation is that the world is moving increasingly toward larger social and political units, and that what is "small" makes no sense. True, there is formation of bigger units—witness creation of the European Union—but we are also seeing the breakup of empires and the decomposition of states.

What we call the unstoppable process of globalization is neither lineal nor simple. The state is one of the strategic places in which social scientists note the effects of these processes. We now speak of the crisis of the nation-state. This is not a crisis involving its disappearance, but rather one of complexity. In the Modern Age, the nation-state is the level on which the fundamental social processes converge, so the nation-state rationale becomes the totalizing and monopolistic logic of society. The crisis of the nation-state is the loss of this monopoly. New logics are making their appearance: the logic of globalization from above as well as the challenges from below, usually in the form of social movements, such as ethnonationalist ones, that compete with the preexisting nation-state logic. Despite this competition, the state logic persists, even as an effect of the logic of globalization that elsewhere I have called *standardizing* (Pérez-Agote 1996, 25–26). That is, today every country that wants international standing must first organize itself as a territorial state, legitimized in democratic-national terms (a legitimacy that it is difficult to achieve in many countries that have emerged recently from colonization).

Totalizing, the other logic of globalization, leads, on the one hand, to world interdependence and, on the other, to the formation of larger social and political units. This is not a mathematical law, but if we bear in mind that in the larger social units it is more difficult to construct meaning socially, we will be able to perceive how the individuals immersed in that process will attempt to build smaller units to give greater sense to their existence. Alain Touraine, in part, suggests this when he says that the nation-state is too small for the big problems and too large for the small ones (Touraine 1997: 60). Jordi Borja and Manuel Castells agree with this viewpoint when they note that the local and the regional have strategic importance as management centers of the global within the new techno-economic system. This is reflected in three principal areas: economic productivity and competitiveness, sociocultural integration, and political representation and management (Borja and Castells 1997, 14). Economic activity tends to transpire in places where the three factors coincide strategically. Arguably, the involved individuals enjoy a higher standard of living and degree of social integration.

We could think of Euskadi as a privileged place in such strategic terms, but only if the marked social and political schism that currently exists in our society does not persist. We possess a strong tradition of industry and management. Basque identity, which is what interests us here, could be a fundamental ingredient for producing sociocultural integration, as well as for giving the meaning to life and identity that the globalizing forces are incapable of producing. The same is true with respect to political representation and management inasmuch as Euskadi has the basis of a democratic political system and the potential for a reasonably high level of professional formation.

In Durkheimian terms, the formation of the nation-state as a democratic, urban, industrial, and secular society led to anomie for the individual, particularly for those who migrated from the traditional countryside to modern urban settings. Anomie is a lack of correspondence between what is known by and what affects a person. It is the sense of being powerless and influenced by things that one does not know and cannot control. In this sense, globalization produces anomie. It distances the decisions that affect individuals not only because of the increasing complexity of the organizations making them, but also because the decisions transcend the meaningful territorial boundaries of individuals. The territory is the space carved out by experience and affects. In this sense, globalization is deterritorialization. In general, we can say that modernity produces a chronic deficiency of meaning for the individual because of the systemization of the world and the privatization of the processes of production of life's meaning. Postmodernity, with its distancing through globalization and systemization and through deterritorialization and anomie, further exacerbates the individual's sense of deprivation. But this panorama of progressive abstraction, of loss of meaning, enhances the importance of those social institutions and elements that can assist the individual in acquiring a meaningful existence. It is within this context that I wish to situate the virtualities and possibilities of identity, specifically, of the various Basque identities.

Luis Michelena says that the true mystery of the Basques is not so much their origin as their survival (Michelena 1977). The origin is a mystery for anthropologists, linguists, prehistorians, and historians alike. Since time immemorial (that is, beyond what our collective memory can recover), the Basques have inhabited the land called Euskalherria and spoken a language unrelated to the Romance ones of surrounding areas.

Throughout history, our sailors, our travelers, and, above all, our emigrants have explored and settled in very distant latitudes. While some have sown those lands with their names—in the registers, the toponyms, and the street names—the majority of these emigrants have been lost without a trace. More recently, Basque emigrants to the Americas formed their own associative framework that symbolically recreates their land of origin, allowing members to maintain a new form of identity, yet referring to their Basque origins through the mythical and ritual structures that underpin any and all collective identity(ies).

This current of emigration to the Americas occurred from the mid-nineteenth century until the First World War and coincided with the industrialization of the Basque Country. Thanks to *Amerikanuak* (1975), the excellent book by William A. Douglass and Jon Bilbao, it is no mystery why, for those emigrants, America was dearer to rural Basques, in cultural terms, than the more urbanized and industrialized nuclei of the Basque Country itself. Indeed, the arrival of migrants from other parts of Spain seeking industrial employment posed a perceived threat to the continuity of a Basque way of life.

It is worth noting here that, in the Americas, the Basque centers constituted the most visible form of the socially plausible Basque identity, but not the only one. We have conducted research into the forms of Basque identity in Argentina that are not articulated through a particular Basque center, but rather expressed through less formally institutionalized structures, at least at the outset (Pérez-Agote, Azkona, and Gurrutxaga 1997).

These immigrant communities, grouped around the Basque centers in the main, received new input into their Basque colony and identity when, as a result of the Spanish Civil War and the subsequent dictatorial regime of Francisco Franco, many Basques adopted an American country as their land of exile. This renewed flow introduced into the already consolidated network of Basque centers a new symbolic relationship between the diaspora and Euskalherria. The political vicissitudes of the motherland acquired a restored presence, immediacy, and significance for generations of Basques who had been born in the New World. That this should occur, at a time in human history when improved transportation and communications had already substantially reduced the distances between continents, strengthened the collective identity of the diaspora.

In this respect, I would note a categorical response I received when conducting interviews in the 1980s with the members of the Laurak Bat Basque Center of Buenos Aires. They were the adult members of Basque families who had gone into exile forty years earlier in the post-war period. The interviewees refused, unanimously, to speak of a "diaspora" because, they said, this would mean the divine punishment of having no motherland. They did have one, but politics prevented them from being there. This provides us an inkling into the degree to which political exile strengthened, rather than weakened, the ties to their land of origin.

This diasporic Basque identity was substantially modified by: 1) a new input of direct contacts with the society of origin; 2) an interest of the immigrants' descendants in the politics of the society of origin; 3) a new organizational drive in the Basque centers; and 4) the revitalization of a general diasporic Basque identity by reference of all to a common core, the Basque Country or motherland.

This strengthening of the diasporic Basque identity through political exile was to achieve an even higher level with the end of Franco's dictatorship and the reestablishment of the democratic order in Spain. With the creation of an Autonomous Community of the Basque Country—that is, of a certain Basque political empowerment (although imperfect and incomplete)—it became possible for the new Basque government to provide political and financial encouragement to the diaspora.

The relationship with a center, endowed with a certain symbolic power and certain economic-administrative means, confers the possibility of conducting a policy of identity formation, as well as one of ethnically-conditioned, international economic development. Besides, the existence of this institutional anchor undoubtedly will increase the possibility of personal relations (contacts, trips, etc.) between Old World and New World Basques, including the possibility of organizing collective rituals of identity in both the motherland and the diaspora.

In the Basque Country itself, the original and symbolic center of "Basqueness," Basque collective identity is also played out in several scenarios and along several axes of alterity or, at least, of relationship. The more it is institutionalized, the more identity becomes visible and delimited. Of the five relevant politicoadministrative levels of government, three are internal to the Basque Country (municipal, provincial, and Basque governmental), and two are external (Spanish national and the European Union). All are affected by the institutionalization of a Basque Autonomous Community within a federal Spain.

If we consider the so-called "Basque sociometric" (public opinion poll), there is evident skewing in favor of local controls. Indeed, the closer to home, the more popular the level of government. Thus, the municipal councils receive a 64 percent approval rating; the provincial deputations, 61 percent; and the Basque government, 57 percent. There follows then a precipitous drop to 30 percent for the Spanish government and to 28 percent for the European Union (*Sociómetro Vasco* 1998). It should be noted that relations with Europe and the political institutionalization of these relations are both quite recent. Basque nationalist politicians place great emphasis on European ties as a possibility for effecting suprastate institutionalization that would accommodate direct political relations between the Basque Country and Europe while circumventing Madrid. But, apart from the fact that, for now at least, Europe is a union of states and not one of *ethnies*, democratic politics at the Continental level are nascent and deficient. Therefore, the Basques, for the time being, do not place their trust in that political structure.

The central government, as the incarnation of the Spanish state, has been the most important form of political alterity for Basque identity. Hence my discussion about the future of that identity will focus on a double axis: the historical conflict with the state center and the internal relations within Basque society itself.

As an authoritarian system, Francoism prevented the expression and reproduction of the Basque language, culture, and nationalist ideology in the public sphere (the political arena, the educational system, the mass media). Their reproduction therefore withdrew to the private circles of social life: family and friends, the microsocial facets of the Catholic Church, and the framework of seemingly apolitical associations (but ones that concealed a broad range of nationalist political socialization). In these private arenas, a progressive, affective identification with the violence of Euskadi Ta Askatasuna (ETA) emerged. ETA was the most visible part of the response of the first nationalist generation of the postwar period, which, in general, became radicalized in nationalist and ideological terms with respect to its parental generation.

Throughout the 1960s, the two social processes of confrontation (the violence between the state and ETA) and reinforcement (ETA's violence and collective support of it) increased the pressure within the Basque intersubjective framework, which, under Franco, had been reduced to silence. About 1970, the public expression of collective discontent emerged. After 1970, the *cuadrillas* (groups of friends) and the memberships of some associations take to the streets during the crucial dramatic moments of social life (political protests, funerals of ETA activists, etc.). The occupation of the streets, in spite of its intermittent character, supposes the emergence and display of Basque symbology: i.e., nationalism and other symbols of difference become public. There is a process in which public expression increasingly is given to a consciousness that heretofore had been guarded in private. In general, Basque nationalism came to enjoy dominance of the streets, and other public spaces, that was disproportionate to its electoral strength.

This process, whereby collective life becomes politicized, intervenes in and influences the confrontation and reinforcement of the previous period. There is now mutual reinforcement of collective life, occupation of the streets, and the violence of ETA, and these solidly interlocked three elements confront state violence. This complex social dynamic culminates in the first years of post-Francoism, creating difficulties for the political rationalization and normalization of Basque society in this period of political reform. Beginning in 1970, the political venue of this dynamic was the street, and, therefore, in initial post-Francoism it proved difficult to insulate politics from collective street life in order to situate it in a different social sphere, i.e., where the representatives of the people (the professional politicians) act (representation as both political delegation and in the theatrical sense). This constitution of politics into a differentiated social sphere is, after all, the Western political model, the one to which Spanish society adjusted by means of the so-called political reform or democratization of Spain.

Following the death of Franco, the progressive establishment of the so-called Statute of the Autonomous Communities (of Spain) set in motion a series of events. First, it became possible to form political parties. In general, this led almost immediately to the rupture of the unanimity among the forces of anti-Francoism, i.e., their common front during the dictatorship. It also created a split between ethnonationalist parties (Basque, Catalan, etc.) and Spanish nationalist ones. Different political alternatives have emerged and the citizens must opt for one of them, particularly at election time.

Another consequence of the functioning of these institutions for channeling political demands is, logically, a reduction of the political pressure on society in general. As a result, there is a shift in the social attitudes toward political violence. A progressive splintering occurred within the Basque political continuum over attitudes toward the violence of ETA. It is a continuum that was, and is, configured by the existence of a social mechanism that we might call reason-sentiment ambivalence. That is, within the nationalist world, a person who was politically opposed in principle to ETA's tactics could nevertheless, and because of his personal experience under Franco-ism, harbor positive affective feelings toward the violence. The super-position of disparate political discourses would progressively force social actors to choose between them, i.e., to support or oppose the violence.

Beneath the process of progressive political institutionalization (that is, the channeling of political demands by the parties, the con-centration of political life in the new political institutions, the de-crease in the importance of the street as the place where politics are realized, and the rupture of the reason-sentiment schism because of the social penetration of the political discourse) there nonetheless continues to exist an important bastion of radical nationalism that does not accept the institutional centering of politics (upon the new Spanish state and the autonomous Basque government). This bastion, besides being important in numerical terms (its political party, Herri Batasuna (HB), receives some 16 percent of the votes in the Basque Autonomous Community), exercises a certain attraction for the younger generations. Above all, this is because of its capacity to at-tract the votes and active political participation of the members of the new youth movements in general, as well as the antimilitarists, anti-nuclearists, ecologists, and gay rights' advocates in particular.

The second fundamental element put in motion by the constitution of a Basque autonomous political power has been a certain cultural, symbolic, and linguistic liberalization. In the first place, this produces a strengthening of the internal (i.e., to the Basque nationalist world) dimension of the conflict. The Francoists' repression of the Basque language gave rise to a traumatic awareness of its imperiled and frag-ile state. This consciousness, in turn, produced a positive political overvaluation of the language, one that defined the linguistic conflict as primordially a political one with the Spanish state. The setting in motion of democratic political institutions internal to Basque soci-ety—ones that have the legal, administrative, and economic means for effecting cultural and linguistic recovery—produces internal de-bate over what should be done and how, and by which of the afore-mentioned means.

In the Basque Country there has been a strong decline in the social cohesion of the intersubjective and affective framework, such that the process of progressive privatization of life has accelerated in spite of the fact that certain social phenomena continue to constitute a brake. In particular, there is the periodic recourse of political actors, at times of various persuasions, to public political demonstrations organized in a professedly nonpartisan spirit.

This decline of social density, in relation to the associative world, has two facets. The first is quantitative, which might be debatable because of the current proliferation of new associative forms. The second, which is fundamental for this discussion, is the redefinition of the associations whose aims were ostensibly cultural (sporting, gastronomic, etc.). While, during Francoism, under the appearance of pursuing their stated aims, these associations systematically harbored the hidden function of political socialization, at present, we find that, generally, they restrict themselves exclusively to their explicit (nonpolitical) activities.

If we return to the political associations that were created (or that became visible) during the Transition, the political parties currently do not have a strong capacity to recruit the new generations. It is a fairly widely held opinion that the most radical sector of Basque nationalism has the greatest capacity for attracting the youth. Of course, this does not mean that the majority of the young are adopting more or less organized radical positions. What we wish to point out is that the word "youth" constitutes a plural world in terms of attitudes, values, and beliefs, and that most of the young fail to join any political party, although they may inscribe in other types of organizations that have political effects. On the other hand, there is a youthful minority within the current of radical nationalism.

At present, it is possible to speak of a very profound decline in this social world of the *cuadrillas* and their collective ritual. The private world of social actors is becoming increasingly important. It now occupies the time and energy that was previously devoted to the collective intersubjective world, to one that had considerable public-political projection.

As we have contended in other works (Pérez-Agote 1987, 1992), the legalization of associative liberties and the creation of Basque autonomous political power substantially modified the future of the symbolic political conflict between Basque nationalism and the central

Spanish state. While the conflict did not disappear entirely, of course, a new political space was etched out within the Basque Country itself, with attendant competition among the Basque political forces over control of the new economic, legal, and symbolic-political resources. On the one hand, as noted, anti-Francoist unanimity shattered and, within it, Basque nationalist unanimity threatened to rupture as well. Onto the habitual tensions between the parties of the left and right within Spanish politics were grafted the tensions between these parties and the Basque nationalists, as well as the internal tensions of the latter. This produced a complex array of institutional political actors. Pivotal is moderate nationalism—at times confronting the Spanish State parties in tandem with the other Basque nationalist forces, while at others confronting the radical nationalist world, which can even entail a degree of rapprochement with the Spanish. As if the situation were not complicated enough, there is also a contemporary split within moderate Basque nationalism. In what follows, we will try to establish the tendencies toward fission and toward fusion within the Basque nationalist world.

Tendencies toward Fission within Basque Nationalism

1. The element that most divides the symbolic nationalist universe is the present ethical and political debate over ETA's violence.

In other works (Pérez-Agote 1984, 1992), we show how, during Francoism, ETA's violence achieved strong affective support within broad sectors of the Basque population, given the total prohibition on public expression of discontent or of any ideological or cultural manifestations that differed from the official ideology. This state violence, symbolic and physical, provided legitimacy to the political violence of ETA. This sentiment was experienced by a society that was both very small and very dense. With the Transition, the political discourse of the moderate nationalist parties has gradually reduced the legitimacy of ETA's violence. However, a mechanism—the one we have referred to as the reason-sentiment schism—was at work within Basque social life, which meant that, within nationalist circles, even those for whom the violence was politically incorrect, there was, nevertheless, a certain sentimental acceptance of it, based on biographical memories. Eventually, the political discourse of moderate nationalist individuals and institutions rejected this stance. Now moderate nationalists refer to the violence in absolutely negative terms.

In the public sphere, tension is increasing at the local level, and the disagreement between HB and the remaining political parties (not only Basque nationalist ones), is evident.

This institutional isolation of radical nationalism is increasing in part because of the violent actions of ETA against individuals, but also because of the attacks on political party offices as a part of the campaign of street violence.

2. *This internal struggle within Basque nationalist ranks (although not exclusively within nationalism) has posed, in the public mind, the danger of the possibility of a general civil conflagration. At certain times and places, collective confrontations are already taking place.*

But, in addition to the personal and collective confrontations, we can point to the strong ritualization of the civil confrontation with the appearance of certain pacifist groups and their rituals, particularly those of the organization *Gesto por la Paz*. Its periodic silent rallies in every district and village, including ones following a death by an armed action, led to countermanifestations by radical nationalist individuals at the same time and in the same place. These ritualized confrontations do not appear—at least, not frequently—to have reached the point of physical conflict, in spite of the moments of very dramatic tension between those observing silence and those shouting radical nationalist slogans.

3. *Another of the elements contributing to a certain schism in the nationalist world is the appearance of a new form of quotidian urban youth violence, one that does not derive from mass mobilization.*

The street struggle has evolved in recent years. There has always been a certain degree of street violence associated with the world of radical youth. But it was usually the final outcome of a mass rally, a kind of concluding ritual violence. In this regard, it was predictable action and, in principle, unplanned. Nevertheless, at present, there is a new and ominous development: the arrival in a village or district of a group of youths who, wearing hoods, carry out violent acts, such as burning bank automated teller machines, buses, and business establishments. This is not a spontaneous mass action, but rather one that is planned, orchestrated, and led.

4. *The fusions provoked by the tension within Basque nationalism: its fissions produce fusions in other areas.*

In every situation of social stress, an increase of tension implies greater fusion at each of the extremes and produces a certain capacity for coexistence and political agreement between the Basque moderate nationalist currents and the Spanish political forces. On the other hand, the radical nationalist world is becoming denser. There is evident strong fusion and greater cohesion internal to it:

- the rupture of the mechanism of the reason-sentiment schism obviates, at least partially, the plausibility and efficacy of broad mass mobilizations merely through radical slogans. The radical political organizations must undergo a functional change in order to adapt to the situation: from the attempt to mobilize sympathetic masses to the formation of nuclei that are more motivated by a coherent focal doctrine.
- the central discourse, progressively self-centered and without fissures, corresponds to a feeling of isolation.
- there is a greater ideological coherence in relationships among peers.
- the radical nationalists' capacity to attract youths is greater, relative to that of other political organizations, given the generally greater political-religious pluralism of the interpeer youth groups.
- it has a greater power to attract and provide support regarding social conflicts in general.
- the radical world constitutes an authentic one, in the sense of its being a network of attraction and indoctrination. (For the present concern of Jarrai, the youth movement supporting ETA, with education and indoctrination within this world, compare *El Correo*, 1 April 1998.) It is also a network of logistical plausibility for the actions of the youth movement (politically denoted bars and social centers).

Tendencies toward Fusion within Basque Nationalism

In a schematic, and certainly hypothetical, way we can now enumerate certain elements that could induce a tendency toward fusion within the Basque nationalist world. This is not to say that we see fusion as a dominant tendency; to the contrary, fission predominates. However, we will now consider certain phenomena of nationalist conflation.

a. The movement to bring Basque prisoners held in Spanish prisons closer to the Basque Country constitutes one of the axes of agreement across the Basque nationalist-political spectrum.

b. Another of the elements that is inducing a nationalist fusion is the agreement between LAB and ELA, the two most powerful trade unions in the Basque Country.

c. Other types of plausibility of nationalist conflation could come from the use of the Basque language, Euskera: both from new structures of pluralist coexistence with a predominance of Euskera in public and private life and from certain pragmatic (nonideological) positions of Euskera's promoters on political negotiation with respect to ETA's violence.

d. And, last but not least, another factor of Basque nationalist fusion is the ever-increasing, evident Spanish nationalism of our times.

Bibliography

Borja, Jordi and Manuel Castells. *Local y global: La gestión de las ciudades en la era de la información.* Madrid: Taurus, 1997.

Douglass, William A. and Jon Bilbao. *Amerikanuak: Basques in the New World.* Reno: University of Nevada Press, 1975.

Michelena, Luis. "El largo y difícil camino del Euskera." *El Libro Blanco del Euskera.* Bilbao: Real Academia de la Lengua Vasca, 1977.

Pérez-Agote, Alfonso. *La reproducción del nacionalismo: El caso vasco.* Madrid: Centro de Investigaciones Sociológicas—Siglo XXI, 1984.

———. *El nacionalismo vasco a la salida del Franquismo.* Madrid: Centro de Investigaciones Sociológicas—Siglo XXI, 1987.

————. "Silence collectif et violence politique. La radicalisation sociale du nationalisme Basque." *Espaces et Sociétés*, vols. 70–71, 57–72, 1992.

————. "La sociedad se difumina, el individuo se disgrega. Sobre la necesidad de historizar nuestras categorías." *Complejidad y teoría social.* Edited by A. Pérez-Agote and I. Sánchez Incera. Madrid: Centro de Investigaciones Sociológicas, 1996.

Pérez-Agote, Alfonso, Jesus Azkona, and Ander Gurrutxaga. *Mantener la identidad: Los vascos del Río Carabelas.* Bilbao: Servicio Editorial Universidad del País Vasco, 1997.

Sociómetro vasco. Vitoria-Gasteiz: Gabinete de Prospecciones Sociológicas, Gobierno Vasco, 1998.

Touraine, Alain. *¿Podremos vivir juntos? Iguales y diferentes.* Madrid: PPC, 1997.

Iñaki Zabaleta

The Basques in the International Press: Coverage by the *New York Times* (1950–1996)

In this world of increasing globalization, where direct personal experience and knowledge are being replaced by indirect and mediated social interaction via mass media and on-line networks, we have to address seriously the role mass media play in creating, maintaining, and transforming the images and stereotypes of social groups and nations, such as the Basques. At the same time, we must reassess the importance, effect, usefulness, and convenience of such images and stereotypes.

Image Creation by the Media

No one would deny the importance of establishing a clear conceptual difference between the *image presented* by the media through news items, opinion articles, and advertising about a social group or nation and the *image perceived* by the audience. In both concepts, there are elements of social categorization and stereotyping, but the fundamental viewpoints are different. The image presented can be described through analysis of the information flow; the image perceived must be inferred using social psychology.

It is also well known that the image an audience holds about a nation is the product of numerous sources of information and interaction, ranging from visits to the country in question and contacts with its citizens to secondhand information obtained from, for example, media, literature, film, art, education, and acquaintances. Of all these image-making factors, the news media are widely credited with playing a particularly significant role, (*cf.* "Media Dependency Theory"[1]) (Ball-Rokeach and Defleur 1976).

Nevertheless, as David K. Perry, William H. Melson, and Tammie Howard said in their 1997 experimental research, although international news flow stresses "bad news" (events of conflicts, violence, accidents, and disasters), such coverage may not have a constant and correlated effect on the audience. They concluded that "the research adds to suspicions that the whole debate about negative news is overstated or misdirected" (1997, 16). Several correlational studies support this line of argumentation (Korzenny et al. 1987; McNelly and Izcaray 1986; Perry 1990; Perry 1989; Semetko et al. 1992).

Perry, in another study (1996), brings new evidence to the hypothesis that the nature of the news' content does not inevitably determine its effects upon audiences. More specifically, *schema theory* for cognitive processing suggests that infrequent and negative coverage of underdeveloped countries may sometimes, but not always, contribute to negative stereotypes.

In order to understand this statement, we should focus on the concept of "bad news" and realize that, *grosso modo,* there may be two kinds: one mostly ruled by *inevitability*[2]—or perceived as such, as in the case of earthquakes, accidents, natural disasters, and even those domestic political and economic crises with no direct effect upon the audience—and another produced by society and individuals, as in crimes, violence, and terrorism. The first type of bad news does not suppose any risk to the interests of the government and the people served by the media (and, in that case, Perry's conclusions can be valid). It could even be argued that such news may promote solidarity within the audience, often mixed with a touch of contempt toward that "inevitably-bad-news-driven" country because of its lack of apparent knowledge or expertise. In the 1997 research by Perry and his colleagues, the "non-dangerous" bad news items were earthquakes and economic crises in Libya, Nigeria, and Mexico.

Finally, we should remember that negative information has more impact on a person's evaluation of a country if he or she has little prior knowledge of, or contact with, it. As a person's familiarity increases, "dangerous negative information should have less effect" (Perry 1996, 13).

Media Coverage of Terrorism

George Gerbner, an American media scholar of international repute, stated that the U.S. media and government policy put increasing emphasis on terrorism. He studied the media coverage and the research done on the subject and, based on M. Cherif Bassiouni's (1982, 1981) and others' studies, pointed out that "although international terrorism against states receives most attention, terrorist acts by states and in a national context are far more numerous" (Gerbner 1992, 95).

David L. Paletz et al. (1982) analyzed the *New York Times* coverage of the Irish Republican Army (IRA), the Italy-based Red Brigades, and the Puerto Rican group, Armed Forces of National Liberation (Fuerzas Armadas de Liberación Nacional [FALN]) between 1977 and 1979 and found no grounds for the charge that coverage tried to legitimize the cause of a terrorist organization. To the contrary, 70 percent of the stories did not mention either the cause or the objectives of the group. Another study of U.S. networks (M. A. Milburn et al. 1987) noted the same absence of causal explanations in the stories and the frequent attribution of mental instability to the perpetrators of terrorist acts that affected the United States.[3]

Robert G. Picard, author of *Media Portrayals of Terrorism: Functions and Meaning of News Coverage* (1993), sets forth some research findings upon which most scholars agree:

1. State terrorism is generally ignored, and the criticism of this reality by scholars and observers has been mostly forgotten by the media.

2. The amount of nonstate terrorism covered is limited. Only 2 or 3 percent of the incidents of nonstate terrorism that occur annually worldwide receive coverage in the U.S. press. According to Michael J. Kelly and Thomas H. Mitchell (1981), this is due to the fact that the media mostly focus their attention on the region they are located in, ignoring terrorism that occurs outside.

3. News coverage concentrates on incidents and government issues, to the detriment of background explanatory information.

4. The coverage among different media is similar.

As Picard points out, the problem of understanding reality is particularly salient when dealing with sociopolitical issues, such as terrorism, because, in some instances, "one man's terrorist is another man's freedom fighter" and, according to some research, even journalists have particular difficulty determining the differences between irregular warfare and terrorism (1993; 96–97)

Studies on the labeling of terrorist acts and perpetrators have found that, in general, the American media appear to make an effort to be neutral or balanced in reporting terrorism that does not affect American interests (but when bias enters coverage, it tends to favor social order and the status quo) and that there is a similarity in how terrorist violence is covered by different media (Picard 1993; Simmons 1991).

Picard and Adams (1991) studied the subject of terrorism coverage by three standard elite newspapers during 1980–1985[4] and found that the journalists and editors used *terrorist*, the label with the highest negative connotation, only 7.8 percent of the time, a far smaller percentage than the 38.1 percent usage of the equivalent labels with moderate or slightly negative connotations (*gunman, guerrilla, rebel, leftist, extremist, armed man*).[5]

But the results in Simmons's study (1991) of weekly magazines[6] were quite different. He found that the most commonly used term was *terrorist* (a 65 percent frequency). The second was *gunman* (7 percent), and the rest of the labels (*guerrilla, attacker, extremist,* and *radical*) had respective frequencies in the 3–5 percent range. This evident discrepancy may have to do also with the distinctive nature of daily newspapers versus weekly magazines. In any case, the figures differ.

Simmons further observed that "when those opposed to U.S. policy committed a terrorist act, [these] news magazines labeled them as *terrorists* 72% of the time. However, the same term was used only 55% of the time when the act was committed by those neutral toward U.S. policy" (Simmons 1991, 30).

Finally, John Martin's study (1983) of the words *terrorism* and *terrorist* in the U.S. press found that the terms would be used in headlines only if there was a prevalent disposition against the group involved, which resembles Simmons's findings and the idea that American interests play an important role in media labeling of terrorism.

These findings will have greater relevance when we look at international media coverage of the Basques because most of it refers to terrorist acts by the Basque guerrilla group, Euskadi Ta Askatasuna (ETA).

International News Flow

Thomas Ahern (1984) developed a *factor typology*[7] to explain international news flow. It distinguishes between *intrinsic factors*, those that pertain to the event itself—that is, to the newsworthiness of the story (relevance, consequences, etc.)—and *extrinsic factors*, those characteristic of the broader context, such as geopolitics, foreign policy, national interests, and trade.

Ahern found that the most relevant extrinsic factors affecting coverage were *gross national product* (GNP), *trade,* and *political relations.* Together, these three variables accounted for 59 percent of the variance. However, the relationship between trade and foreign news is not totally clear, as other scholars suggest.

The statistical analysis conducted in the Canadian press by Herbert G. Kariel and Lynn A. Rosenvall (1984) of the factors influencing international news flow showed that four—*population, trade, gross national product,* and *eliteness*—were statistically significant in predicting news coverage of about twenty-four countries. *Eliteness* appeared as the most significant predictor of international news flow.

The notion of *"eliteness,"* a term mentioned by Johan Galtung and Mari H. Ruge (1965), was defined in a quite ambiguous way by Kariel and Rosenvall (1984) as "the relative standing of nations in the eyes of others" (p. 511). Some authors identify *elite nations* as those highly developed countries that are also dominant in world politics.

However, in a survey conducted by Tsan-Kuo Chang and Jae-Won Lee (1990) among U.S. newspaper editors, the results suggested that, when making international news coverage decisions, editors' primary concerns were with both the U.S. *geopolitical interests and involvement abroad* and *world peace threats.* Economic factors, such as U.S. trade relations and a country's level of economic development, were of little significance. Catherine Cassara, in her 1995 study, reached the same conclusion.

The factor of *cultural affinity* gets mixed results and that of *physical distance* seems to have no import in coverage when referring to distant places.

Finally, among the explanations for the inadequate and unbalanced coverage of certain areas of the world, some scholars argue that *struc-*

tural factors, such as the geographic distribution of the personnel of the bureaus of the news agencies (Associated Press, for example), influence international coverage inasmuch as these bureaus generate most of the wire copy for the small and medium-sized media.

Looking more specifically at the international news flow in the U.S. media, Daniel Riffe said that the foreign news flow is decreasing significantly, particularly regarding First-World news (1993). On the other hand, Third-World coverage is increasing. More precisely, from 1969 to 1990, the mean percentages of news flow in the *New York Times* for the so-called "three worlds" were: First World 43 percent, Second World 14 percent, and Third World 43 percent.

In that same study of the "bad news" about the Third World in the *New York Times* over a twenty-two-year span, Riffe concluded that 50 percent of the Third-World coverage is *bad news,* compared with only 22 percent in the First World, and 27 percent in the Second World. The differences are significant.

Coverage of the Basques in the International Media: The Representative Case of the *New York Times*

In this study, we analyze the information flow and type of news about the Basques[8] in the *New York Times,* one of the most influential and international newspapers in the world. The reason for choosing this newspaper is that many other scholars use it in similar studies.

The specific research questions refer to quantitative information flow about the Basques, the nature of the news content, and the labeling of the violent group ETA. We will look also at the effect news of the Basques has upon the total coverage of Spain.

Our study takes into account the Basques in general, regardless of their region of residence (southern France, northern Spain, or even the Basques of the United States). Nevertheless, it is quite evident that practically all of the news flow about the Basques in the *New York Times,* and in other international media, refers to the Basques of Spain. This is so even though some Spanish Basques, or the events related to them, are located in the French region (as refugees, members of ETA, or the victims of terrorist acts by the Spanish govern-ment–supported Grupo Antiterroristas de Liberación (GAL)).

The time span considered for the analysis of Basque information extends from 1950 through 1996, forty-seven years of extraordinary significance, extending from the Cold War almost to the present and including Spain's transition to democracy after dictator Francisco Franco's death in 1975.

The methods we have used are content[9] and linguistic analysis[10]: the first for categorizing the news and the second for studying the adjectival characterization of ETA.

The category system used here for the news-content analysis is based on other scholars' previous work (Burgoon et al. 1984; Potter 1987) and it has been slightly modified to accommodate the Basque reality, especially in the case of the subcategories of "conflict."

1. *Government:* any activity by any government department includ-ing military; foreign, local, national and international politics; political parties and leaders and their activities.

2. *Conflict:* terrorism, street and police violence, demonstrations, right-wing activities, labor conflicts, strikes, natural disasters and accidents, and drug traffic. This category is similar to Bur-goon's "sensational" category[11] (Burgoon, et al. 1984). We divide this general category of "conflict" into four subcategories: a) *sociopolitical*—social and political demonstrations and conflicts, strikes, labor conflicts, trials for sociopolitical activities, crime, and drug smuggling; b) *terrorism*—terrorist and violent activi-ties by ETA and Spanish state-supported terrorist groups, such as GAL; c) *torture*—news about this activity practiced by the police on Basques, according to the newspaper; d) *other*—any other type of tense event, such as natural disasters or accidents.

3. *Economy:* Economic (but not governmental) activity, money, la-bor agreements, business, market, agriculture, and industry. *Sub-categories:* agriculture, industry, finance, other.

4. *Science-technology:* education, modernization, innovations, tech-nology, health, environment. *Subcategories:* education, environ-ment, health, technology, other.

5. *Popular:* sports, travel and vacations, art, culture, amazing fea-tures, tourism, lifestyles, popular figures (writers, artists, fa-

mous people), gastronomy, bullfighting, entertainment. *Subcategories:* sports, culture, travel, people, entertainment, other.

Results of the Coverage of the Basques

First we examine the quantity of news stories about the Basques in the *New York Times* between 1950 and 1996 (see table 1). Are there differences over time? How intense is the international media attention regarding the Basques?

Between 1950 and 1996, there were 674 news items on the Basques in the *New York Times,* the vast majority of them bits of information along with a few op-eds. The average is twenty-five items per year, i.e., one news item every fifteen days. We can discern five periods in the table:

1. *1950–1970:* average of ten items per year (standard deviation of eight). A period of very low coverage. It was the time of the Cold War. The Basques were silent about themselves and, apparently, did not produce internationally newsworthy events. The year 1955 sticks out with only one news item. At the end of this period, in 1970, we observe the beginning of a trend change: the average increases to twenty-two news items annually (which also raises the standard deviation of the period by three points). This evident increment of the journalistic weight of the Basques is due to their violent political struggle for their freedom, entailing opposition to Franco's dictatorship.

2. *1975–1981:* average of fifty-three items per year (standard deviation of ten). The period of greatest reportage. It seems that the international media monitored the Basque reality closely, paying special attention to terrorist violence and, to a lesser degree, to political turmoil. Probably, the *New York Times* considered that the Basque reality affected the Spanish political transition unfolding at the time in a relevant way.

3. *1982–1987:* average of twenty-eight items per year (standard deviation of ten). An important reduction in information flow, with an average almost equal to the general one (twenty-five items per year). This period started with the 1982 victory of the Socialists

TABLE 1. *Quantity of Basque Information Flow (1950–1996)*

Year	Basque News Flow	Mean	Standard Deviation
1950	12		
1955	1		
1960	9		
1965	6		
1970	22	10	8
1975	59		
1976	49		
1977	62		
1978	39		
1979	68		
1980	47		
1981	50	53	10
1982	23		
1983	15		
1984	43		
1985	26		
1986	36		
1987	22	28	10
1988	7		
1989	14		
1990	8		
1991	4		
1992	7		
1993	8		
1994	3	7	4
1995	19		
1996	15	17	3
Total	674	25	20

Numbers represent news items; mean and standard deviation values are rounded up.

in the general elections of Spain. It seems as if the Basques lost some international media attention.

4. *1988–1994:* average of seven items per year (standard deviation of four). This is the period with the least coverage; indeed, it is quite similar to the 1950–1970 period. During the transitional Cold War years, it is evident that the Basques were not newsworthy at the international level. As we will see later in the tables on content types, almost all the news was about violence and conflict.

5. *1994–1996:* average of seventeen items per year (standard deviation of three). Although this two-year span does not seem long enough to form a period of its own, we decided to highlight it because it seems to reflect a new trend, a news flow recovery in the *New York Times.* This trend may have continued until the 1997 opening of the Guggenheim Museum in Bilbao and some other recent newsworthy events.

We may now consider the information content of Basque news items in the *New York Times* over the same 1950–1996 period (see table 2).

The vast majority of the information on the Basques is related to the category of "Conflict." With an astonishing 93.8 percent, this category requires closer scrutiny. The second category, "Government," has a general mean of only 4.0 percent, and "Popular," a mere 1.7 percent. The category of "Science-technology," including education, is practically absent.

We can observe that media attention to the category of "Government"—one that includes not only any government action but also the life and activities of political parties and their leaders—clusters during the period 1977–1985, the time of the creation of Basque autonomy with its regional government and parliament, as well as of the political transition in Spain. During those eight years, the average of "political information" articles in relation to total flow was 13.3 percent. After 1985, the *New York Times* covers practically no Basque political or governmental activity. (A note of caution: the 100 percent value of "economy" in 1955 corresponds to a single news item, the only one about the Basques published during that year.)

Clearly, in order to penetrate further into the analysis of the media

TABLE 2. *Basque Information Type, 1950–1996*

Year	Conflict	Government	Popular	Economy	Total
1950	*100.0%*	*0.0%*	*0.0%*	*0.0%*	*100.0%*
1955	*0.0%*	*0.0%*	*0.0%*	*100.0%*	*100.0%*
1960	*100.0%*	*0.0%*	*0.0%*	*0.0%*	*100.0%*
1965	*100.0%*	*0.0%*	*0.0%*	*0.0%*	*100.0%*
1970	*95.5%*	*0.0%*	*4.5%*	*0.0%*	*100.0%*
1975	100.0%	0.0%	0.0%	0.0%	100.0%
1976	100.0%	0.0%	0.0%	0.0%	100.0%
1977	83.3%	16.7%	0.0%	0.0%	100.0%
1978	100.0%	0.0%	0.0%	0.0%	100.0%
1979	85.7%	14.3%	0.0%	0.0%	100.0%
1980	75.0%	25.0%	0.0%	0.0%	100.0%
1981	77.8%	11.1%	11.1%	0.0%	100.0%
1982	88.9%	11.1%	0.0%	0.0%	100.0%
1983	100.0%	0.0%	0.0%	0.0%	100.0%
1984	83.3%	16.7%	0.0%	0.0%	100.0%
1985	75.0%	25.0%	0.0%	0.0%	100.0%
1986	100.0%	0.0%	0.0%	0.0%	100.0%
1987	100.0%	0.0%	0.0%	0.0%	100.0%
1988	100.0%	0.0%	0.0%	0.0%	100.0%
1989	50.0%	0.0%	50.0%	0.0%	100.0%
1990	100.0%	0.0%	0.0%	0.0%	100.0%
1991	100.0%	0.0%	0.0%	0.0%	100.0%
1992	100.0%	0.0%	0.0%	0.0%	100.0%
1993	*100.0%*	*0.0%*	*0.0%*	*0.0%*	*100.0%*
1994	*100.0%*	*0.0%*	*0.0%*	*0.0%*	*100.0%*
1995	*100.0%*	*0.0%*	*0.0%*	*0.0%*	*100.0%*
1996	*100.0%*	*0.0%*	*0.0%*	*0.0%*	*100.0%*
Total	93.8%	4.0%	1.7%	0.6%	100.0%

Total N = 177 items. During the years marked in italics, all of the news items about the Basques published by the *New York Times* were coded (1950, 1955, 1960, 1965, 1970, and 1993–96). For the rest of the years, 1975–1992, we used adequate samples. Notwithstanding, the use of samples can produce slight errors of around 5 percent in the results. Consequently, it is quite probable that some 0 percent sample results might really have a value of up to 5 percent had we coded the total number of articles.

coverage of Basques, it is absolutely necessary to look more closely at the general category of "Conflict." For that purpose, we subdivided it into four subcategories: (a) *sociopolitical*—any kind of social and/or political conflict such as demonstrations, strikes, crimes, and trials; (b) *terrorism*—violent activities by ETA and any other group, and that which is directly related to them; (c) *torture*—news about this practice by the police; (d) *other:* accidents, disasters, etc. Here are the results.

In table 3 the subcategory that dominates the information flow about the Basques in the *New York Times* is "terrorism," constituting 65.5 percent of the total Basque coverage. Next is "sociopolitical" conflict, with 24.3 percent of the total flow. For the category of "terrorism," there are three periods:

1. *1950–1965:* during this first period there were no information items on this subject because there were no terrorist acts due to the fact that ETA was not operating in a violent fashion as yet.
2. *1970–1985:* in this second period terrorist news makes up 64.3 percent of the total coverage.
3. *1986–1996:* with a mean of 90.9 percent in relation to the total flow of these years. During this third period the pattern of information flow on "terrorism" is constant and increasing, except for the year 1989.

These figures require some consideration. It is quite significant that, during the last eleven years of the study (1986–1996), 90.9 percent of the Basque-related coverage was about terrorism, or much more than in the previous period from 1970 to 1985 (64.3 percent). It looks as if the Basques lost international newsworthiness and informative weighting as a people and nationality in their own right. It was as if their regular social, political, and economic life—including the workings of their regional autonomous political institutions—were not worth media coverage. The sole exception is terrorism, a subcategory of bad news that the audience usually perceives to be linked to so-called Third-World coverage.

In the subcategory of "sociopolitical" conflict there are also three periods:

1. *1950–1965:* the dictator Franco's years, with a mean of 70.8 percent in regard to the total flow of that period. They were the

TABLE 3. *Types of Conflict in the Basque Information Flow 1950–1996*

Year	Terrorism	Socio-political	Torture	Others	Total Conflict
1950	0.0%	100.0%	0.0%	0.0%	100.0%
1955	0.0%	0.0%	0.0%	0.0%	0.0%
1960	0.0%	100.0%	0.0%	0.0%	100.0%
1965	0.0%	83.3%	16.7%	0.0%	100.0%
1970	68.2%	27.3%	0.0%	0.0%	95.5%
1975	66.7%	16.7%	0.0%	16.7%	100.0%
1976	20.0%	40.0%	40.0%	0.0%	100.0%
1977	50.0%	16.7%	0.0%	16.7%	83.3%
1978	50.0%	50.0%	0.0%	0.0%	100.0%
1979	85.7%	0.0%	0.0%	0.0%	85.7%
1980	75.0%	0.0%	0.0%	0.0%	75.0%
1981	77.8%	0.0%	0.0%	0.0%	77.8%
1982	77.8%	11.1% ·	0.0%	0.0%	88.9%
1983	100.0%	0.0%	0.0%	0.0%	100.0%
1984	50.0%	33.3%	0.0%	0.0%	83.3%
1985	50.0%	0.0%	25.0%	0.0%	75.0%
1986	100.0%	0.0%	0.0%	0.0%	100.0%
1987	100.0%	0.0%	0.0%	0.0%	100.0%
1988	100.0%	0.0%	0.0%	0.0%	100.0%
1989	0.0%	50.0%	0.0%	0.0%	50.0%
1990	100.0%	0.0%	0.0%	0.0%	100.0%
1991	100.0%	0.0%	0.0%	0.0%	100.0%
1992	100.0%	0.0%	0.0%	0.0%	100.0%
1993	100.0%	0.0%	0.0%	0.0%	100.0%
1994	100.0%	0.0%	0.0%	0.0%	100.0%
1995	100.0%	0.0%	0.0%	0.0%	100.0%
1996	100.0%	0.0%	0.0%	0.0%	100.0%
Total	65.5%	24.3%	2.3%	1.7%	93.8%

Total N = 166 items. The final column, "Total Conflict," represents the "Conflict" column of table 2 (with 93.0 percent as the final total). Also, in the years marked in italics, all of the news items about the Basques published by the *New York Times* were coded (1950, 1955, 1960, 1965, 1970, and 1993–96). For the rest of the years, 1975–1992, we used adequate samples. Notwithstanding, the use of samples can produce slight errors of around 5 percent in the results.

years of the beginning of the Basque uprising against Spanish rule, and the news items were about, for example, demonstrations and the trials of Basque priests for defending the use of their forbidden language and culture.

2. *1970–1978:* the second period, with an average of 30.1 percent of the total flow of those years, had similar content in the news items (political demonstrations, trials, etc.), but there is a notable reduction from the previous period, due to an increment of the category of terrorism, mentioned above. This period corresponds to the last years of Franco's dictatorship, which ended in 1975, and the first part of the Spanish political transition (1976–1978), dominated by Francoist politicians such as Adolfo Suarez, Fraga Iribarne, and Martin Villa who became democrats. It is worth noting that the Spanish army and various police forces were under the total command of Francoist officers who, in both the public and scholarly view, accepted the political transition to democracy, provided that they were not to be removed, challenged, discharged from their posts, or prosecuted for unlawful actions (torture, assassinations, etc.) during Franco's dictatorship.

3. *1979–1996:* with an average of 5.2 percent coverage with respect to the total of the period. This is a long period in which the Basque sociopolitical conflicts (strikes, demonstrations, crime, etc.) practically disappear from newspaper coverage. It spans the time when the Basque Autonomous Statute is passed (1979) and the Basque regional government and parliament are constituted and begin their activities. In the rest of Spain, political democracy becomes the norm.

The subcategory of "torture," practiced by the police and considered epidemic when related to the Basque conflict, gets some meaningful attention during only three years: in 1965, 16.7 percent; in 1976, 40 percent; and in 1985, 20 percent. The many subsequent complaints, even as reported by the United Nations and other international human rights organizations, have not generally reached the U.S. and international media. This practice has not yet disappeared, as attested to by annual international reports on human rights in Spain.

Now that we have examined the amount and type of coverage the

TABLE 4. *Basque Economic and Social Variables in Comparison to Spain*

	Basque Region	Navarra	Total Basque
Foreign investments			
(1993–96)	2.9%	2.9%	2.9%
GNP (1990–93)	5.9%	1.6%	3.7%
Population (1996)	5.0%	1.3%	6.3%

Sources: *Anuario El País* (1994, 1995), *Anuario El Mundo* (1995).

Basques receive from this international newspaper, we can establish a comparative frame of reference as provided by the *New York Times's* treatment of Spain. For this area of the research, the period analyzed is from 1975, the year of Franco's death, to 1996.

But before effecting an analysis of what percentage of the total coverage of Spain pertains to the Basques (including the Navarrese), let us first consider the relative social and economic weight within Spain.

From the data in table 4, we can affirm that the relative social and economic weight of the Basques with regard to the entirety of Spain is in the mid-single digits. Neither should we forget, as mentioned earlier, that some of these entries—GNP, for example—seem to affect the international news coverage and are considered partial predictors of that flow. Keeping this in mind, making a single linear translation, and taking no other social or newsworthy considerations into account, we could hypothesize that the Basque information coverage would be close to a 6–7 percent figure. The results follow (see table 5).

Looking at the "Basque" column, we can see that over the twenty-two years studied, the average Basque coverage is 16.3 percent of Spain's total. We also can distinguish five periods:

1. *1975–1977:* the average Basque contribution to Spain's information flow is 14 percent, almost equal to the overall average of 16.3 percent.

2. *1978–1981:* the presence of Basque information in the *New York Times* increased dramatically, and so did its contribution to Spain's total, as we can see from its mean of 33.9 percent. This

TABLE 5. *Comparison between Basque and Spanish Information Flow (1975–1996)*

Year	Basque	Spain	Total	Basque Mean
1975	11.4%	88.6%	100.0%	
1976	11.0%	89.0%	100.0%	
1977	19.7%	80.3%	100.0%	14.0%
1978	28.9%	71.1%	100.0%	
1979	42.8%	57.2%	100.0%	
1980	33.1%	66.9%	100.0%	
1981	30.9%	69.1%	100.0%	33.9%
1982	18.5%	81.5%	100.0%	
1983	9.9%	90.1%	100.0%	
1984	21.6%	78.4%	100.0%	
1985	13.4%	86.6%	100.0%	
1986	18.3%	81.7%	100.0%	
1987	15.7%	84.3%	100.0%	16.2%
1988	6.4%	93.6%	100.0%	
1989	10.4%	89.6%	100.0%	
1990	8.0%	92.0%	100.0%	
1991	6.2%	93.8%	100.0%	
1992	4.9%	95.1%	100.0%	
1993	7.7%	92.3%	100.0%	
1994	3.5%	96.5%	100.0%	6.7%
1995	19.2%	80.8%	100.0%	
1996	15.5%	84.5%	100.0%	17.3%
Total	16.3%	83.7%	100.0%	

N = 3,819 news items.

unusual pattern coincides with the turbulent period in the Basque homeland (including Navarra), where Spanish political transition did not take firm root and the political violence and terrorism were serious.

3. *1982–1987:* the Basque news contribution to Spain's information

flow decreases markedly again to 16.2 percent, almost equal to
the overall average.

4. *1988–1994:* this is a period when Basque news flow, in regard to
Spain's, sinks to its lowest level, 6.7 percent. It about equals the
relative social and economic weight that the Basques have in
Spain.

5. *1995–1996:* the Basque coverage rises to 17.3 percent, slightly
above the general average of 16.3 percent.

These results seem to reinforce the idea that gross national product
is not an adequate variable for predicting international news flow, as
some studies mentioned earlier suggest. Rather, some intrinsic factors
referred to as event *newsworthiness* and other extrinsic ones, such as
U.S. interests and *peace threats,* may be playing a role in our case.

There is another interesting comparison to be made: the effect of
the Basque coverage of Spain's total with regard to content type. In
this fashion, we can know what would happen if the "conflict-ruled
Basque news flow" were not included in that of Spain.

From table 6, we can see that, for the whole 1975–1996 period,
Basque information flow only affects Spain's coverage significantly in
the category of "conflict," shifting it from 17.5 percent to 28.6 percent.
In the rest of the categories the variation is small, or insignificant.

At this point, we consider it important to contextualize and compare these findings with others dealing with world coverage. The
question is: how do Spanish and Basque *conflict* information flows,
equated as "bad news," compare with First-World and Third-World
"bad news" data provided in a study done by Riffe (1993)?

In table 7, compiled by combining Riffe's data (1993) with that of
our own study, we have equated our category of "conflict" with
Riffe's category of "bad news," given the fact that the definitions for
both are almost identical. In Riffe's study, the category of "bad news"
comprises the subcategories of internal and between-nation conflicts,
displaced persons and refugees, and miscellaneous crimes, accidents,
and disasters, which coincides remarkably with our category of "conflict." That said, we can deduce very interesting results:

1. *Spain without Basques, a First-World country.* Spain, without including Basque information, is treated as a First-World country

TABLE 6. *Effect of Basque Information on Spain's Coverage (1975–1996)*

	Government	Conflict	Economy	Science	Popular	Total
Spain without Basque information	36.2%	17.5%	17.7%	3.7%	24.9%	100.0%
Spain with Basque information	31.8%	28.6%	15.1%	3.2%	21.3%	100.0%

N = 853 news items.

TABLE 7. *Comparisons of* "Bad News" *or* Conflict *Information (1975–1990)*

Year	Total World*	First World*	Third World*	Spain Only	Spain + Basque	Basque
1975	32.4%	17.8%	49.6%	11.6%	30.9%	100.0%
1976	31.6%	21.5%	43.9%	34.2%	41.9%	100.0%
1977	29.6%	25.8%	32.0%	20.0%	32.3%	83.3%
1978	32.9%	20.0%	44.7%	44.4%	61.5%	100.0%
1979	33.0%	16.6%	48.9%	33.3%	56.3%	85.7%
1980	33.6%	21.7%	47.6%	40.0%	50.0%	75.0%
1981	35.0%	23.1%	45.2%	57.1%	62.5%	77.8%
1982	40.3%	36.3%	46.7%	20.0%	45.8%	88.9%
1983	31.6%	14.9%	48.6%	15.4%	21.4%	100.0%
1984	38.6%	17.2%	57.1%	18.8%	28.9%	83.3%
1985	46.0%	37.7%	57.8%	31.3%	36.1%	75.0%
1986	38.0%	25.4%	50.9%	6.3%	21.1%	100.0%
1987	32.6%	19.4%	49.6%	20.8%	26.9%	100.0%
1988	31.3%	17.2%	49.6%	5.6%	10.5%	100.0%
1989	39.3%	25.4%	55.4%	10.5%	15.0%	100.0%
1990	26.2%	14.9%	37.8%	0.0%	6.3%	100.0%
Total	34.5%	22.2%	47.8%	23.1%	34.2%	91.8%

Note that the data of the columns marked with the asterisk (*) have been taken from Riffe's work (1993).

in its coverage in that it has an almost identical "bad news" percentage (23.1 percent), as does this category in the First World (22.2 percent).

2. *Spain with Basques, proximate to a Third-World country.* Spain, with Basque information flow included, receives coverage similar to that of a Third-World country in that the percentage of "bad news," or "conflict" news, in the nation-state of Spain is 34.2 percent, approaching the coverage of the Third World (47.8 percent), and almost equal to the average percentage in the whole world (34.5 percent).

3. *Basque only, the worst coverage.* It is worth repeating that more than 90 percent of the international coverage of the Basques is "bad news," almost twice as much as the percentage of the Third World (47.8 percent).

These findings make it necessary to analyze the main subject of Basque news flow, that is, ETA, with regard to its labeling by the *New York Times*.[12] In fact, we addressed this issue of terrorist labeling by the media at the beginning of this study, and the question is clear: what kind of adjectival characterization has the *New York Times* used to define ETA?

ETA has been characterized by the *New York Times* in very different ways,[13] as we can see in table 8. Roughly half the time (54.5 percent) the main characterization employs the adjective "separatist." This label was used during almost the entire period analyzed, with an increase during the last few years (from 1984 to 1996).

The second most common characterization is "terrorist" (20.8 percent). Its use is steady after 1985. Often, in the same news item, the newspaper designates the violent acts carried out by ETA as "terrorist acts," and the organization is characterized as "the separatist group ETA," "the separatist guerrilla group ETA," or something similar. Then, later in the text, the journalist comes to terms with journalism's rule of brevity and refers only to "ETA," leaving out the adjectives.

Third comes the denomination "guerrilla" (13.9 percent), particularly during two noticeable periods: from 1979 to 1983 and from 1993 to 1996. It is also used in composite labeling such as "Basque separatist guerrilla group ETA" or "Basque nationalist guerrilla group ETA."

Fourth comes "nationalist" (6.9 percent), used basically during

TABLE 8. *ETA Labeling (1970–1990)*

Year	Separatist	Terrorist	Guerrilla	Nationalist	Extremist	Marxist-Leninist	Rebel	Underground	Total
1970	30.0%	0.0%	30.0%	10.0%	10.0%	0.0%	10.0%	10.0%	100.0%
1975	0.0%	50.0%	0.0%	50.0%	0.0%	0.0%	0.0%	0.0%	100.0%
1976	0.0%	0.0%	0.0%	100.0%	0.0%	0.0%	0.0%	0.0%	100.0%
1977	50.0%	0.0%	0.0%	50.0%	0.0%	0.0%	0.0%	0.0%	100.0%
1978	50.0%	50.0%	0.0%	0.0%	0.0%	0.0%	0.0%	0.0%	100.0%
1979	50.0%	0.0%	50.0%	0.0%	0.0%	0.0%	0.0%	0.0%	100.0%
1980	50.0%	0.0%	0.0%	0.0%	0.0%	50.0%	0.0%	0.0%	100.0%
1981	33.3%	50.0%	16.7%	0.0%	0.0%	0.0%	0.0%	0.0%	100.0%
1982	40.0%	0.0%	60.0%	0.0%	0.0%	0.0%	0.0%	0.0%	100.0%
1983	50.0%	0.0%	50.0%	0.0%	0.0%	0.0%	0.0%	0.0%	100.0%
1984	100.0%	0.0%	0.0%	0.0%	0.0%	0.0%	0.0%	0.0%	100.0%
1985	0.0%	100.0%	0.0%	0.0%	0.0%	0.0%	0.0%	0.0%	100.0%
1986	60.0%	40.0%	0.0%	0.0%	0.0%	0.0%	0.0%	0.0%	100.0%
1987	100.0%	0.0%	0.0%	0.0%	0.0%	0.0%	0.0%	0.0%	100.0%
1990	80.0%	20.0%	0.0%	0.0%	0.0%	0.0%	0.0%	0.0%	100.0%
1993	37.5%	37.5%	25.0%	0.0%	0.0%	0.0%	0.0%	0.0%	100.0%
1994	100.0%	0.0%	0.0%	0.0%	0.0%	0.0%	0.0%	0.0%	100.0%
1995	70.6%	17.6%	11.8%	0.0%	0.0%	0.0%	0.0%	0.0%	100.0%
1996	86.7%	13.3%	0.0%	0.0%	0.0%	0.0%	0.0%	0.0%	100.0%
Total	54.5%	20.8%	13.9%	6.9%	1.0%	1.0%	1.0%	1.0%	100.0%

N = 101 news items.

1975–1977, the period of Franco's death and Spain's political transition.

Finally, several labels show a residual percentage of 1 percent: "Marxist-Leninist," of strong ideological remembrances and connotations; "extremist," employed in 1970; "rebel," used in some compound labels; and "underground," an adjective of the 1970s.

Conclusions

The Basques, as a nation without a state and as a marginal society, have little capacity to produce internationally newsworthy events. Their rather inconsequential economic and social weight, even within Spain, makes them of scant interest to the international audience. Nor are standard Basque politics, whether regarding a degree of parliamentary self-government within a federal Spain or as a highly circumscribed regional player in Spanish and European affairs, worthy of much outside attention. As a consequence, negative news, mostly related to terrorism, will continue to dominate Basque coverage within the international news flow, at least until such time that peace is attained.

However, the alleged negative impact of "bad news" upon the perception of the international audience should not be overestimated nor intuitively stated as a scientific fact. In spite of such coverage, Basque society and its institutions and social actors should try to increase the news flow regarding topics such as "economy," "popular culture," and "science-technology." These topics provide the type of good news that helps to increase tourism, trade, and social interaction, while providing the counterbalance to the bad news. However, we should also keep in mind that "good news" does not necessarily convey a sense of nation to the international audience, but rather just a profile of a region with a peculiar people named "Basques," who live in the borderlands of Spain and France.

In any event, we should not give too much credence to the international news flow. Contrary to common perception, image and portrayal are seldom the key factors in any political or economic decision making. Above all, the Basques should just continue to be themselves if they want to remain open to the world and become part of the global community, for the international audience most values what is both original and authentic.

Notes

1. The Media Dependency Theory predicts that the media influence on the conception of social reality is reduced when the audience has personal experiences with such reality, with the people of such a social group.

2. The definition of *inevitability* might be sharpened with the aid of another concept, that of *responsibility*. Hence, the agent responsible for inevitable bad news may be nature, as in the case of earthquakes and droughts, or responsibility may become diffused or directed at "society's lack of expertise/knowledge," as in economic crises.

3. Cited in Raboy and Dagenais (1992).

4. The three newspapers were the *New York Times,* the *Los Angeles Times,* and the *Washington Post.* The data sample was taken from the following index headings: *assassinations, airline hijackings, bombings, hostages, kidnappings, murders, shootings,* and *terrorism.* As is evident, they were content categories and not geographical or people categories such as *Ireland, Nicaragua,* or *Palestinians.* This fact probably excluded from their data some regional conflict items, such as that of the Basques. Nevertheless, the results are quite significant.

5. Labeling in the press carries connotations that may affect the shaping of the image or stereotype of a newsmaker. For example, studies have shown that U.S. media use the word *government* to label legitimate, legal, and even "morally" constituted (nation-state) institutions and the words *regime* and *dictatorship* for less legitimate and legal ones (as was the case with the Communist countries). However, as scholars point out, the labeling is inconsistent inasmuch as these negative words are not frequently used with, for example, pro-U.S. authoritarian regimes of Latin America.

6. *Time, Newsweek,* and *U.S. News & World Report.*

7. Cited and used by Catherine Cassara (1995) in her study.

8. There is a previous, more limited study by the same author, covering the period 1975–1987 (Zabaleta 1991–1992).

9. For the content type research the *unit of analysis* was the informational item, be it a news or an opinion article. We considered that the computations and results of the study would be better based on *information item counting,* rather than *size measuring,* following the same approach

used by other scholars (Potter 1987; Ramaprasad 1993; Riffe 1993). For the selection of the diverse *sample sizes*, the more recent methodological contributions to sampling techniques were taken into account (Riffe et al. 1993; Riffe et al. 1996; Stempel 1952). Since the amount of news items varied through the years, we made several sampling decisions that are explained here. *Sample during period 1950–1970:* all the information items of every fifth year were analyzed, that is, all the Basque news items in the years 1950, 1955, 1960, 1965, and 1970. *Sample during period 1975–1981:* one information item in every ten was included due to the large quantity of information items during those years. *Sample during period 1982–1992:* one information item in every five, due to the decrease in the quantity of information items during those years. *Sample during period 1993–1996:* all the information items were coded. The validity of the sample sizes was checked several times by comparing the results from samples against the results for all the items. This was done for the years 1975 and 1983. The results of the samples were very close to the total results, within the 5 percent range. Then again, the results of the total information items of 1994 were compared to those of a sample of items constructed in the same fashion as the previous ones and they were significantly similar. However, we should mention that, due to the fact that during some years the number of information items was so few, the results derived from samples may hide small percentage values that some infrequent categories might access (Basque politics, science, and economy for example). Finally, *Holsti's inter-coder reliability* was 94 percent.

10. For the ETA labeling, the technique is based on the selection of the most prominent or salient denomination per news item, situated at its beginning in the headline or the first paragraphs. This is similar to the method used by Picard and Adams (1991), who coded the first three characterizations, made by both the newspapers and by the witnesses or officials.

11. A very broad category of news events that, because of their relation to life and death situations, arouse emotions and sensations in the audience: earthquakes, war, crimes, terrorist attacks, accidents, and so on.

12. In each news item only one denomination, one adjective, was chosen, the most relevant one, located usually in the headline or at the beginning of the news item. This coding procedure, considered methodologically adequate in content analysis of message styles (as explained before), does not mean that in any specific news item no other adjectives were used to characterize ETA. On the contrary, several adjectives might occur, but we considered that basically one of them set forth the tone and the characterization sought by the newspaper. At times, there were even

combinations of adjectives, such as "separatist terrorist," and "separatist guerrilla." In such cases, we coded both.

13. The noun phrases used by the *New York Times* to label ETA, in addition to its initials, are the following (order has no meaning here): 1) ETA, ETA members; 2) Basques; 3) Basque guerrilla, Basque guerrilla organization ETA; 4) Basque nationalists, Basque nationalist guerrillas, Basque nationalist guerrilla group ETA, Basque nationalist group ETA; 5) Basque separatists, Basque separatist organization ETA, Basque separatist group ETA, Basque separatist guerrillas, separatist guerrilla group ETA; 6) terrorists, Basque terrorists, Basque terrorist members of ETA, Basque terrorist organization ETA, Spanish terrorists; 7) Marxist-Leninist organization ETA; 8) rebels, Basque rebels; 9) underground group.

Bibliography

Ahern, Thomas. 1984. Determinants of foreign coverage in U.S. newspapers. In *Foreign news and the New World information order,* edited by Robert L. Stevenson and Donald Lewis Shaw. Ames: Iowa State University Press.

Ball-Rokeach, Sandra, and Melvin L. Defleur. 1976. A dependency model of mass media effects. *Communication Research* 3: 3–21.

Bassiouni, M. C. 1982. Media coverage of terrorism: the law and the public. *Journal of Communication* 33, no. 2: 128–143.

———. 1981. Terrorism, law enforcement and the mass media: perspectives, problems, proposals. *Journal of Criminal Law and Criminology* 72, no. 1.

Burgoon, Judee K., Michael Burgoon, and Miriam Wilkinson. 1984. Dimensions of content readership in 10 newspaper markets. *Journalism Quarterly* 60: 74–80.

Cassara, Catherine. 1995. International news in six American newspapers: last look at a bipolar world? *International Communication Bulletin* 30, nos. 1–2 (spring): 1317.

Chang, Tsan-Kuo, and Jae-Won Lee. 1990. Factors affecting gatekeepers' selection of foreign news: a national survey of newspaper editors. Paper presented at the annual meeting of the Association for Education in Journalism and Mass Communication, Minneapolis.

Galtung, Johan, and Mari H. Ruge. 1965. The structure of foreign news. *Journal of Peace Research* 2: 64–91.

Gerbner, George. 1992. Violence and terror in and by the media. In *Me-*

dia, crisis and democracy: mass communication and the disruption of social order, edited by Marc Raboy and Bernard Dagenais. London: Sage.

Kariel, Herbert G., and Lynn A. Rosenvall. 1984. Factors influencing international news flow. *Journalism Quarterly* 61: 509–515.

Kelly, Michael J., and Thomas H. Mitchell. 1981. Transnational terrorism and the western elite press. *Journal of Political Communication and Persuasion,* no. 1: 269–296.

Korzenny, Felipe, Wanda Del Toro, and James Gaudino. 1987. International news media exposure, knowledge and attitudes. *Journal of Broadcasting & Electronic Media* 31 (winter): 73–87.

Martin, L. John. 1983. The media's role in international terrorism. Paper presented at the Association for Education in Journalism and Mass Communication convention, Oregon.

McNelly, John T., and Fausto Izcaray. 1986. International news exposure and images of nations. *Journalism Quarterly* 63: 546–553.

Milburn, M. A., C. Bowley, J. Fay-Dumaine, and D. A. Kennedy. 1987. An attributional analysis of the media coverage of terrorism. Paper presented at the Tenth Annual Conference of the International Society of Political Psychology, San Francisco.

Paletz, David L., John Z. Ayanian, and Peter A. Fozzard. 1982. The I.R.A.: the Red Brigades and the F.A.L.N. in the *New York Times. Journal of Communication* 32: 162–172.

Perry, David K. 1989. World news and U.S. public opinion about the Soviet Union: a panel analysis. *Communication Research Reports,* no. 6 (1989): 65–68.

———. 1990. News reading, knowledge about, and attitudes toward foreign countries. *Journalism Quarterly,* no. 67: 353–358.

———. 1996. *Theory and research in mass communication: Contexts and consequences.* Mahwah, NJ: Erlbaum.

Perry, David K., William H. Melson, and Tammie Howard. 1997. The impact of negative news on audience attitudes toward less developed countries: an experimental study. *International Communication Bulletin* 32, nos. 1–2: 13–17.

Picard, Robert G. 1993. *Media portrayals of terrorism: functions and meaning of news coverage.* Ames, Iowa: Iowa State University Press.

Picard, Robert G., and Paul D. Adams. 1991. Characterizations of acts and perpetrators of political violence in three elite U.S. daily newspapers. In *Media coverage of terrorism,* edited by A. Odasuo Alali and Kenoye Kelvin Eke. London: Sage.

Potter, W. James. 1987. News from three worlds of the world's press. *Journalism Quarterly* 64: 73–79.

Raboy, Marc, and Bernard Dagenais, eds. 1992. *Media, crisis and democracy: mass communication and the disruption of social order.* London: Sage.

Ramaprasad, Jyotika. 1993. Content, geography, concentration and consonance in foreign news coverage of ABC, NBC & CBS. *International Communication Bulletin* 28, nos. 1–2 (spring): 10–14.

Riffe, Daniel. 1993. The stability of "bad news" in Third World coverage: 22 years of the *New York Times* foreign news. *International Communication Bulletin* 28, nos. 3–4 (fall): 6–12.

Riffe, Daniel, and Eugene F. Shaw. 1982. Conflict and consonance: coverage of Third World in two U.S. papers. *Journalism Quarterly* 59: 617–626.

Riffe, Daniel, Charles F. Aust, and Stephen R. Lacy. 1993. The effectiveness of random, consecutive day and constructed week sampling in newspaper content analysis. *Journalism Quarterly* 70, no. 1: 133–139.

Riffe, Daniel, Stephen R. Lacy, John Nagovan, and Larry Burkum. 1996. The effectiveness of simple and stratified random sampling in broadcast news content analysis. *Journalism Quarterly* 73, no. 1: 159–168.

Semetko, Holli A., Joanne Bay Brzinski, David Weaver, and Lars Willnat. 1992. TV news and U.S. public opinion about foreign countries: The impact of exposure and attention. *International Journal of Public Opinion Research,* no. 4: 18–36.

Simmons, Brian K. 1991. U.S. newsmagazines' labeling of terrorists. In *Media coverage of terrorism,* edited by A. Odasuo Alali and Kenoye Kelvin Eke. London: Sage.

Stempel, Guido H. 1952. Sample size for classifying subject matter in dailies. *Journalism Quarterly* 29 (summer): 333–334.

Zabaleta, Iñaki. 1991–1992. Imagen y tratamiento informativo del País Vasco y España en el *New York Times,* 1975–1987 (Desde la muerte de Franco hasta las elecciones europeas). *Journal of the Society of Basque Studies in America* 11–12: 57–83.

Cameron Watson

Imagining ETA

"The Party's course is sharply defined, like a narrow path in the mountains. The slightest false step, right or left, takes one down the precipice. The air is thin; he who becomes dizzy is lost."

—Arthur Koestler, *Darkness at Noon*

"We believe that, so far as the actual world is concerned, truth is the most important criterion, whereas we tend to think that fiction describes a world we have to take as it is, on trust. Even in the actual world, however, the principle of trust is as important as the principle of truth."

—Umberto Eco, *Six Walks in the Fictional Woods*

In September 1998 a cease-fire was declared by the armed resistance group ETA (Euskadi ta Askatasuna—Basque Land and Freedom) which, at least to date (summer 1999), shows signs of holding. This paper deals, however, with the violent history of ETA or, more accurately, with perceptions and images of that violence and how these have been projected to create and articulate a discourse of terrorism.

There is no "eternal terrorist" but rather terrorism is imagined, that is, formed and transformed within and in relation to representation. In his influential study on nationalism, Benedict Anderson argues that nations are "imagined communities." Even members of the "smallest nation," he writes, "will never know most of their fellow-members," they will never meet or "even hear of them, *yet in the minds of each lives the image of their communion.*"[1] I argue that terrorism, like the nation, is imagined and I explore here some of the ways in which ETA lives in the minds of people.

We cannot refer to ETA from a fixed point of thought and being,[2] for it is imagined in many different ways. Perhaps the most pervasive of these images is that of the universal (almost "exoticized") terrorist.[3] It is an image which has been created and sustained by an entire network of information, including the popular media, educational institutions, and governments in the Basque Country, the Spanish state, and beyond. This imagining, I believe, is a form of Koestler's "Party" or Eco's "truth"; in other words, a way of creating specific categories as universal truths.

I would like to challenge these categories (and their policing by the network mentioned above) through an examination of the twin processes of discursive representation and categorization. Specifically, I will address how three loci of representational power—Hollywood, the media, and ETA itself—promote and sustain an image of the universal terrorist.

Following Emile Durkheim,[4] I will take representation to mean a discourse sustained by a number of elements such as narrative, continuity, foundational myths, the invention of tradition, and ideological purity. In particular, narrative (both discursive and visual) is a powerful element in the process of imagining because it translates events into a simple, yet crucial, beginning-middle-end sequence. Narrative empowers, sustains, and differentiates. It is, in fact, *the* weapon of systems of cultural representation.

Categorization is a form of representation and an exercise in power. The category of universal terrorist has, I believe, been imagined and created from an institutional viewpoint. This creation sees ETA from a specific political or ideological perspective yet claims its own point of view as the one, universal true opinion. Robert Darnton maintains that "we order the world according to categories that we take for granted simply because they are given. They occupy an epistemological space that is *prior to thought,* and so they have an extraordinary staying power."[5] I contend that we too frequently accept the universal terrorist on the assumed premise of a terrorism discourse created and sustained by specific interests. It is this acceptance, in many ways redolent of a time prior to critical thinking, that gives the universal terrorist concept its staying power.

Hollywood, the media, and ETA obscure a critical understanding of political violence. Instead, they promote convenient stereotypes based on simple binary oppositions such as good versus evil. This stereotyping results in totalizing Manichean discourses that simplify the issues, reify the actors, and obscure the reality of political violence. My aim, then, is to challenge the standard and accepted discourse on terrorism. I will therefore conclude by exploring the genealogy of ETA—an exploration of past realities, present uncertainties and future possibilities. One such possibility, I suggest, is a reimagining of ETA.

Finally, while recognizing the potential ethical problems involved in attempting to understand terrorism in its own terms, I contend that although all types of political violence destroy human lives, we should not allow this to somehow situate such violence outside history and therefore make it immune to analysis. Close scholarly attention does not devalue or trivialize what is a fundamentally human horror and tragedy. In fact there is a greater danger in viewing terrorism as an ahistorical force, something so awful that we cannot, or should not, attempt to comprehend it, for this only accommodates the convenient narratives purveyed by the network of institutional forces mentioned above.

Such narratives, I believe, have two serious implications: they obscure critical understanding by creating and ordering a series of simple paradigms; and they seduce those of us receiving the information into not thinking, but simply accepting. Michael Ignatieff reminds us that "the horror of the world lies not just with the corpses, not just with the consequences, but with the intentions, with the minds of killers." For Ignatieff, "the temptation to take refuge in moral disgust is strong indeed. *Yet disgust is a poor substitute for thought.*"[6] If nothing else, I hope that this exploration might serve as an exercise in critical reflection.

Hollywood and ETA

Returning to the original considerations of discourse and representation, I suggest that Hollywood provides an obvious starting point in the quest to examine institutional frames of reference regarding terrorism.[7] Consider the following narrative:

There are forces in the world as powerful as nations. They have the ability to declare war and the resources to carry it out. Their motives may be political, financial, or personal. But the goal is always the same: deliver a public message, soaked in blood, to strike fear in the hearts and minds of those who, for whatever reason, they regard as their enemy.[8]

There is a conscious effort here, articulated in simple, expressive and emotional terms, to conjure up images of terror. It is a straightforward indictment of terrorism—both terrorism in a general, abstract, and universal sense and, more specifically, international terrorism, seen as a genuine threat to an undefined "normal" state of being.

The forces mentioned are not nations. They are as powerful as nations but they are not nations. Their goal is to deliver a blood-soaked message intended to "strike fear in the hearts and minds" of those they regard as their enemy. These forces must, in effect, be terrorists. This view of international terrorism echoes most of the academic discourse on the subject. Terrorism is a performative symbolic endeavor—it is violence perpetrated to effect a response in a target audience rather than the violence of opposing armies attempting to overcome one another in open warfare. Such is the perception of terrorism commonly purveyed by both academia and the popular press: an unseen, deadly presence, which seeks to undermine the good work of nation-states. It would seem natural, then, to suppose that the preceding statement comes from a university textbook or a newspaper editorial. This is not the case.

It is in fact from the official Web site of a 1997 Universal Pictures film, *The Jackal*, starring Bruce Willis and Richard Gere. The film, a visual narrative that reveals much about the imagining of terrorism in the late 1990s, features one character of particular interest to the current topic: former ETA member Isabella Zancona, played by French actress Mathilda May.

Two statements from the movie are especially worth noting. In one scene Zancona recalls her previous life as an ETA operative, when she was romantically involved with IRA member Declan Mulqueen (played by Gere): "I suppose we were all dangerous people but he [Willis as the hired assassin, the Jackal] was different. . . . Declan was fire, all passion. He had a cause. This man was ice. No feeling. Nothing." Later, Mulqueen is warned by a Russian Secret Service agent that "Basques live by the vendetta. If they hate someone it is to the death. It's the same when they love."

A cursory examination of this film prompts three responses:

1. That terrorists are fiery and passionate for their cause, in contrast, for example, to rational, cold, and calculating assassins.
2. That terrorists are sexually attractive.
3. That Basques are violent.

Hollywood apparently views the terrorism of the IRA and ETA as linked in the sense of the *cause.* It is this cause which gives the Irish and Basques their passion and fire—an attempt, perhaps, in the case of the Irish, to placate the imagined feelings of Irish-American filmgoers sympathetic to the historical struggle of the IRA. Terrorism is, though, an obviously irrational way to serve the cause and throughout the movie neither of the two former terrorist characters actually defends their previous life. IRA terrorist Mulqueen has paid a heavy price by serving a long-term prison sentence. Isabella Zancona has seen the error of her ways, laid down her arms, married, and is living the American dream with husband and child in a nice house by a lake. By contrast, the Jackal has no cause; for him, the act of killing represents a business transaction to be completed. As opposed to its statements about terrorism, the movie never actually morally condemns the actions of the Jackal. As a consequence, one might conclude that terrorists in general (including ETA operatives) are fiery, hot-headed, quick-tempered, and irrational.

Secondly, both Isabella and Declan are portrayed in a consciously sexual way. Indeed, given the nature of female roles in such films, it seems as if May has been asked to portray a character whose sexual proclivity, throughout every moment of her brief appearances in the movie, is constantly evident. Quite apart from an obvious incarnation of Simone de Beauvoir's essential and absolute "Other," the (dangerous and threatening) *Eternal Feminine,* the character of Zancona embodies the danger and threatening presence of terrorism, and resonates with sexual symbolism. "To pose Woman," contends de Beauvoir, "is to pose the absolute Other, without reciprocity, denying against all experience that she is a subject, a fellow human being."[9] My immediate response to viewing this character prompted a similar conclusion: that, in the imagining construction of Hollywood, the danger and "otherness" of terrorism is reinforced by locating it within a female character.[10] Understood this way, terrorism as an illicit practice of power might be conceived as a convenient metaphor for sexual behavior and adventure, a seductive and potent mix.

It would also appear that Hollywood unproblematically reduces Basques to a single discursive category: they are violent. Basques love a vendetta, and either love or hate a person to the death. In the movie this was a description of Basques in general, not just members of ETA. The message, then, is that the terrorism of ETA is in some way linked to Basque culture in general with, once again, open allusions to its fiery, vindictive nature.[11]

What might we conclude from Hollywood's imagining of ETA? The mass entertainment industry is essentially concerned with the smoothest and most efficient transition from production and marketing to consumption. It thus eschews complicated analysis or critical understanding. It wants to imagine in as simple, easy, and understandable forms as possible, so as to appeal to the lowest common denominator of public opinion—the very substance of mass cultural and commercial forms.[12] What is at stake, therefore, is not necessarily understanding, analyzing, or thinking about ETA or terrorism, but rather a basic formula of cultural production—a system of production and consumption arranged for profit—and the formation of aesthetic judgments which reinforce dominant cultural and institutional values.[13]

The consequences of this are clear to see in *The Jackal*. The name Isabella Zancona, for example, is neither Basque, Spanish, nor French. Little research seems to have been done to establish credibility or accuracy in the development of the character. Furthermore, the acronym ETA is never actually mentioned in the film. The dialogue relies, in fact, on the term "Basque terrorist"—yet another simple and causal link between Basques, as a people or particular ethnic group, and terrorism. Finally there is an explicit reference to the importance of the vendetta for Basques, a notion entirely absent in Basque culture. Instead the filmmakers have chosen to subsume Basque culture within a broad and stereotypical image of southern Europe and the Mediterranean, the principal loci of vendetta cultures.

With respect to ETA, then, the important imagining premises for

Hollywood are that Basques are terrorists and that the universal terrorist is to a certain extent a femme fatale for the 1990s. This is a
straightforward representational system devoid of debate, analysis,
and understanding, which instead relies on simple, though trenchant,
images to sell a product.

Media Representations of ETA

Together with popular film, a dominant locus of representational authority in the late twentieth century is the media. Adapting a series
of questions posed by Stuart Hall in his thorough investigation of ideology and the media,[14] I ask the following: How is the active work of
privileging *some* explanations and descriptions (at the expense of others) as *the* explanations and descriptions accomplished in modern societies, in which the dominant mechanism doing the privileging is
undoubtedly the media? I will attempt to answer this question by exploring ETA's representation in the Spanish media. Specifically, I will
argue that this representation is intended to cast a dominant discourse as *the* account, an attempt to effect a limit, ban, or proscription
over alternative or competing discourses. It is therefore an assault on
a critical or objective imagining of ETA.

Figure 1 contains two images taken from the Spanish daily *El
Mundo* which establish a link between ETA and the political party
Herri Batasuna (the radical Basque nationalist party). The top sequence (Figure 1a) blends the two organizations through the potent
and effective symbol of blood. The cartoon suggests that there is
blood on the hands of HB, and that together the two groups are destroying the Basque Country, as represented by the log. The context
of the scene, however, reveals another level of representation. *Aizko-
laritza*, or woodcutting, is a traditional endeavor which forms part of
Basque rural sports. Of course the cartoonist needs to locate the subject, but there is a potential message here that conflates a feature of
Basque culture in general with the violence and terrorism of ETA.
Two ideas are consequently presented: Basques are terrorists and
ETA/HB represent all Basques.

In the second cartoon (Figure 1b) the striking image is the face
of the individual. Curiously (and paradoxically, considering Holly-

Figure 1. a. Cartoon from El Mundo, *July 21, 1997.*
b. Cartoon from El Mundo, *July 16, 1997.*

wood's approach), all ETA members represented in the Spanish media are male, unshaven, and unsavory-looking—a typical discursive
strategy in demonizing the dangerous terrorist, making him seem as
morally offensive as possible. This obscures both the role that women
play in ETA and the very normalcy of successful terrorist operatives.
Furthermore, as in the first image, an intimate connection is established between ETA and HB. HB is, unproblematically, ETA and
vice versa. No attempt has been made to provoke a more objective
understanding of the phenomenon of Basque political violence which
might, for example, include a critical questioning of the precise links
between HB and ETA.

In Figure 2, I originally intended to compare two images: a photo
from the (now defunct) Europe-wide weekly, *The European,* and a cartoon from the Spanish daily, *El País.* Unfortunately, *El País,* perhaps

the mediatic symbol of post-Franco Spain, would only give permission for the cartoon to be reproduced in this non-profit, educational publication for what can only be described as a highly exorbitant fee. Without being able to reproduce the original cartoon, then, let me describe it as best I can: Taken from *El País* of 21 May 1996, it shows a hooded ETA member with gun in hand stating, "La patria con sangre entra" ("The *patria* is learned with blood"—a play on the traditional Spanish proverb "Letters are learned with blood").

Both images make the same point: that the danger of ETA, indeed the danger of terrorism in general, lies in its unseen face. Facelessness both empowers ETA and disempowers the onlooker. There is danger lurking behind the masks. That space, beyond the mask, is somehow beyond the human sphere, beyond the boundaries and limits of normal human interaction as viewed or seen through human eyes.[15] Quite apart from unilaterally demonizing terrorism as the only unseen enemy in today's world (one might make mention here of the litany of "faceless" actions, from police brutality and torture to indiscriminate military operations, on the part of the modern state) there is an interesting and important parallel here. Namely, as we shall now see, both the media and ETA itself use this imaginative discourse.

ETA Imagines Itself

One need only view the controversial video, the *Alternatiba Demokratikoa* (Democratic Alternative), or examine any "official" photo release by the organization, to see how ETA itself is intimately involved in the control and perpetuation of a singular or unitary representation of Basque political violence.

Two elements of this video are especially striking: the location—an outside "wild" and "Basque" setting, free from the constraints of the Spanish state; and the narrative discourse of the activists themselves— strong and defiant, adding *Eusko Gudariak* (Song of the Basque Warrior) at the end of the video to reaffirm their status as *gudariak,* soldiers in a war. Ironically, what the video also demonstrates is ETA imagining itself in the same way that it is imagined by the Spanish media.

The three ETA figures in the video are covered from head to toe. The viewer cannot see their human faces. It seems as if ETA has an

Figure 2. Photo from The European, *July 17–23, 1997.*

interest in promoting the hidden threat of terrorism. I would thus contend that, in its own contemporary imagination, ETA shares some common ground with those forces that imagine it from the outside; that, indeed, the imagining of ETA is to some extent the shared experience of the terrorists, their enemies in government, and the media which both shapes and reflects the public opinion of democratic society.

Imagining ETA: A Speculation

Both the subject matter and tools of investigation commonly used in critical cultural analysis tend to prevent neat explanation or suitable solutions. Imagining the response, then, of some critics to my own exploration of ETA's genealogy and the phenomenon of Basque political violence, I offer the following. ETA is imagined, through the dominant discursive media of today's society, in two principal ways:

1. ETA appears as a category interchangeable with Basques, so that the eternal terrorist surfaces through the condition of being Basque. Imagining ETA is, in the minds of many people, an exercise in imagining Basques. Put another way: know ETA and you know Basques.
2. ETA's terrorism is the great unseen threat—a threat to the very existence of the Spanish state (or nation). With a threat of such proportions, extreme measures are needed and justified to counteract its power.

However, what is also apparent, though never mentioned or discussed, is the symbiotic relationship between ETA, official ideology (governments, educational institutions, and so forth), and the media which actually sustains each element. ETA achieves the goal of getting its violent message across through its actions being reported in detail by the media, which in turn sells these stories to a frightened or outraged public. The Spanish government, responding to citizens' fears, can thus refuse to talk to ETA, basing its decision on both the ethical principle of being against terrorist violence (though not, of course, other forms of political violence such as state-sanctioned war) and the outraged response of its citizens.

By way of a more independent-minded critical observation, then, we might consider the view that

> the more one accepts that how people act will depend in part on how the situations in which they act are defined, and the less one can assume either a natural meaning to everything or a universal consensus on what things mean—then, the more important, socially and politically becomes the process by means of which certain events get recurrently signified in particular ways. This is especially the case where events in the world are problematic (that is, where they are unexpected); where they break the frame of our previous expectations about the world; where powerful social interests are involved; or where there are starkly opposing or conflicting interests at play. The power involved here is an ideological power: *the power to signify events in a particular way.*[16]

The power to signify is neither a neutral nor ambivalent force in modern society. Indeed it seems that this power, expressed through the latent classificatory schemes and ideological matrices of competing institutions, has unilaterally condemned the representation of ETA to a single, simplified, and unitary category. I have attempted to highlight how some of the representations of ETA—how ETA is imagined—reflect an articulation of ideology through language, image, and discourse. This leads to a kind of "production of consent," or a shaping of consensus while at the same time reflecting it.[17] Just as Hall points to a "rediscovery" of ideology, so my concern is for a reimagining of ETA. A critical reimagining of the phenomenon of Basque political violence not only undermines the very sources of its power, but, should it lead to a greater freedom of imagination—that is to say, independent, critical thought—might even expand the discourse and debate. Furthermore, such an approach would, I believe, address real issues instead of playing to preconceived notions and stereotypes, themselves redolent of specific ideological constructions which never attempt understanding or analysis, but only condemnation.

In the preparation of the current discussion, I was questioned by a young Basque as to what I would say about ETA's victims. Would I be showing pictures of the car bombs, the hostages, the grieving families at funerals? The answer was no, but not for any desire to somehow lessen the impact of ETA's actions. It is now just a little over thirty years since ETA killed the first of its several hundred victims. This is the context—these past thirty years—by which institutional frames of power (the Spanish media, for example), and even ETA itself, promote and sustain the imagining of the organization. As an example, in a document available on-line, ETA limits discussion of its own historical origins to four sentences:

> The moderate actions of the Partido Nacionalista Vasco (P.N.V., Basque Nationalist Party) during the Franco regime prompted the emergence of another nationalist group by the name of EKIN (to act), which was created by several young activists from Bizkaia and Gipuzkoa who wanted to move the Basque cause forward with more energy. EKIN tried to get the support of the PNV but the opposition of some of its leaders prevented cooperation.

In 1958, EKIN became Euskadi Ta Askatasuna (E.T.A., Basque Homeland and Freedom). ETA was the only armed group that emerged in the Spanish state during Franquism.[18]

Why would ETA want to obscure its own history? The answer, I suspect, is that an examination of the organization's origins metaphorically unmasks ETA. Critical inquiry of this nature undermines the monolithic image (of violence, power, threat, and danger, for example) that ETA as well as the Spanish government and media construct and promote as universal of the organization.

Space precludes a detailed analysis of these origins here.[19] Briefly, ETA did not emerge spontaneously in the late 1950s as some kind of simple dialectical response to the PNV. Rather, a reimagining of ETA should see its historical genealogy as the result of three broad trends: the historical development of Basque nationalism in general (including the PNV); the specific social, cultural, and economic circumstances of post–Civil War Basque society; and, crucially, the important but forgotten role that post–World War II European philosophical trends (especially existentialism) and cultural preoccupations—that is to say, creative narrative discourses—played in its formation.

The original members of Ekin, the student group that would ultimately become ETA in 1959, drew direct inspiration for their political and cultural activities from the great names of the existential tradition: Kierkegaard, Heidegger, Sartre, Camus, and Marcel among them. If there was one dominant intellectual principle which underscored the formation of ETA it was—according to Txillardegi, one of the organization's founding members—the search for *authenticité*.[20] This search did not imply a given Basque essence. Rather, according to those original members of ETA, the Basque essence had to be *created*. Furthermore, the existential creation of a Basque essence implied a threefold personal and communal experience: the search for the meaning of Basqueness itself, the unavoidable anguish that this search implied, and, ultimately, the negation (of all things Spanish) required to achieve the quest.[21] This, in my opinion, is the original concept of *ekintza*, or action, so seminal to ETA's own mythification—ekintza as an original quest to define and resist through both thought and deed, most vividly expressed in Ekin/ETA's promotion of the Basque language, *Euskara*.

Additionally, if any dialectical relationship was paramount in the original formation of ETA it was not that of reaction to the PNV, but rather one of accommodation between nationalism and existentialism as a means of resolving the intrinsic problem of individual and group identity.

In cultural terms this was reflected in ETA's appreciation of Basque sculptor Jorge Oteiza's artistic theory of the disoccupation of space. Oteiza had formulated a theory whereby the many cromlechs which dotted the Basque countryside constituted a metaphor for the prehistoric freedom of the Basques, a freedom whose ultimate expression was nothingness. According to ETA, the political answer to the severe questions facing Basque society in the 1950s and 1960s was thus the dismantling of Spanish occupation or containment, as a means of restoring the Basque Country to its original void—that is, disoccupied, empty, and free space.[22]

A creative reimagining of this sort, I believe, challenges not only the dominant ideologies of contemporary society as perpetrated by governments and media, but also ETA's self-mythification based solely on its destructive history since 1968. Breaking this mythological construction of fear, which is articulated through the ekintzak, the (violent) actions, of ETA—a construction still actively sponsored by the organization in 1998—would be an important step towards a valuable reimagining of Basque political violence, even terrorism in general. To the young Basque, then, who questioned my motives in discussing ETA without mention of its victims, I would respond that this type of discourse—ETA as threat, society as victim—is the very life and soul of the organization.

By way of contrast I advocate a reimagining of ETA by addressing the conclusions presented earlier:

1. ETA does *not* represent all Basques, and Basques should not be simply reified as terrorists. When a whole people are condemned for the actions of some, then we have entered a different type of discourse, one of condemnation of, and attack upon, a specific people for no other reason than they *are* that people. It is the discourse of racism and genocide.

    Furthermore, while political violence does exist in the Basque Country, there is also violence—political, social, or otherwise, and on the part of both official and unofficial groups and individuals—in many other countries both to much greater and much lesser degrees. To cite European examples, Northern Ireland was, until recently, certainly more violent than the Basque conflict, and both situations pale in comparison to recent events in Kosovo.

2. In real terms ETA does not present a physical threat to the presence of the Spanish state. And I wonder whether the demonizing of terrorism in general allows for the modern democratic state to forget its obligation to open, free, and critical discourse.

If society wishes to address the phenomenon of political violence in a meaningful way, a first step toward the freedom of imagination required for this must begin with a skeptical approach to both official ideological images of ETA—from government and the media, for example—and ETA's own self-portrayal, coupled with a firm resolution toward dialogue, debate, and interaction.

We live today in a volatile world which emphasizes the value of instantaneity and disposability. This probably explains the form in which ETA is imagined by the institutional systems mentioned above. Such volatility makes a reimagination difficult, for, after all, how does one respond to rapid change? To the latest "terrorist outrage," for instance? The dominant institutions, be they governments or the media, tend toward short-term responses masked as long-term solutions. It is a seductive approach, but in so doing they obfuscate past realities and current predicaments. In fact, the past has a role to play in this time- and space-compressed contemporary age—not the past of romantic nostalgia nor present-affirming modernity, but rather an incorporated past. This is a difficult task, given the paradoxically powerful, ephemeral, yet consistent image production of the modern world as evinced above. By advocating an incorporated historical context, though, such imagining loses its communicating power.

Returning to ETA, then, and the question alluded to at the outset of the present discussion about its future possibilities, I conclude that an incorporation of the past into the discourse of Basque political violence allows for a more appropriate expression and articulation of the phenomenon. Indeed, I would argue that such an incorporation, seen as a reimagining of ETA, and spurning grand narrative (offering formulaic and fixed solutions, for example, to complex questions) might actually offer the possibility for limited and positive action in relation to Basque political violence. At the very least, a reimagination of ETA might highlight the infinite quality of the world in which we live. And such recognition can only individually empower us as members of a society faced with the challenge of dominant and unitary frames of reference, which are fostered by the institutions that potentially control us. As Walter Benjamin cautions,

> in every era the attempt must be made anew to wrest tradition away from a conformism that is about to overpower it. The Messiah comes not only as the redeemer, he comes as the subduer of the Antichrist. Only that historian will have the gift of fanning the spark of hope in the past who is firmly convinced that *even the dead* will not be safe from the enemy if he wins. And this enemy has not ceased to be victorious.[23]

Without critical approaches or any attempt to understand, I believe that even the dead, even the victims, will not be safe from the victory of the real enemy, the eternal terrorist.[24]

Epilogue: Cultural Reimagination and the Basque Political Process

In September 1998, barely two months after delivering this paper, ETA announced a cease-fire which, at least to date, has held. I would argue that both the cease-fire and the tentative *abertzale* political alliance of the PNV, EA (Eusko Alkartasuna), and EH (Euskal Herritarrok, a new organization comprising former members of HB) together represent a significant reimagination of the Basque political process. Furthermore, it seems to me that this reimagination has integrated a decidedly postnational view of the political process, and that this strategy has, in many respects, significantly altered Basque politics vis-à-vis the Spanish state.

Discussion of postnationalism in relation to Basque politics is nothing new.[25] However, I contend that such views have, in many respects, missed the point of the postnational debate. For, as Richard Kearney

rightly cautions: "In endeavouring to go beyond negative nationalism one must be wary . . . not to succumb to the opposite extreme of
anti-nationalism. Those who identify all forms of nationalism with
irredentist fanaticism habitually do so in the name of some neutral
standpoint that masks their own ideological bias."[26] Postnationalism
does not, as many observers seem to think, imply the end of nationalism, but rather, I suspect, a kind of accommodation (much like that
of postmodernity with the modern condition) between nationalism
and changing social, economic, political, and cultural realities. "Beyond the 'modern' alternatives of national independence ['Spain' for
example] and multinational dependence [global capitalism?]," argues Kearney, "lies another possibility—a postnational model of
interdependence."[27]

Between October 1997 and September 1998, I believe a critical reimagination of the Basque political process took place along postnational lines. In October 1997 a joint political demonstration, organized by the Basque nationalist labor unions ELA and LAB, occurred
which significantly altered the Basque political landscape. The joint
declaration of these labor unions paved the way, in fact, for a closer
cooperation between the disparate elements of Basque nationalism,
recognizing much common ground amid their political agendas. And
central to this critical reimagination was a recognition that dialogue
should take center stage in addressing the issue of ETA and Basque
political violence. This would, perhaps, seem a simple enough
strategy to invoke, but, as I hope I have demonstrated, critically unmasking terrorism has proved to be a difficult exercise for many
observers.

I ultimately contend that the so-called "third way" proposal of
Eusko Langileen Alkartasuna (ELA) and Langille Abertzalean Batz-
ordea (LAB), the cease-fire of ETA, and the formation of the all-
Basque nationalist coalition government at the end of 1998 indicate,
in however embryonic form, a "liberatory discursive strategy"[28]
which, taken together, are indeed going some way toward critically
rethinking ETA. And in critically addressing ETA—through the issue
of returning Basque political prisoners to the Basque Country, for example—the combined forces of the three Basque nationalist political
parties have actually begun the process of a move toward a postna-

tional model of interdependence. As emphasized earlier, postnationalism does not imply a mythical end of nationalism, but rather an accommodation with changing terrains, strategies, and discourses of nation and identity. By way of contrast, it seems that the advocates of Spanish nationalism, those who remain locked into a fear of fanatical minority ethnonationalism at the end of the twentieth century (surely representative of modernity's inherent sense of melancholy), are at present less aware of postnational settlements, sensibilities, and strategies.

Of the many telling moments that have marked the current process of Basque political reimagination and the move toward postnational political identities, I would highlight the common front advocated by all Basque nationalist political leaders (many of them former bitter adversaries) during the multitudinous demonstration in early 1999 in favor of the return of Basque political prisoners to the Basque Country, an event little reported in the Spanish nationalist press. Followed a few months later by a tentative electoral pact between the three Basque nationalist parties, it would seem that the terrain of imagining Basque political violence is shifting and that, with a wealth of future possibilities before it, Basque nationalism has actually begun the process of critically unmasking the eternal terrorist.

Notes

1. Emphasis added. Benedict Anderson, *Imagined Communities: Reflections on the Origin and Spread of Nationalism.* Rev. ed. (London and New York: Verso, 1991), p. 6.

2. Such fixity, it is argued here, is reflective of the modern project in general, which itself stems from the Enlightenment ideal that "there was only one possible answer to any question. From this it followed that the world could be controlled and rationally ordered if we could only picture and represent it rightly." David Harvey, *The Condition of Postmodernity: An Enquiry into the Origins of Cultural Change* (Cambridge, MA and Oxford: Blackwell, 1990), p. 27.

3. Cf. Partha Chaterjee's assertion that the West, specifically through the collusion of governments and media, views nationalism as a dark and unpredictable threat to the peace and order of its societies, like drugs,

illegal immigration, and terrorism. See "Whose Imagined Community?" in *Mapping the Nation,* ed. Gopal Balakrishnan (London and New York: Verso, 1996), pp. 214–16.

4. Durkheim views representation as a system of beliefs, values, and symbols that serves as a means of articulating the world meaningfully to members of a particular cultural group. See, for example, Emile Durkheim, *The Elementary Forms of Religious Life: A Study in Religious Sociology,* trans. Joseph Ward Swain (London: George Allen & Unwin; New York: The Macmillan Company, 1915), pp. 370–371, 377–388.

5. Emphasis added. Robert Darnton, *The Great Cat Massacre: And Other Episodes in French Cultural History* (New York: Vintage Books, 1985), pp. 192, 193.

6. Emphasis added. Michael Ignatieff, *The Warrior's Honor: Ethnic War and the Modern Conscience* (New York: Metropolitan Books, 1998), pp. 24–25.

7. According to Frederic Jameson, film is not only "the first distinctively mediatic art form" but also a powerful location of culture which, despite some examples to the contrary, remains modernist in both form and sensibility. It thus serves as a central discourse or narrative in creating and sustaining essentialist cultural values and categories. See *Postmodernism: Or, the Cultural Logic of Late Capitalism* (Durham: Duke University Press, 1991), p. 68.

8. *The Jackal* Web site (http://www.thejackal.com).

9. Simone de Beauvoir, *The Second Sex,* trans. and ed. H. M. Parshley (New York: Alfred A. Knopf, 1964), p. 253.

10. Cf. an excellent article by Irit Rogoff which explores the gendering of another "threatening" discourse—fascism (*the* index of fear and horror for the West, argues Rogoff)—through the curious binary positioning of male and female objects and artifacts in a German museum. Rogoff argues that the museum display, supposedly the representation of a very real human tragedy (the period of National Socialist rule in Germany), is enacted through the "ahistorical arena of women's lives and written via the representation of women's bodies and fetishized parts of the female anatomy." See "From Ruins to Debris: The Feminization of Fascism in German-History Museums," in *Museum Culture: Histories, Discourses, Spectacles,* eds. Daniel J. Sherman and Irit Rogoff (Minneapolis: University of Minnesota Press, 1994), p. 247.

11. Lest we might think that *The Jackal* represents an isolated case, I point to two other recent Hollywood films which reduce Basque characters to similar basic stereotypes. *A Time of Destiny* (Columbia TriStar Pictures, 1988), the tale of an immigrant Basque family in California during

World War II, contains a plot-line that hinges on the importance of honor and a vendetta-like revenge of the central character, Martin Larrañeta, played by William Hurt. *Grosse Pointe Blank* (Buena Vista Pictures, 1997) includes a minor role of an ex-ETA terrorist, who is described by Dan Aykroyd's hitman character as "some Basque whacker from the Pyrenees," hired to kill the leading man, played by John Cusack.

12. Cf. Harvey's argument that "corporations, governments, political and intellectual leaders, all value a stable (though dynamic) image as part of their authority and power . . . This becomes, in effect, the fleeting, superficial, and illusory means whereby an individualistic society of transients sets forth its nostalgia for common values. The production and marketing of such images of permanence and power require considerable sophistication, because the continuity and stability of the image have to be retained while stressing the adaptability, flexibility, and dynamism of whoever or whatever is being imaged" (*The Condition of Postmodernity,* p. 346).

13. Ibid.

14. Stuart Hall, "The Rediscovery of 'Ideology': Return of the Repressed in Media Studies," in *Culture, Society and the Media,* eds. Michael Gurevitch, Tony Bennett, James Curran, and Janet Woollacott (London and New York: Methuen, 1982), pp. 67–68.

15. Cf. Joseba Zulaika and William A. Douglass, *Terror and Taboo: The Follies, Fables, and Faces of Terrorism* (New York and London: Routledge, 1996), p. 204.

16. Hall, "The Rediscovery of 'Ideology,'" p. 69.

17. Ibid., p. 87.

18. At http://osis.ucsd.edu/~ehj/html/birtheta.html.

19. For a more complete articulation of this argument, see Cameron J. Watson, "Sacred Earth, Symbolic Blood: A Cultural History of Basque Political Violence from Arana to ETA," Ph.D. Diss., University of Nevada, Reno, 1996.

20. José Luis Alvarez Enparantza [Txillardegi, pseud.], *Euskal Herria helburu* (Tafalla: Txalaparta, 1994), p. 140.

21. For an expansion of this argument see Watson, "Sacred Earth, Symbolic Blood," pp. 549–556 and ff.

22. Joseba Zulaika argues that in Basque the concept of *aska,* implying a "container" and "emptiness," comes from the same root as *aske* or "free," also found in the words *askatasunez* (freely, spontaneously), *askatu* (to free), and *askatasuna* (freedom). See *Basque Violence: Metaphor and Sacrament* (Reno and Las Vegas: University of Nevada Press, 1988), pp. 282–283.

23. Walter Benjamin, *Illuminations: Essays and Reflections*, ed. Hannah Arendt, trans. Harry Zohn (New York: Schocken Books, 1968), p. 255.

24. Cf. Zulaika and Douglass's assertion that they have "engaged themselves in scrutinizing terrorism discourse in order to challenge both the inquisition and the witches. As the world moves forward into uncharted political waters, it is well to deprive both sides unchallenged access to, and control of, terrorism discourse, since ultimately it is we, the public, who are the real targets (and victims) of the manipulation. If we take away their witches from the self-styled, emblematic protectors of the moral order, elected or otherwise, then they must justify their activities in other terms. Stripped of their scapegoats, the architects of the New World Order and its flawed democracies will have to explicate and defend their agendas in terms of political rather than terroristic discourse. Similarly, by dissolving the category and unmasking the rhetorics of terrorism, the 'terrorists,' denied their roles within a plausible script would cease to be actors capable of a credible apocalyptic performance. Terrorism discourse must be disenchanted if it is to lose its efficacy for all concerned" (*Terror and Taboo*, pp. 238–239).

25. In 1994 the secretary general of the Partido Socialista de Euskadi–Euskadiko Ezkerra (the Spanish socialist party) in Gipuzkoa, Jesús Eiguren, observed that "the theory of post-nationalism had become reality" in the Basque Country through a "social and political legitimizing of the non-nationalist vote" (*El Correo Español*, June 19, 1994, p. 21, col. 1); cf. Jon Juaristi's observation that postnationalism implies a situation in which other forms of social loyalty debilitate the strength of nationalism. See "Postnacionalismo," in *Auto de Terminación (Raza, nación y violencia en el País Vasco)*, eds. Juan Aranzadi, Jon Juaristi, and Patxo Unzueta (Madrid: El País/Aguilar, 1994), p. 97.

26. Richard Kearney, "Postnationalism and Postmodernity," in *Postnationalist Ireland: Politics, Culture, Philosophy* (London and New York: Routledge, 1997), p. 58.

27. Ibid., p. 60.

28. To borrow a phrase from Homi K. Bhabha, *The Location of Culture* (London and New York: Routledge, 1994), p. 178.

Begoña Aretxaga

A Hall of Mirrors: On the Spectral Character of Basque Violence

What matters when one tries to elaborate upon some experience,
isn't so much what one understands, as what one doesn't understand.

—Lacan, *The Seminar of Jacques Lacan, Book 1*

I begin with a story that most people in the Basque Country probably know.[1] It is about things that happen somewhere midway between dream and reality, in the space some would regard as the unreal materialized or that others might consider to be inapprehensible reality, the domain of trauma and fantasy. December 10, 1995, Mikel Otegi, 23 years old, took the shotgun hanging on the wall of his farmhouse, went outdoors, and killed two *ertzainas* (Basque policemen) who had come to inquire about his fast driving. He then called the authorities to report the crime and surrendered. In his deposition, Otegi testified that he could not remember what had happened, and only recalled that he "lost it" (*se salió de sus casillas*). He said that he saw the two policemen by the side of the road while driving. When he arrived home he went to bed. Then he heard the dogs barking, came out to see what was happening, and saw the two policemen, one of them near his car. He testified that he told them to go away, but the *ertzainas* ignored him. He then "lost it," went inside the house, and could not remember what happened next. Otegi also stated that the Basque police had harassed him over the previous two years, that he was beaten by them once, and that, since then, he had felt constantly accosted (Forest 1997: 247–248).

This episode touched a deep nerve within an already nervous political world of the Basque Country. It became a symptomatic event, one triggering heightened emotions and deeply contested interpretations. I begin with this episode in order to talk about the violent exchange between radical Basque nationalist youths and the young *ertzainas* that has dominated the political climate during the late 1990s until ETA's recent cease-fire. During the last decade, the *ertzaintza* (Basque police force) has progressively assumed the police functions accorded previously to the Spanish national police, including riot control and conducting the anti-terrorist campaign. One consequence has been that young activists coming of age during this decade frequently encountered the power of the state in the guise of the *ertzaintza*, and therefore made it a target of the violence within an escalating strategy of rioting and sabotage against the state. Because the violence occurring between Basque police and radical-nationalist activists falls within the "imagined community" of the Basque nation (in contrast to a former symbolic structure in which the "Basque people" was opposed to the "Spanish state"), such violence has evoked for many Basques the specter of fratricide and a corresponding deep anxiety over national (Basque) identity. After Otegi's killings, for example, the phantom of fratricide haunted the reports, editorials, and articles published by the *Diario Vasco* newspaper.[2] The brother of one of the policemen killed voiced it by saying that "we are killing ourselves,"[3] meaning the Basques. Professional experts reinforced this specter of civil confrontation.[4] Whether created or reinforced, the anxiety of fratricide has been fed by the mass media in its ongoing reports referring to monstrous ethnic violence and active metaphorical comparison of the Basque Country with the Balkans.

While anxieties over violence occur across the nationalist political spectrum, moderate and radical nationalists blamed each other for generating it and thereby jeopardizing the nation-building project. This opposition between nationalists has changed with ETA's cease-fire, a development that has given rise to a regrouping of all nationalist forces in the struggle for self-determination, and that has re-established the older opposition between Basque nationalists and the Spanish state. Yet, despite this shift, young activists have continued to deploy the kind of urban violence called *kale borroka*, which has been infused more than before with the aura of fratricidal spectrality. The street violence is a threat to the recent nationalist alliance (and the current structure of political opposition between Basque nationalists and the Spanish state) because it underscores an inherent tension within nationalism. Inasmuch as the Basque institutions assume state powers in the development of government and its security apparatuses, opposition to the state by radical activists continues to fall within the mission of their version of Basque nationalism, or at least within the contested space of "Basqueness," thereby framing national identity as split and shifting construction. I would suggest that the realization of a divided and conflicted national identity has a traumatic impact, one that gives political violence its spectral form.

In this article I am interested in tracking the ghostly character of this violence between Basque police and young radical nationalists, its structure and manifestations for those who engage in it and whose everyday lives are marked by its presence. I will argue that for those agents and sufferers of the violence whom I interviewed—*ertzainas* and young activists alike—violence is engendered, materialized, and reproduced as, and within a realm of, violence and terror woven by the rumors of abuse and death circulating within the Basque Country's dense public sphere—that is, in the bars and streets, in posters and newspapers—as well as through the ritualized interactions and performances of young *encapuchados* (hooded activists) and masked police. In this sense I suggest that violence in the Basque Country is better understood as a fantastic reality than as an ideological product. To speak of violence as fantastic reality is not to say, however, that it is illusory, or the product of some kind of social pathology; rather, it means that in the Basque Country the experience of violence corresponds to a *different* mode of reality, one whose visibility is that of the invisible, a spectral mode not unlike that of witchcraft. I use fantasy here in a psychoanalytic sense—that is, neither as a deformation of an original event nor as a purely illusory construction, but as a form of reality in its own right, one that structures the lives of subjects and that might become, in fact, the only truly *Real*.[5] Otegi's feelings of persecution by the police might or might not correlate with actual police harassment, but the violence of being accosted was for him—as it is for many other youths—real, and it produced its own reality effects and its own corresponding violence. The same, I will argue, can be said about the *ertzaintza*, whose feelings of harassment by young *encapuchados* were/are as real, and are equally capable of triggering their own forms of institutionalized (albeit illegal) violence.

This spectral space of trauma and fantasy constitutes what Benjamin saw as a kind of no-man's land of the modern state, where the police cease to maintain the law but instead take it into their own hands.[6] Yet the ghostly violence of the police is undergirded by a profound ambivalence toward the law, which is simultaneously maintained, transgressed, and experienced as a punitive agency. Basque police share with their radical youth counterfoils the experience of Law as oppressive agency. In articulating collective anxieties about Basque national identity, the mimetic exchanges between these opposing forces engender violence as another reality, a presence that erupts into the order of normality, disrupting it and giving it a sense of surreality.

The Space of Trauma

I. THE SPECTER OF THE STATE

I first heard about Otegi in the course of a whispered conversation held as we walked through the bars and streets of Bilbao, invested with the political intimacy of secret knowledge that can become dangerous in the possession of the wrong person. My friend Antonio had introduced me to two other young men, and told them that I was interested in writing about "street fights."[7] He was careful not to say "street violence," as young activists attribute that term to the attempts of the mass media and the state to discredit them. As we walked through the labyrinthine streets and plazas of the old part of the city, Jesus suddenly began to talk about the *ertzaintza*, as if prompted by memories sprouting up out of the urban landscape: "The *ertzaintza* are crazy," said Jesus, "they are ready to repress anything that goes out of their control. The other day, for example, the *parados* (the unemployed) were in this plaza having a meeting like they do every week and the police appeared all of a sudden with their vans and their sirens, dressed in riot gear, and gave them two minutes to disperse. For no reason! They had always met there. The police are increasingly belligerent and aggressive."

I heard many stories about the "craziness" of the Basque police during those first months of 1997. "The way the Basque police are acting is excessive," said Jesus. "I think they are experimenting with some towns, like Hernani and Renteria." Itziar, a girl from Hernani, told me on another occasion that they used to laugh at the Basque police, but "now we don't laugh anymore. We are frightened. With the national police or the civil guard you always knew what they were up to, they either beat you or they didn't, but with the Basque police you never know . . . you can be doing nothing and they come and beat the hell out of you—they're crazy."

We entered a bar. There were very few people within or, indeed, out in the streets, but Jesus was whispering and looking over his shoulder from time to time as if to make sure that nobody was listening. "They broke my arm after a demonstration," he said. "There was not even a riot or anything, and suddenly this *ertzaina* throws me to the ground, *puto vasco de mierda,* and started beating me with his wooden baton. And they are Basque! I haven't gone to a demonstration since then. I'm too scared." His friend said that he had also been followed by the police. "For three months," said Jesus. "You got into the car and it was you and three other cars behind. You could go through a road block with no problem, they will see the police cars behind you and let you pass. There were constantly several plain clothes policemen behind me all the time, no matter where I went. It creates a lot of panic and paranoia. It's very frightening and it is difficult to remain calm. Some people react violently and just go and get a gun." This is when I heard about Otegi for the first time, in the company of Anuk, a young member of ETA who claimed to have been abducted by the *ertzaintza.* Jesus continued, "This poor guy, Otegi, who shot two *ertzainas* . . . it could have happened to anybody . . . it is terrible that there are two persons dead, but it's not strange. The presence of the *ertzaintza* is very suffocating."

As he spoke, I remembered the conversation the night before in one of the radical bars in the old part of Bilbao. Somebody had told a story about the *ertzaintza* waiting for some high school students in front of their houses, intimidating them with threats of violence should they continue with their radical activities. The story provoked the outrage of all those present and prompted a string of similar tales. "That is what they are doing now," said Marga, "and they have taken to strip searching women detainees, that is how they terrorize the girls." "People don't know about this," stated Jesus, "because you don't see it, it is never reported; the mass media is distorting reality. They are manipulating what is happening. What happened to this guy, Anuk, was terrible." "What happened?" I asked. "He was kidnapped by the Basque police and they did all sorts of things to him, experimented with him by giving him drugs and using psychological techniques. They let him go, but they were following him all the time. He managed to send a letter to the leadership of ETA—you see he was a militant—in which he told what was happening. He appeared a few days after they had taken him with a toy gun in his hand in front of an old garage, and almost immediately the *ertzaintza* and the Spanish police appeared on the scene and fought among themselves [for the right] to arrest him. It was clear that they were waiting for him, that this was something prepared. And then the national police took him to their station and, obviously, he couldn't take it anymore, so he threw himself out of the window." "Have there been more cases like this one?" I asked. Javi produced a cynical smile and said, "Well, now they hang themselves with a rope," alluding to a Basque political prisoner (Jesus Aranzamendi) who had been found hanging dead in his cell, his feet and hands tied, his eyes covered with a kerchief. The next day the town was plastered with posters denouncing the death as political assassination by the state. Prison authorities said he had committed suicide.

Antonio had his theory of suicide as the new form of dirty war after the GAL[8] scandal, which implicated Spanish state officials in paramilitary assassinations of Basque radicals, had made overt killing difficult. "Nobody believes the suicide! They [the state authorities] are trying to create terror, send a message to Basque radicals that says 'this is what awaits you.'" In the discourse of the everyday speech of radical nationalism, the state is a phantom, an authoritarian and violent agency that is everywhere yet nowhere in particular; a ghostly presence that haunts the political imagery of Basque radicalism and organizes it around stories of violence and death.

For the young *encapuchados* involved in defacing the state with Molotov cocktails, the *ertzaintza* has become, alongside the Spanish police or Civil Guard, the embodiment of the state. For the radicals, the state's ghostly power permeates the actions of the *ertzaintza*, cloaked in the black masks that they call the *verdugillo*. For Tasio—an *ertzaina*—the mask is self-defeating because it betrays fear and manifests, all too iconically, the blurred line between terrorism and policing, between the terror of Law and the law of Terror. "When you see the images of the police with masks and the arrested leaders of Herri Batasuna without them, you realize that the police has failed as such," says Tasio. For him, the masked police emblematize the state as outlaw and signify its mimetic performance of terrorism.

The power of the state circulates in the form of rumors and stories about the sudden appearances of the police, their abuses, and their unfathomable motives. Ekaitz, an old radical, thinks that the Basque police is totally infiltrated by the CSID (the Spanish Secret Service) and that nothing Basque or autonomous remains in it. Like Ekaitz, young radicals also think that the body of the *ertzaintza*, which once represented the clearest image of an imagined Basque state, has been possessed by the Spanish state. Therefore, for them, the Basque police force is simply not Basque anymore, it is another state's body. And like the body of the possessed, the *ertzaintza* speaks and acts as someone else (De Certeau 1988: 246). Consequently, for radical nationalists it becomes doubly alien, an object of fear and resentment, a powerful shadow that is and isn't, a familiar figure turned stranger, a betrayer that has to be uncovered by unmasking its duplicitous identity with the derogatory designation: *cipayo.* The term *cipayo* refers to the soldiers of Indian origin serving in the British colonial army, and therefore conveys the implicit meaning of betrayal.

These rumored stories of unpredictable police violence and dirty wars circulate freely in the dense public sphere of Basque politics—in the bars, on the streets, and in informal conversations. My friend Maria assures me as we walk along the ocean in San Sebastián that a couple of young guys disappeared in the area of Mondragon, reappearing hours later without knowing where they had been. She has no doubt that this was the work of the Basque police, even though she cannot answer any of my concrete queries about when, how, and who.

In this maze of rumors it is not truth that counts, for it cannot be extricated from the narratives. What matters are the stories themselves, delineating as they do a traumatic space where the uncanny sense of the real erupts in the form of spectral exchange. Like the police, whom they violently engage, these young activists have a ghostly reality as well. Appearing and disappearing with their faces covered, they suddenly strike against a building or a police van, like an eruption of another *reality* upon the mundane surface of politics, their masks mirroring those of the police in a hide-and-seek game, a repetitive *fort da,* that iconizes the power of concealment.

II. A HALL OF MIRRORS

The *encapuchados* are the agents of a new form of political violence focused on the defacement of the state and performed by radical youngsters ranging from 14 to 22 years of age. In the years before the cease-fire, it became an increasingly quotidian occurrence for a pack of these youngsters to invade the central streets and plazas, their faces covered with hoods and kerchiefs and their hands bearing the Molotov cocktails that were destined to burn public buses, police vehicles, telephone booths, ATM machines, the headquarters of conservative political parties, court houses, and other public buildings, only to disappear as swiftly as they had appeared. For the *encapuchados,* this was sabotage of the state. During 1995 and 1996, according to the counts by Gipuzkoan authorities,[9] there were 408 and 440 such acts in the province respectively, and they increased by a further 25% during 1997. More so than the violence of ETA, the presence of the *encapuchados* has struck a deep nerve in Basque society.

Like the police, the *encapuchados* trigger all sorts of rumors about their identity. Jayone, who is a patrolling *ertzaina,* thinks that the *encapuchados* are manipulated by older radical nationalists. "Some of those people are dogmatic, they are like a sect and you cannot talk to them because they do not listen or think by themselves." She thinks that some might be idealists, but others are simply hired to create trouble. "A fellow officer told me," she said, "that his sister was caught in a riot and took refuge in the entry hall of an apartment building, along with a group of young guys; and then an older man entered the building, took his wallet out of his pocket and gave 5,000 pesetas [approximately $40] to each person. The officer's sister took the money and left, afraid to say anything." Jayone is convinced that at least some *encapuchados* are paid and she said that most *ertzainas* think so too.

As she talked, I remembered the story told by my neighbor, a woman in her fifties who, like many of her generation, does not approve of the sabotages and arbitrary rioting, even though she sympathizes with radical nationalists. She, too, wonders about the identity of the *encapuchados* and thinks some of them might be paid by the "state" to create bad press for radical nationalists. "They are not our people," she says. And her story followed the same plot as that of Jayone, even though they occupied opposed positions within the political spectrum. My neighbor assured me that she personally once saw how, after a riot in the old city, an old man gave 5,000 pesetas to a young fellow. She said she told them they were shameless and they both lowered their heads. This was how she knew that it was payment for stirring up trouble.

Those studying political violence know that the story of "agents" being paid for organizing riots is a common one in many places (Tambiah 1997). Juan, a savvy cultural activist, laughs at the story when I ask him what he thinks about the rumors of paid *encapuchados*. "Oh sure, I have also heard them, all the stories have the same plot," he says as he repeats it right down to the 5,000 pesetas. "So you, too, have heard them?" I ask. "Of course, it's part of the political folklore." To me it seems like an attempt to seize the ghostly reality of violence. For the *ertzaintza*, such spectral violence has crystallized into what has been called "*grupos Y.*"

These spectral *grupos Y* organize the experience of being a Basque police-person as one dominated by fear.

> The central experience as patrolling *ertzainzas* is fear. The *encapuchados* are a source of fear. With the *encapuchados* you have a sense of helplessness, a sense that you can be attacked at any moment and you cannot do anything, because they are the ones who throw stones or explosives or Molotov cocktails at you. And you are in there trapped in the small space of a van or a car and are just an easy target. And if you hit somebody you can be punished. You feel very impotent and vulnerable, particularly with the judicial system because they are anxious to find a culprit and the penalties are then higher than the ones they give to these youths.

Jayone tells how the *ertzaintza* was called one night to a small town, "because somebody had set ablaze a trash container." A police van responded and it turned out to be an ambush. More than a hundred *encapuchados* emerged, suddenly throwing stones. The *ertzaintza* started firing rubber bullets and somebody hit one of the *encapuchados* in the eye. There was a thorough investigation that supposedly discovered which officer had caused the injury, which is something very difficult to know because "there are several people shooting at once and all of them are wearing masks." Jayone tells the story of the ambush as an illustration of the *ertzaintza*'s vulnerability in the face of both social transgression and the Law which she herself embodies. Thus, in her story, the Basque police force appears as a particularly alienated body: at once the agent of the Law and the subject who fears it, a split subject, who is at once the Law and the outlaw.

Jayone's story mirrors, remarkably, the rumors of young radicals. Like the latter, the *ertzaintza* experiences the *encapuchados* as spectral subjects of violence, a reality governing their lives, yet inapprehensible. As in the case of the *encapuchados,* such spectral violence can erupt unexpectedly at any moment and works through the production of fear, which then circulates within a strange cultural economy spawning a universe of mimetic practices between the young radical *encapuchados* and the police (the other *encapuchados*), a ritualized *fort-da* play that futilely attempts to master the absent presence of the other. An example is when Tasio says that there is an urgency among *ertzainas* to "do something" about the *encapuchados*. "And what do you do? You go and try to unmask them, even though you might know who they are, because that unmasking gives you the feeling of doing something, of having some control, some power. Even though you haven't done anything, it gives you the sense that 'at least now we know who they are.' But you see in most towns you know already who they are before the unmasking. However, you get sucked into that game."

So the *ertzainas* also resent and distrust the Law which, in the form of judicial restraints, can turn against them. As with the young radicals, for the police the production of, and need for, a culprit is an arbitrary process that renders them vulnerable. There is a measure of arbitrariness in the detention and charging of radical youngsters, since the activists are hooded and generally have their faces uncovered only upon being arrested. So there is little chance of determining who was doing what. Jayone's description of the production of a culprit after the shooting of a young man with a rubber bullet echoes, ironically, the same predicament.

The sense of defenselessness that the police feel in the face of the

Law reached the level of paroxysm upon the outcome of Mikel Otegi's trial. In a shocking verdict the jury found Otegi not guilty, heeding the defense's argument that Otegi's killings were the consequence of a heightened feeling of persecution that translated into a moment of mad rage. Otegi was set free. "That was *very, very* hard," said Jayone, "it hurt very deeply because you felt totally vulnerable and impotent, totally at their mercy, it is like *they* [the Law] had given *them* [radical nationalists] impunity to do anything. There are two persons dead and he is *free!!* He is not in a psychiatric hospital or anything like that, he is free. And next day you are on the street on duty and see a demonstration of young radicals shouting *"Mikel Askatua"* (Mikel Free) and applauding, and you have to be there listening to it, and you cannot do anything because they are not doing anything illegal, they are just shouting! I saw my fellow officers cry out of anger."

Anger and fear organize the structure of feelings of the Basque police and young radicals alike. They constitute the experience of violence as a mimetic relation that makes the sense of what is *real* for the Basque police and for the *encapuchados* mirrors of each other. This *reality* of violence is not ordinary reality but rather is what seeps through the order of reality and ultimately shapes it as a space of trauma and terror. This *reality* of violence makes reality a play of surfaces and what some call political madness a reality.

Notes

1. The research for this article was funded by grants from the American Council for Learned Societies (ACLS), Wenner-Gren Foundation for Anthropological Research, and the George Lurcy Educational and Charitable Trust. A version of this piece has been published in Spanish in *La Cuestión Vasca: Claves de un Conflicto Socio Cultural,* edited by Josetxo Beriain and Roger Fernandez (Barcelona: Proyecto A Ediciones). The names of people used in this article are pseudonyms.

2. An editorial in *El Diario Vasco,* 12/11/95, p. 3, explicitly invoked the phantom of fratricide: "The demonstrations in support of the aggressor accompanied [by] threats to the *ertzaintza* brings to the surface how the cancer of fanaticism is weaving a fratricidal strategy with very perverse effects on the future."

3. *El Diario Vasco,* 12/13/95, p. 1.

4. Javier Elzo in *El Diario Vasco*, 12/12/95.

5. See Laplanche and Pontalis (1989 [1966]).

6. See Walter Benjamin's essay "Critique of Violence."

7. The names of people used in this article are pseudonyms.

8. From 1983 to 1987, a new right-wing paramilitary organization called GAL (Grupos Antiterroristas de Liberación) claimed the assassinations of more than thirty Basque activists. In 1994, two policemen revealed the implication of the Spanish government and the military in organizing the GAL.

9. For more information, see the annual reports of the Fiscalia de la Audiencia Provincial de San Sebastián, years 1995 and 1996.

Bibliography

Benjamin, Walter. 1978 [1920]. "Critique of Violence." In *Reflections. Essays, Aphorisms, Autobiographical Writings*, 277–300. New York: Harcourt Brace Jovanovich.

De Certeau, Michel. 1988. *The Writing of History*. New York: Columbia University Press.

Forest, Eva. 1997. *Proceso al Jurado?: Conversaciones con Miguel Castells*. Hondarribia: Argitaletxe.

Laplanche, Jean, and Jean-Bertrand Pontalis. 1989 [1964]. "Fantasy and the Origins of Sexuality." In Ed. V. Burgin, J. Donald, and C. Kaplan, *Formations of Fantasy*. New York: Routledge.

Tambiah, Stanley. 1997. *Leveling Crowds: Ethno-Nationalist Conflicts and Collective Violence in South Asia*. Berkeley: University of California Press.

Navarra: Historical Realities, Present Myths, Future Possibilities

When in 1998 Euskadi ta Askatasuna (ETA) laid down its arms, the status of Navarra suddenly became news again. An issue that, to many, had long seemed settled quickly returned to the fore, and has since stayed there. There is a strong sense of déjà vu to this debate. For amid the formulation of some new possibilities, it is striking how many old ideas are being rejuvenated and established rivalries rekindled. Thus, though I wish to discuss the present reality of Navarra in this chapter, I have first to examine the negotiations during the Transition, which led to Navarra's constitution as an "autonomous province," as so many of the positions adopted and arguments wielded then are directly relevant to the Navarra of today and the immediate future.

Negotiating the Transition

Like any area with a deeply divided population undergoing significant constitutional change, the political history of Navarra during the Transition is complex, labyrinthine, and, above all, tortuous to follow, for all but the most committed of onlookers. For these reasons I shall try to be brief. I do not wish to oversimplify, but nor do I want to drown the main points in a sea of details.

Within a short time after Franco's death, the main political divisions within Navarra could already be outlined. On the far right was "the bunker," headed by the Franquist president of the province's Deputation, Amadeo Marco, and several of its deputies. On the right and center right stood *navarristas:* those deeply opposed to any inclusion of the province in a broader Basque polity. The center left was mainly occupied by the Partido Socialista Obrero Español (PSOE) and the Carlist Party, which were both at this time in favor of inclusion. A spectrum of Basque nationalist parties ranged from the center right to the far left.

When in August 1977 the first proposal for Basque preautonomy (which proposed the inclusion of Navarra) was made known, the Deputation agreed to seek "full foral integration," that is, "restoring the traditional institutions of the Old Kingdom of Navarra," which had existed until 1839, when the leaders of Navarra had pacted with the central government to surrender much of its time-honored autonomy.[1] This seemingly bizarre proposal was seen as a maneuver by the Deputation to protagonize, to take the lead over the political parties, and to prevent Navarra being considered in any form of Basque preautonomy.

In contrast to this reactionary bid, all parties (bar the Navarran Foral Alliance, a platform for "the bunker") were agreed that the government had to be modernized, that is, democratized. In October the navarristas controlling the provincial branch of Unión de Centro Democrático (UCD) put forward their own program: the new Deputation was to be elected by a representative Foral Council (the legislative chamber of the province). Stressing the importance of the 1839 Foral Pact, the program said that any negotiations had to be between the government and the Deputation, assisted by the deputies to Madrid who had won office in the general elections of June 1977. To the Navarran UCD, the possible integration of Navarra into Euskadi could not be tackled *until* the foral institutions had been made much more democratic.[2]

Because the Navarran UCD was so determinedly navarrista, the government tried to have Navarra excluded from the preautonomy.[3] The Navarran UCD rebuffed the approaches of the Partido Nacionalista Vasco (PNV) and PSOE, refusing even to discuss preautonomy with them.[4] Adolfo Suárez told Basque deputies that negotiations would not start if Navarra was included in the preautonomy text.[5] But both the Navarran UCD and the Deputation were very worried when the text was made known, for it stated that the integration of Navarra would be decided by "the competent foral institution"; that is, it neither stated *which* organism it was referring to nor how it would be democratized. The Navarran UCD, worried that a democratic Foral Council might approve integration, argued that it was a right of the Navarran people to be consulted on the issue in a referendum, to be held *before* "the competent foral institution" discussed the issue.[6] Amid stories that the Navarran UCD was thinking of splitting with its national body, numerous people began to call at the headquarters of the party in Madrid to see if the rumor was true that the integration of Navarra had already been agreed on.[7]

This reactionary outcry effectively halted the negotiations over preautonomy, whose content had been almost completely resolved until the navarristas went on the offensive. Suárez and his ministers were being forced to seek a formula that could satisfy both Navarran and Basque deputies.[8] The Navarran UCD deputies, apparently under pressure from Madrid, then agreed to join the Council of Navarran Parliamentarians (CNP).[9] The fundamental objective of this new body was the study of, and the negotiation with Madrid over, foral reintegration and democratization of the foral institutions.

The response of the Deputation was to dig in its heels. The foral deputies did not attend the initial meetings of the council. Instead those in the bunker tried to advance their own proposal for full foral reintegration, and journeyed to Madrid to lobby their cause.[10] They then made the radical, and dangerous, gesture of calling a demonstration for "Navarra, foral and Spanish, yes." The gesture was radical because the Deputation felt able to criticize even the navarrista deputies then negotiating the status of Navarra. The Navarran UCD, as a party, would not attend the demonstration, but its leaders felt obliged to support publicly its objectives, and many participated in a personal capacity. The gesture was dangerous, as the Navarran leader of the PSOE warned, because of the emotional tension resulting from the ETA killing a few days before of a police commander in Pamplona. On that day, Marco spoke to a crowd of about 8,000 from the balcony of the Deputation. Meanwhile armed demonstrators attacked spectators who shouted antifascist slogans. The final balance was twenty wounded. At the same time, in Madrid, 3,000 members of a newly formed navarrista association of Navarrans resident in Madrid demonstrated against the integration of Navarra: some gave the fascist salute; an *Ikurriña* (Basque flag) was publicly burnt.[11]

In reply, fifteen (mainly left-wing) parties and six trade unions

staged a much larger demonstration five days later for "the democratization of the foral institutions."[12] The Assembly of Basque Parla-
mentarians, worried by the increasing violence and polarization of
the debate, agreed in late December that the three Navarran deputies
(two PSOE, one PNV) who attended their meetings could negotiate
with the six Navarran UCD deputies in the Council of Navarran Par-
lamentarians the details of "the competent foral institution" and its
means of deciding on the integration of Navarra.[13] In other words, the
parliamentary opposition to the Navarran UCD had accepted the idea
of a referendum.

Two days later the CNP, after two daylong meetings in Madrid,
finally agreed that "the competent institution" would be the Foral
Council, once it had been elected democratically. Any affirmative decision by the council had to be ratified by simple majority in a referendum of the Navarran people. The Madrid Council of Ministers then
met and immediately agreed to the preautonomy regime for the
Basque Country.[14] However, the "Decree-Law for the application in
Navarra of the Decree-Law on the preautonomy regime of the Basque
Country published three days later did not mention a referendum by
simple majority but stated that "the decision will be ratified by the
Navarran people by direct popular consultation via proceedings and
in the terms which the Government decides, in agreement with the
Deputation." In other words, the decisive majority needed could still
be two-thirds. The Navarran UCD deputies had swiftly engineered
this before the Council of Ministers had met to approve preautonomy.
In reaction, the PNV and PSOE threatened to reject the preautonomy
decree if the referendum on Navarra was *not* based on a simple majority. The CNP met again but could not come to an agreement.[15]

It took six meetings, held in January 1978, between the PNV, PSOE,
and UCD at the state level before they could reach agreement that
only a simple majority would be needed in the proposed referendum.
Many Navarrans in the UCD were very unhappy with this agreement, and felt that ministers in Madrid had pressured Navarran UCD
deputies into toeing the party line. Some were clearly unsatisfied by
the statement of their provincial leaders that PNV and PSOE had at
last agreed with the UCD that the referendum would never be held
in a climate of violence, that Navarra would never be "blackmailed
by terrorism."[16] This, perhaps, was a crucial moment in the negotia-

tions, for given the size of the PSOE electoral base in the province, which way PSOE swung would decide whether any referendum took place. Small wonder, then, that radical nationalists reacted vociferously against the PSOE in the immediate aftermath of its joint decision with the PNV.

Though the democratic forces with interests in Navarra were now finally beginning to come to a conclusive agreement, members of the Deputation complained that they had been excluded from discussions about the referendum.[17] On the same day that the decree approving Basque preautonomy was published, the Deputation chose to make known its own conception of full foral integration. This proposal was so patently anachronistic that even members of the UCD dubbed it "satirical."[18] In the next meeting of the Foral Council, held a month later, Marco prevented the reading of a document (once backed by the majority of the political parties) that demanded the democratization of the foral institutions. He also interrupted, and allowed the public (mostly of the extreme right) to boo, any intervention referring to the incorporation of Navarra or even just mentioning the word "Euskadi."[19] The Franquist Deputation was continuing as it had begun—in a flagrantly nondemocratic mode.

Throughout 1978 (a year particularly marked by political violence in Pamplona), the government continued to lean on Marco and his deputies to agree on formulas for the democratization of the foral institutions. But any concessions Marco and his men did make were made only grudgingly and after much sustained pressure.[20] What seems to have coaxed Marco into finally entering serious negotiations was the government's threat to constitute a Navarran "management team," for which there was historical precedent, and which, on its constitution, would have promptly demanded the resignation of the incumbent foral deputies.[21]

This new, more amenable style of the Deputation, prepared to engage in constructive discussions with the Foral Council and the CNP, suited all concerned, as since 1978 the Constitutional Committee had been debating the proposed Constitution for the country, several of whose provisions referred to Navarra. While the Navarran bunker, the navarristas of the UCD, and Basque nationalists could not easily agree on many issues, at the very least they needed to debate them together thoroughly in their home area, before state-level politicians, frequently working according to different agendas, decided them in Madrid. For example, a joint Deputation–Foral Council committee twice visited the capital to lobby senators to defend the proposals of the council.[22]

After much negotiation between the parties, the Senate approved the following version of the Additional Provision:

> The Constitution supports and protects the historic rights of the foral territories. The general modernization of said foral regime will be carried out, in its own terms, within the frame of the Constitution and the Statutes of Autonomy.

Members of the Deputation-Council committee were unhappy because, in their opinion, the approved version left "the theme absolutely unclear." They had wanted Navarra dealt with separately so that its negotiations with the government would not be linked with those of the Basque Country. Their proposal for the second sentence of the Additional Provision had been: "The reintegration and modernization of these (historic) rights will be carried out in agreement with the representative institutions of said territories."[23] The Navarran UCD deputies had tried to present an amendment that incorporated the proposal of the Deputation and the Council, but had been unable to do so because of PSOE intransigence. They claimed, however, to be satisfied and defended themselves against the charge that they had ceded to pressure from their party at the national level, by arguing that "for the first time in our constitutional history, the foral regime of Navarra is protected and respected by the Constitution." It had been agreed in the constitutional debates that the second sentence of the provision did not apply to Navarra.[24]

The version of the Fourth Transitory Provision approved by the Senate mentioned

> the integration of Navarra into the Basque General Council or the autonomic regime which would substitute it, whose requisites are the approval by majority of the foral organ and the ratification in a referendum by the majority of votes validly cast.

Fears that any Basque-wide referendum on the incorporation of Navarra might lead to the relatively large populations of Bizkaia and Gipuzkoa overriding Navarran opinion were allayed when a UCD senator from Huesca successfully proposed a modification to the Constitution that any proposed statute of autonomy had to be approved in each province of the projected autonomous community.

Jaime Ignacio del Burgo, a leader of the Navarran UCD, had proposed in the Senate that the majority needed in this provision be qualified, not simple. But fellow UCD senators on the Constitutional Committee did not support him. Jesús Aizpun, the other leader of the Navarran UCD, was not so prepared to compromise. He complained that Madrid ministers had treated the Navarran wing of their party badly and had failed to fulfill the agreements earlier pacted by the CNP. He believed the "Basqueness" of Navarra should never be put to plebiscite and so resigned from the UCD. Shortly afterward he launched a new party, which was to be called Unión del Pueblo Navarro (UPN).[25]

The effects of these debates were shown clearly in the following general elections of 1 March 1979 and the local elections to town halls and the Foral Parliament (successor to the Foral Council) of a month later. The results of these elections showed a growing polarization of the Navarran electorate, with the UCD losing votes to the UPN, and the center-left parties (PSOE and the Carlist) losing them to different Basque nationalist groups. To the disappointed Carlists, it seemed everything was going to be reduced to the issue of Navarra's relation with Euskadi.[26]

They were not far wrong, as, for Navarran politicians, the end of 1979 was mostly taken up with the negotiations over the Basque Statute of Autonomy. The Navarran UCD deputies had already complained that the first draft of the statute presented by the Basque General Council was antiforal and anticonstitutional, because it prejudged the situation by automatically including Navarra within Euskadi. Aizpun claimed that the decision to include Navarra in the statute and not to consult Navarran deputies about the matter came from "higher up" than the Minister of Regions, who would normally have dealt with the matter. He strongly implied that the government had managed to reach agreement over the preautonomy text with the Basque parties (which had been threatening to boycott the negotiations otherwise) only by not presenting UCD candidates in Gipuzkoa and by including Navarra in the text.

The statute, ratified by the Cortes in mid-December, stated that if the Navarran people approved incorporation, a second referendum about the incorporation would be carried out in Navarra, Araba, Gipuzkoa, and Bizkaia together. It was left unclear whether the results of this referendum would be calculated globally (as the PNV claimed), or separately in each province (in accordance with the earlier modification of the Constitution).

In reaction, two Navarran UCD deputies, Pegenaute and Monge, promptly left the party because its leaders—the ministers of the government—would not state openly their interpretation of the statute with respect to the second referendum. Pegenaute then publicly protested that Suárez had only ever paid attention to the Navarran deputies of his party when they had adopted positions of firmness. In letters to Suárez, the Navarran deputies had complained that he had not taken their ideas into account when negotiating with Basque deputies and, for that reason, they had said they were ready to defend their position "until the very end." Pegenaute then released details of the much-rumored pact between his former party and the PNV. Suárez and Carlos Garaikoetxea, leader of the Basque government, had signed it on 21 July 1979 "behind the backs" of the Navarran deputies for the UCD. On its signing, Suárez is reputed to have said, "The Statute is good. I will sign it though the matter of Navarra is not too clear."[27] In the senatorial debate over the statute, a pact between the UCD and other parliamentary groups prevented Monge from speaking. Unzueta, a senator for the UCD, told him that the Navarran UCD deputies should quietly drop the subject of Navarra, because they should already be very satisfied with what they had won.[28]

However, the Organic Law for the Regulation of Referendums, approved by the Senate in mid-January 1980, established that the results of a referendum for the incorporation of a province into an autonomous community would be calculated separately in each of the provinces affected.[29] PNV senators were so put out by this that Villa Arregui, UCD spokesman, said his party did not consider itself bound to calculate by province the results of a second referendum on Navarran incorporation. The UCD wanted to leave the form of the second referendum vague to please the PNV; if a referendum on the incorporation of Navarra was to be held in all Euskadi, then the Navarrans could take the matter to the Constitutional Committee.[30] This statement so displeased UCD senators that del Burgo was able to get Suárez to deny publicly that the UCD had pacted secretly with the PNV over Navarra, and that the second referendum would regard the vote in each province. At the same time, Villa tried to mollify the navarristas further by stating that giving priority to the Improvement of the Fuero was the best way to conserve Navarran self-government and to forestall any attempted integration of the province into Euskadi.[31]

Thus, at the end of this long process, the finally determined, full procedure for any attempted integration of Navarra into the Basque Autonomous Community stands as follows:

1. approval of the initiative by an absolute majority of the Foral Parliament;
2. a referendum in Navarra to ratify this initiative;
3. a conjoint convocation of Congress and the Senate to determine the requirements necessary for the reform of the Basque statute;
4. negotiation between the Foral and Basque Parliaments over the reform of the statute;
5. approval by the Foral Parliament of the reformed statute;
6. approval by Congress and the Senate of the reformed statute; and
7. a referendum of all four provinces affected.

Though this procedure did not fulfill all the navarristas' aspirations, its complicated series of seven stages ensured that, in any event, incorporation could not occur easily. Moreover, since the Parliamentary Committee of the Foral Regime had rejected the motion about integration in December 1979, the Foral Parliament could not debate the issue and it could not be raised again for another five years.[32]

To sum up: outlining, as I have done, the twists and turns of these, at times, tempestuous negotiations should not be seen as a somewhat tedious exercise in one corner of Basque political history, for it demonstrates (a) the passions this debate can generate, (b) the positions different groups maintain or shift around (and still mostly maintain and shift around), and (c) the fact that an agreed-on outcome was reached only after years of intense politicking and maneuvering between all the interested parties. Perhaps most important of all is the obvious corollary of this sketched chronology: that any fresh, determined attempt to join Navarra with Araba, Bizkaia, and Gipuzkoa would, most probably, result in a similarly tortuous, impassioned, and prolonged debate.

Talking the Transition

Navarristas and Basque nationalists could be so strongly opposed because they had such very different conceptions of "Navarra" and all it entailed. In 1976, nationalists, contemporary bearers of a long-established ideology, already had a popular base on which they could rely and a host of arguments supporting their position. In contrast, as del Burgo admitted, at that time "the Navarran consciousness was asleep." It was largely thanks to the efforts of himself and a few other energetic right-wing Navarran politicians that a modern *navarrismo* was successfully created during the Transition. Theirs was an essentially reactionary ideology, one fabricated in response to the Basque nationalist challenge and deployed by navarristas to dispute their rivals' arguments point by point. The disputes between these blocs thus broadened into a wide-ranging ideological battle where each side provided its own conceptions of Navarran prehistory, history, "race," religion, territory, language, and political destiny.[33]

BASQUE NATIONALIST NAVARRA

To nationalists, Navarra *was* Euskadi, and an Euskadi without Navarra was a "mutilated" Euskadi, a "monster," for Navarra was the "cradle," the "mother," the "trunk," and the "root" of Euskadi. Even to question whether Navarra was part of Euskal Herria was "offensive," "insulting."[34] Navarrans were Basques "of pure stock." Following the ideas of Jos Miguel de Barandiarán, the revered Basque scholar, contributors to the nationalist newspaper *Egin* spoke of Navarra as "the natural and anthropological enclave of Euskal Herria," a land inhabited by Basques for 6,000 years. "The quasi-totality of the Navarran population has the features of the denominated Basque race, and this taking the upper Paleolithic as point of reference."[35] The original inhabitants of Navarra were Basque; those who came later were "colonizers." Though the aboriginals had been culturally affected by these incomers, the "primordial reality" of the Navarrans was Basque.[36]

The earliest known language of Navarra is Euskera, the only tongue with "the right to call itself Navarran, because all the others have been imported." In a much-quoted phrase originally used by Navarran bishops at the Council of Letran, Euskera was *"linguae navarrorum."*[37] It was only in the last centuries that southerly Navarrans had stopped speaking it. To stress the Basque nature of Navarran culture, nationalists referred to the existence in the province of Basque surnames, toponyms, names of football teams, sports, traditional songs, musical instruments, dances, and rites. They also liked to emphasize the many original contributions made by Navarrans to Basque culture in general.[38]

Most nationalists did admit that the only good example to be found in history of the union of the Basques was the short-lived kingdom of Sancho the Great. But this shortage of precedents did not matter, for history was not to be regarded as "a mirror in which we ought to contemplate the reflection of our present image, but rather the frame which shows us to what extent the historical facts . . . (reveal) . . . the frustration of our community." Some suggested that all difficulties could be overcome if, following the example of Sancho the Great, the grouping of the four Basque provinces was collectively called "Navarra." Navarristas might be against the incorporation of Navarra, but how could they be against the "Navarrization" of Euskadi?[39]

Some navarristas called for "full foral integration." But why were they not making irredentist claims for Lower Navarra, the "sixth *merindad* (historical district)" of Navarra, on the other side of the Pyrenees? Part of the Navarran kingdom from the tenth century to 1503, it was "essential for the territorial, ethnic and historical integrity of Navarra." For nationalists, pointing to this omission in the navarrista program was a way of underlining the division of the Basques by an international boundary, and of reminding others that del Burgo and his colleagues operated only within a Spanish framework.[40]

Though Navarra is famed for the number of clergy it has produced, one Navarran nationalist priest attacked the Catholicism of the province as always "belligerent, aggressive, wild." All "good" navarristas, he claimed, were Tridentine Catholics, as evidenced in 1979 by their open criticisms of the newly installed Archbishop of Pamplona, a

Basque.[41] If Navarra was distinctly Catholic in comparison with an aconfessional Euskadi, was this a form of religiosity one could be proud of?

Navarra was linked to the other three Basque provinces not just historically and culturally, but economically as well. The four territories were integral elements of the same economic structure since they were economically complementary spaces mixing industry and agriculture, and since they developed among themselves a much more intense network of economic interrelations than with neighboring provinces. In turn this network created an interdependence and solidarity of communal interests.[42] Navarra alone would have too small a base from which to construct a viable autonomous community in the modern Spanish state.

Radical nationalists also stressed the differences between themselves and navarristas by conjoining cultural dispute and class conflict. Their conception of Euskadi was socialist and, to them, the navarristas represented the interests of the local bourgeoisie. They were *caciques* (local bosses) who

> have possessed this old kingdom like a private reservation of their political domination, of their dirty business, of their extortions of the Navarran peasantry. . . . A Navarra outside Euskadi is a Navarra of the Right. For that reason, the Right try to gain time, to prevent by any means the unification of Navarra with the rest of Euskadi because they know that, integrated in Euskadi, their power would be weakened.[43]

These bosses were manipulating the consciousness of Navarrans, for the reality was that the Spanish nation had exploited Navarra in the past, and continued exploiting it in the present.[44] In the late 1970s, "Bosses out!" became a common graffito on Pamplonan walls.

NAVARRISTA NAVARRA

To navarristas, Navarra is not singularly Basque; it is plural. They acknowledge that the Basques are the oldest inhabitants of the region; they deny that Basque culture should be regarded as definitive for the whole province. Instead they like to emphasize the demographic and cultural contributions of the ancient Romans, Franks, later French migrants, Jews, and Muslims, as well as the part played by centuries and centuries of pilgrims making their way to Santiago de Compostela. The list of languages spoken in Navarra in the past thus includes Latin, Hebrew, Arabic, Provençal, and Romance as well as Euskera. The Basques, moreover, are as culturally homogeneous as Navarra itself. One UCD advertisement underlined the diversity of Navarran folklore: some were clearly early Basque in origin; others evinced Mozarabic or Roman influences.[45]

Navarristas liked to refer to the work of Claudio Sánchez-Albornoz, a distinguished historian and president of the Republic in Exile from 1962 to 1970. In a much-reprinted article, he argued that the Basques are not historically distinctive in any fundamental sense, given their "intimate kinship" with a great part of the early population of the peninsula. According to him, the aboriginals of Navarra were the Euskera-speaking Vascon people who, sometime between the sixth and tenth centuries, "Vasconized," or colonized, the three tribes to their west, then occupying the areas roughly coterminous with the modern boundaries of Araba, Bizkaia, and Gipuzkoa. In the process, they gave the colonized peoples Euskera and certain forms of life. During the centuries of Muslim occupation, Navarra and the "Vasconized Country" (the *"País Vascongado,"* as Araba, Bizkaia, and Gipuzkoa are sometimes known) lived separately: the destiny of the "Vasconized peoples" was linked to that of the Asturians and the Cantabrians. Sánchez-Albornoz also emphasized that by the tenth century many Basques were living in northern Castile, and that between the twelfth and the nineteenth centuries the Basques never attempted to secede; rather, they were often moved by their enthusiastic patriotism for Spain.[46] Sánchez-Albornoz thus did not disagree with nationalists that Navarra was "the trunk" of the Basques, but what he also did was to expand the Basque frame so broadly that it dissolved within the greater Spanish one.

The main article in which he argued this case was specially reprinted in 1977 by the Committee of Navarrans in Madrid while he himself tried to have his thesis as widely disseminated as possible. Patently navarrista, he liked to claim that the Navarrans had maintained their liberty because they had guts, while the Basques, before colonization by the Vascones, had lived in full barbarity, adoring trees and fire. During the electoral campaign of 1979, the UCD referred to his theories about Vasconia in their advertisements.[47]

Navarristas stressed that from the eighth to the sixteenth centuries Navarra was a historical, political, and regional unity as a kingdom, an independent community. When it was incorporated into the Castilian crown in 1512, this integration was, as stated at the time, "by way of equi-principal union, each retaining its ancient nature, in laws as well as in territory and government." Each monarch of Castile had to swear to uphold this ancient nature and laws of Navarra. Thus Navarra integrated itself fully into Spain and the common task of the Spanish peoples.[48] Navarra maintained its singularity, but within the frame of Spain.

Navarristas could also exploit popular stereotypes of intra- and interprovincial difference. Many people in Navarra speak of its northern inhabitants, living in the Pyrenean valleys, as withdrawn but sincere, and of its southern inhabitants, living on the plain of the Ribera, as exuberant and extremely friendly. Any reference to these dichotomous stereotypes indirectly underlines the cultural heterogeneity of Navarra, for while the Euskera-speaking *montañeros* fulfill almost all of the criteria of almost all the definitions of Basqueness, many *ribereños* do not regard themselves as Basque, and only their very distant ancestors had spoken Euskera. Looking across the provincial borders, people from Bizkaia are caricatured as swaggering boasters and Gipuzkoans as condescending towards Navarrans. In an open letter publicized by the navarrista Junta of Foral Defense and supposedly written by twenty-one Navarrans forced to migrate to San Sebastián for jobs, complaints are made about Gipuzkoans who call themselves pure Basques and use any pretext to insult the migrants.[49] Navarristas also damned large demonstrations in Navarra with sizable Bizkaian and Gipuzkoan contingents as "invasions."

Thus, to the navarristas, Navarra was plural and democratic; Euskadi was racist and totalitarian. Navarra was traditionally Catholic; Euskadi was associated with militant atheism. According to an editorial in the hard navarrista newspaper *El Pensamiento Navarro* a few days before the Deputation demonstration of December 1977, "Navarra will rise again with greatness if it is faithful to its History, if it rediscovers itself in its Christian spirit, the essence of its civilization."[50] There was little chance of that happening, its author implied, if Navarra had to dilute its essence within a greater Basque polity.

Euskadi was industrially congested. Bizkaia and Gipuzkoa were so overcrowded that they wanted to "colonize" the relatively under-populated Navarra, with Basque businessmen setting up factories and bringing their own workforce to fill them. The Basque Government would plan for all Euskadi and might choose certain Navarran areas for massive industrialization. But the industrialization of Navarra had so far been mainly financed by local capital; only 8 percent of the money had come from the Basque provinces. Moreover, in terms of social well-being, Navarra was the fifth best-placed province in the country, while the economy of Euskadi was in decline. Furthermore, it was best for Navarra to defend its own interests by direct negotiations with the government. Navarra would be in a minority within Euskadi. People who used bombs and machine guns to oblige Navarra to enter Euskadi were not going to look after the interests of the province. They were going to exploit it.[51]

FUEROS

If there is one term that sums up the navarrista position during the Transition, it is *fuero.* Originally fueros were simple charters granted by the king or lesser lords to the inhabitants of newly created settlements, guaranteeing them certain rights and privileges. From the fourteenth century the fueros became, in effect, a codified ensemble of juridical provisions that regulated the political and administrative life of the four Basque provinces.[52] The fueros were not a static system but developed over time and, from the fifteenth century, included indigenous customs. From the last decades of the eighteenth century on, however, these fueros were progressively reduced by politicians who saw them as antiquated regional privileges hindering the construction of a modern Spanish state. Navarra, however, managed to keep more of its fueros than did Araba, Bizkaia, or Gipuzkoa, and Franco reinforced its foral system during his rule, in recognition of the Navarran contribution to the war effort.

The fueros were a core symbol in navarrista discourse because the term is so vague. Since fueros have institutional, juridical, political, historical, cultural, and economic aspects, they can be interpreted in a number of separate ways. To some, they became symbolic of the province itself, and what made it distinctive. In the opinion of one local historian, "The fueros are like the SOUL for the immense majority of Navarrans. One cannot say what it is or how far it reaches.

But everything fills it and everything animates it." The fueros could even be viewed as an integral organ of the Navarran body, one that defined the provincial personality and gave it a masculine edge, for in one notorious formulation, they were "los COJONES de Navarra," its balls.[53]

Since "fuero" symbolized Navarran government, the politics of the province were frequently discussed in terms of the fueros. Marco tried to legitimate his own position by calling the Deputation "the only depositary of the unrenounceable legacy of our fueros." To him and others in the bunker, the fueros were based on Christian principles and hence incompatible with Marxism. Dignity, private initiative, and other fundamental liberties of people and social institutions have been in the fueros for centuries. They could be not be made the object of a referendum. Those in the bunker claimed that indiscriminate universal suffrage had never been foral, and they complained of a mania for change at all costs, of applying to the foral "a democratic jacket" that would not fit.[54]

Del Burgo, who called himself "foralist to the marrow," similarly saw the fueros as freedom and justice, as a right to autonomy. Since Navarra had always comprised a racial, linguistic, ethnic, cultural, and sociological mix, its unity was grounded in its fueros. Unlike those in the bunker, however, he (and others in the UCD) did not see the fueros as unchanging, but as open and perfectible. They could be improved, brought more up to date, made more democratic. To him and his confederates, the fuero was the heritage of *all* Navarrans and not just those heading the Deputation. Del Burgo liked to stress that at the core of the fueros lay their pacted nature. To him, this idea of political pact between the Navarran and central governments constituted "the fundament of our national integration and of recognition of our autonomy." Unlike Basque nationalism, his navarrismo was in no way separatist, as "to be Navarran is one of the ways to be Spanish."[55]

The opponents of the Navarrans had other ideas. Though ETA had originally praised the fueros generally, making them centrally important in their idealized conception of the Basque past, radical nationalists said they struggled "not in the name of antediluvian historic rights, but in that of the modern principle of sovereignty of a people." Emphasizing the inherent inequality in any negotiation between Navarra and Madrid, they poured scorn on the famously "pacted" nature of the 1839 Foral Pact. To them, politicians should concern themselves with present problems, plan for the future, and not treat the past as an absolute condition. Fueros were just juridical and political structures; the Navarran people were more than just the fueros.[56]

They were deeply suspicious of the foralist pretensions of some members of the Navarran bourgeoisie. In a joint communiqué, several radical nationalist and left-wing parties criticized "the now 'out and out navarristas and foralists' who have never defended the Navarran laws and fueros, except when they see their personal privileges threatened by the participation and protagonism of the people." In their eyes, those in the bunker were not true foralists but "ritual users of the pseudofuero." Both they and the more democratically inclined foral deputies were merely using the fueros as their own private reserve in order to develop nepotistic networks of sinecures and privileged positions. Those then running the Deputation might proclaim love of the fuero, but it was *their* fuero, not that of the people. To these opponents of navarrismo, the government of Navarra was not "foral" but "fueroid" or "foraloid."[57]

Soul, testicles, dignity, freedom, justice, autonomy, unchanging, dynamic, constitution, mythic mediator, popular charter, universal suffrage, organic democracy, private initiative, compatible with Marxism, based on Christian principles: the fueros can be read in many different ways and translated into other equally ambiguous phrases. This thoroughgoing vagueness was, at the same time, their strength and the reason for their continued use in regional political rhetoric, sometimes in highly novel contexts distant from any traditional conception of the fueros. It's not surprising, then, that this "creative" use of fueros was ironized by some centralists. For example, in the discussions about airports during the negotiations over the Basque statute, the Minister involved asked the Basque representatives if they had also some foral bird?[58]

Consolidation

The "Improvement" of the Navarran Fuero was approved in 1982. Since that date, Navarra has been officially recognized within the

Spanish Constitution as its own separate autonomous community (known as a "foral community"), with its own democratically elected Deputation and Foral Parliament. Navarristas could feel justifiably content with this result, given that it was, to a great extent, their successful and sustained lobbying of the central government that had prevented Suárez and his ministers from offering Navarra up as a sacrificial lamb to please Basque representatives and get a preautonomy statute approved.

And there the matter more or less rested, with both the Basque Autonomous Community (Communidad Autónoma Vasca, CAV) and Navarra establishing themselves more and more over the following years, making integration ever the less possible. People have become, whether grudgingly or not, ever more used to the idea of Navarra as its own autonomous area, albeit one of the smallest, especially via the continued deployment of what the social psychologist Michael Billig calls "banal nationalism": the daily flagging up of distinctiveness through use of its symbols, and through Navarrans being forced to conduct much of local business and matters within a Navarran administrative frame.[59] To this extent, Navarra is a daily lived reality.

The potential attractions of integration were also made dimmer when the Deputation managed to negotiate a particularly advantageous *Convenio Económico* (pacted economic agreement) with the central government: for why would so many Navarrans wish their province to lose this sweetener? Moreover, the electoral reality behind any attempted shift in the status of Navarra is clear: as the results of repeated surveys over the last two decades all show, the majority of the Navarran electorate are not in favor of anything approaching full integration. The latest poll, carried out by *El Diario de Navarra* in September 1998, showed that 65 percent of those asked were against the integration of Navarra into an independent Euskadi and only 18 percent were in favor.[60] Furthermore, with the disappearance of the UCD, many of its erstwhile supporters shifted to the UPN, which, with its staunchly navarrista thesis, has gone on to become the major single party within the province. This political polarization has been exacerbated by the fact that the great majority of nationalists within Navarra do not vote for a moderate nationalist party but for its radical version, which maintains a steadfastly anti-navarrista position. Although, to the great surprise of their common opponents, some navarristas and radical nationalists have been prepared, at certain political junctures, to engage in covert cooperation for the sake of their respective political advantage, neither side has been prepared to compromise its fundamental position with respect to the status of Navarra. For all these different sorts of reasons—economic, social, electoral, political, and "banal"—unless new, highly significant factors surge over the horizon, radical change in Navarra is deeply unlikely.

That does not mean other sorts of change may not be considered, as has occurred in recent years. In early 1995 a schism within the UPN led to some ex-members forming their own party, Convergencia Democrática de Navarra. The CDN was dedicated, among other objectives, to narrowing the gap between navarristas and nationalists, hence the "convergence" in its title. In the elections to the Foral Parliament that year, no party gained an absolute majority. So in July the Navarran wing of the PSOE, CDN, and Eusko Alkartasuna (EA, formed from a schism within the PNV) finally agreed to form a coalition government. The basis of their agreement was a formal pact, which included a commitment to establish "some special and permanent relations with the Basque Autonomous Community, for historic reasons and for the existence of common questions." The idea was to promote a policy of coordination and cooperation between both governments, as well as committing themselves to create a permanent Intergovernmental Committee. This agreement was approved by both the Navarran and Basque governments in the spring of 1996. The following July it was authorized by their respective parliaments, though rebuffed by the UPN in the foral chamber and by its nationwide ally, Partido Popular (PP), in the Basque one. These parliaments then jointly referred the agreement to the Cortes for its authorization. It was sent back.

It was sent back because the tripartite coalition had fractured a few days after the Foral Parliament had authorized it. The UPN had then gone on to form a minority government. As the new president of the province, Miguel Sanz, had forewarned, he had the legislative process for the establishment of the Intergovernmental Committee halted. Although he said that, with certain changes, his executive was prepared to take up the theme again some time and to present the Basque government a new text, it has not so far done so.

In February 1998 the Navarran branch of the nationwide left-wing coalition Izquierda Unida (IU) wished to present a motion to the Foral Parliament aiming to stimulate the Navarran government into formalizing a new agreement with its Basque counterpart. But Sanz and his party would not shift their ground. The Navarran wing of the PSOE stated that it was a theme that could not be put into action without a political consensus. The Navarran PSOE was thus partisan of postponing any new attempts. Ever since his ascent to the secretary-generalship of the Navarran PSOE, Juan José Lizarbe has reiterated that the Intergovernmental Committee is not a priority for his party. On learning that the Navarran PSOE would have abstained in the resulting debate, IU withdrew its motion. The office of the Lehendakari (president of the Basque government) also joined the debate by stating that it did not understand why IU wished to present a motion that would not prosper: "The text agreed between the two governments and ratified by their parliaments is a reference. If a chamber rejects it now it would be spoiled, it would signify a step backwards."[61]

The very next day Juan Cruz Allí, president of CDN, reiterated his party's thesis about the possibility of some kind of convergence between Navarra and the CAV. Reaction was swift: the secretary-general of the UPN accused him of "dancing to the sound of music played by PNV" and of acting as "figurehead and crier" for its leaders. In his opinion, Allí was trying to "undermine what is distinctive about us from the Basque Country, in order to ask if we are not so distinctive, what problem is there for Navarrans and Basques to speak of Navarra. Cousins we will be, but fools never."[62]

And this, of course, is the continuing problem: the well-grounded intransigence of the UPN, for its leaders are fully aware that its attitudes are representative of a very sizable section of the Navarran electorate. Indeed, polls taken prior to the elections of June 1999 suggest that its slice of the vote is set to rise significantly, mainly at the expense of the CDN.[63] The UPN can thus choose to deny, block, and damn any attempt to bring Navarra and the CAV together in however loose or popularly backed a manner, no matter who makes the proposal: the CDN, nationalist-based groups for peace such as Elkarri, or whoever.

It is noteworthy that, rather than diminishing, the UPN's attitude appears to be catching, as shown by the increasingly anti-*vasquista*, unashamedly *españolista* stance of the Araban party, Unidad Alavesa. Indeed the slogan by the party in the campaign for the regional elections of 1999 was "Alava, like Navarra." Its leaders stated that Arabans "are closer to Navarrans than to Gipuzkoans and Bizkaians," and that, imitating the Navarran example, they wish to "promote the sovereignty of the Alavan community so that it decides its own future."[64]

There are, of course, other attempts to draw Navarra and the CAV together. On 7 May 1998, two *etarras* (ETA members) shot dead Tomás Caballero, spokesperson for the UPN, in the town hall of Pamplona. He was the first victim of terrorist violence in Navarra for several years. The next day the nationwide newspaper *El Mundo* printed a cartoon displaying a hooded *etarra* stating "Now we kill Navarran politicians so that it is seen that we consider them as if part of the family." Though deeply cynical, its point is clear: navarristas may wish to have nothing to do with the CAV, but ETA thinks differently. Navarran parties have tried to promote strategies for an end to the violence, but these attempts have usually been in reaction to similar endeavors made by CAV politicians. Usually these attempts have served only to demonstrate the great degree of disagreement between Navarran parties. The Mesa por la Paz de Navarra, created in October 1988 after the example set in the CAV by the Pacto de Ajuria Enea, met spasmodically over the next ten years, with no meetings whatsoever between May 1992 and January 1996. However, since any of its decisions have to be made by consensus, its members (representing all the parties with seats in the Foral Parliament, excepting Herri Batasuna) were rarely able to decide on anything more than a generalized condemnation of terrorism. Its last meeting, held at the end of March 1998, was simply a further example of its internal discord and paralysis. In February 1999, the UPN and the Navarran PSOE rejected a proposal in the Foral Parliament to create a new Mesa por la Paz, which would include HB.[65]

The 1998 declaration of an indefinite cease-fire by ETA bounced the theme of Navarra back on the political center stage. But on the whole, all this move has led to is, so far, the reiteration of old positions by radical nationalists and navarristas. Even Aznar, president of the Spanish government, has joined in the debate, warning that "Navarra is not a trophy which can be hung on the wall." The press has also published an internal document of ETA, which purportedly shows the organization's hopes to establish within the immediate future a separate Basque government covering the seven Basque provinces, on both sides of the border.[66] Such revelations can only help to feed navarrista fears and to strengthen their antinationalist resolve.

There is, however, one very striking difference in the language of debate used by politicians of today and those of twenty years ago: the contemporary lack of any reference to "fueros." To my knowledge, no politician with an interest in Navarra has publicly mentioned the word in the last few years. The term, so central to the arguments of the late 1970s, has come to connote strongly that period, and today's politicians do not wish to be seen as still immured in neo-Franquist times. Instead, they want to be seen as very much today's men and women, able to face today's challenges. Thus they prefer to speak in a modern tongue: of "*autonomías*" and all they entail in the modern Spanish state. In fact, one may even doubt the extent to which the original navarrista talk of "*fueros*" was taken up by the local populace. In the two years (1986–1988) that I did fieldwork in a village in the Middle Zone of the province, and in subsequent trips every year since, I have never once overheard the term in people's conversations. Even in my interviews with a range of selected villagers, on the Navarra/Euskadi debate, very few indeed spontaneously mentioned the word. They were quite ready to talk of threatened "invasion by Basques" or of navarrista denial of the Basque origin, history, and culture of Navarra but not, usually, of "fueros." It would seem that while del Burgo and his confederates were able to generate a Navarran consciousness, they were unable to incorporate this key term of theirs into popular speech.

Europe

But all is not stasis. For the world turns and Navarra, however reluctantly for some of its members, turns with it. I am talking, of course, of the European Union (EU). One effect of the EU has been the creation of multiple transregional and, in some cases, transnational groupings. For instance, the member of the Foral Deputation for Agriculture now meets regularly with his colleagues from the autonomous communities of Galicia, Asturias, Cantabria, and the CAV to form "the Cantabrian Corniche," in order to fight collectively for the interests of their dairy farmers in the European Community (EC).[67] The complementary industrial development of Navarra, the CAV, and Aquitaine is being investigated, so that they may collectively present themselves as a "Euroregion" (and thus compete for funds) in "the new Europe."[68] The possibility of a trans-Pyrenean motorway linking Bayonne and Pamplona, and partially funded by the EU, is now being studied.[69]

Basque nationalists, like many members of other ethnonationalist movements throughout Europe, have long seen the EU as a way to boost their own area at the expense of involved nation-states. For example, in mid-1998 the president of the PNV openly stated to Austrian journalists that "the Basques wish to form their own state within the EU."[70] The new transregional and transnational groupings enabled by the EU (which are seen by some as potential precursors of a broader Basque polity independent of Madrid and Paris) do not, however, necessarily benefit only nationalists. Representatives of the Basque wing of the PP, for instance, have begun to meet with members of similarly minded political groups in Aquitaine in order to develop and fight for their version of this potential Euroregion. They have already made a joint protest against the proposal to unite the three French Basque provinces into a single "Basque département."[71] Further, moves toward European unity may directly go against CAV assertions of its autonomy. The most indicative example here is the recent investigation carried out by the EC into the fiscal incentives offered by the Basque government to attract business investment. For what the Basque government sees as the legitimate exercise of its fiscal independence, the EC regards as unfair competition in what should otherwise be an open market. It seems the time-honored Conciertos Económicos of the area have little place in "the New Europe."[72]

Some of the more visionary-minded see "the European adventure" as the great prospect in which nationalist and regionalist divisions can be resolved. But it is more likely that the European project will at the same time create new arenas for new conflicts, new squabbles. For instance, in April 1999 the presidents of the autonomous communities of the country met in Santiago de Compostela in order to claim a "more active and protagonist" role, compared to that of the Spanish state, in the process of European construction. Also, elections to the European Parliament have created a new electoral arena, in which Basque nationalists join with their counterparts from other regions (Catalonia, Mallorca, Galicia) to form the European Nationalist Coalition. In reaction, Unidad Alavesa, in a meeting with Unión del Pueblo Leonés, proposed a "regionalist front," into which might fit parties such as UPN.[73] Further, the PNV has criticized the PP and the PSOE for refusing to allow the creation of a CAV-bound district for the elections to the European Parliament. Together with EA, it has complained against what it sees as the Spanish government's closing off of "independent means of collaboration" with Europe, and has called for the opening of an office of the EU in Euskadi in order to give material form to the "plurinationality" of the Spanish state.[74]

It is indubitably true that the various operations of the EU are changing the face of the continent. It is also the case that, for reasons discussed above, Navarra and the CAV will remain separate autonomous communities for the foreseeable future. But the series of new, overlapping groupings, stimulated by EU initiatives, each centered on particular socioeconomic themes, suggests some intermediary possibilities between the continuing separation of the two communities and the prospect of a united, independent Euskadi. These possibilities center on the ideas that globalization is a major force of our times, that the traditional concept of the nation-state is increasingly subject to questioning, and that new socioeconomic challenges require new solutions and new forms of cooperation. In the process, the very nature of "independence" and "autonomy" will come under continued scrutiny. The salience of the Spanish state may be diminished, but by the same token, it is improbable that any "greater Basque polity" that may emerge will be able to take on the form of a traditional nation-state. The possible meanings borne by "Navarra" and "Euskadi" will shift accordingly, with the two communities engaging in novel forms of contact with each other and with others. These novel forms will be dynamic, contested, and multifarious. On this reading, the history of Navarra might be singular but its future is plural.

Notes

1. *Diaro de Navarra* (hereafter *DN*), 21 July 1977, p. 1.

2. *DN*, 26 October 1977, p. 13.

3. *DN*, 29 October 1977, p. 4.

4. See the remarks made by Benegas in *El País*, 16 December 1977; *Deia*, 16 December 1977; 21 December 1977.

5. *El País*, 26 November 1977.

6. *DN*, 23 November 1977, p. 1.

7. *DN*, 29 November 1977, p. 1.

8. *DN*, 26 November 1977, p. 3; 30 November 1977, p. 1.

9. Ortzi, 1979, 163.

10. *DN*, 10 November 1977, p. 1; 13 November 1977, p. 1; 16 November 1977, p. 1; 19 November 1977, p. 1; 22 November 1977, p. 1.

11. *DN*, 2 December 1977, p. 24; 3 December 1977, p. 1; 4 December 1977, pp. 13, 17, 18, 32; Ortzi 1979, 164.

12. *DN*, 9 December 1977, pp. 1, 24; *Punto y Hora*, no. 66 (15–21 December 1977): 5–7.

13. *Egin*, 29 December 1977, p. 1.

14. Ortzi 1979, 136; *Punto y Hora*, no. 69 (5–11 January 1978): 5–8.

15. *DN*, 6 January 1978, p. 1; 8 January 1978, p. 17; *Egin*, 8 January 1978, p. 1; *Punto y Hora*, no. 70 (12–18 January 1978): 4–6.

16. *DN*, 27 January 1978, p. 11; 28 January 1978, p. 1; 1 February 1978, p. 6; Ortzi 1979, 167.

17. *DN*, 18 January 1978, p. 1; 31 January 1978, p. 1; *Egin*, 10 January 1978, p. 2.

18. Ortzi 1979, 166; *Punto y Hora*, no. 76 (23 February–1 March 1978): 10.

19. *DN*, 16 February 1978, p. 24; 19 February 1978, p. 28; *Egin*, 16 February 1978, p. 1; Ortzi 1979, 167; *Punto y Hora*, no. 76 (23 February–1 March 1978): 10.

20. *DN*, 16 February 1978, p. 28; 19 February 1978, p. 28; 8 June 1978, p. 1; 14 June 1978, p. 1; 16 June 1978, p. 1; 29 June 1978, p. 6; 30 June 1978, p. 1; *Egin*, 1 February 1978, p. 5; 14 June 1978, p. 6; 28 May 1978, p. 1; *Punto y Hora*, no. 90 (1–7 June 1978): 6.

21. *DN*, 14 June 1978, p. 1.

22. *DN,* 13 September 1978, p. 1; *Punto y Hora,* no. 106 (21–27 September 1978): 13.

23. *DN,* 27 July 1978, p. 1; 6 October 1978, p. 5; Ortzi 1979, 170.

24. *DN,* 10 October 1978, p. 16.

25. *DN,* 10 October 1978, p. 24; 23 October 1978, p. 4; 10 February 1979, p. 18; *Egin,* 18 August 1978, p. 5; Ortzi 1979, 172.

26. *DN,* 5 April 1979, p. 17; *Egin,* 5 April 1979, p. 20; *Punto y Hora,* no. 120 (12–19 April 1979).

27. *ABC,* 13 December 1979; *DN,* 11 December 1979, p. 1; 13 January 1980, p. 13. See also the remarks of Marcos Vizcaya, PNV senator, about the existence of the pact, *Egin,* 3 January 1980, p. 9.

28. *DN,* 13 December 1979, p. 1.

29. *Egin,* 3 January 1980, p. 9; 16 January 1980, p. 1.

30. *DN,* 16 January 1980, p. 1.

31. *DN,* 22 January 1980, p. 1.

32. *DN,* 18 December 1979, p. 32.

33. MacClancy 1993.

34. *Punto y Hora,* no. 11 (1–15 September 1976): 16; no. 12 (15–30 September 1976): 31.

35. *Egin,* 7 September 1979, p. 13; 4 September 1981, p. 14; Nafarrako Biltzarrea 14; *Punto y Hora,* no. 56: 36. For a critique of Barandiarán's approach see Azcona 1984, 56–91; MacClancy 1996.

36. *Egin,* 4 September 1981, p. 14; *Punto y Hora,* no. 57 (13–19 September 1977): 36. See also Larainzar 1979, 11; Nafarrako Biltzarrea n.d., 8.

37. Nafarrako Biltzarrea n.d., 30. For examples of the *"linguae navarrorum"* quote, see *Egin,* 4 September 1981, p. 14; *Lo que debe conocer todo navarro* 1978; *Punto y Hora,* no. 33 (28 April–4 May 1977): 29.

38. *Egin,* 7 September 1979, p. 13; *Lo que debe conocer todo navarro* 1978, 8–9.

39. Nafarrako Biltzarrea n.d., 21; *Punto y Hora,* no. 59 (27 October–2 November 1977): 1.

40. *Punto y Hora,* no. 24 (24 February–2 March 1977): 30, n. 1.

41. *Egin,* 23 August 1979, p. 12.

42. *Punto y Hora,* no. 79 (16–22 March 1978); no. 80 (23–29 March 1978): 40–41; no. 81 (30 March–5 April 1978): 40–41; no. 82 (6–12 April 1978): 40–41; no. 83 (7–13 April 1978): 40–41.

43. *Egin,* 8 November 1979, p. 13.

44. Nafarrako Biltzarrea n.d., 29.

45. *DN,* 15 February 1979, p. 9; 22 March 1979, p. 32; *El País,* 2 August 1977.

46. Sánchez-Albornoz 1984 (1974), 133–153.

47. *DN*, 9 February 1979, p. 9; 15 February 1979, p. 9. A collection of his writings on Navarra, including his public addresses, published in 1984, quickly went into several editions.

48. *DN*, 17 August 1977, p. 11. The quotation is from the *Ley 33 Título 80, Libro 10 de la Novísima Recopilación.*

49. *Punto y Hora*, no. 61 (10–16 November 1977): 31. For a vitriolic exposition of *ribereño* reasons for disliking and feeling alien to Basques, see Larrainzar 1979, 11.

50. *DN*, 10 April 1977, p. 17; 24 May 1977, p. 11; *El Pensamiento Navarro*, 25 November 1977.

51. *DN*, 25 August 1977, p. 11; 26 August 1977, p. 11; 10 February 1979, p. 9; 26 October 1979, p. 13.

52. Collins 1986, 169, 200–201, 220–225, 250–259; Fusi 1984, 189.

53. Jimeno Jurío 1975, 302, quoted in Mina 1981, 171; *El País*, Semanal 31 May 1987, p. 50.

54. *DN*, 2 November 1975; 18 February 1977, p. 13; 10 April 1977, p. 17; 10 May 1977, p. 11.

55. Del Burgo 1976, 19, 23, 25; 1979, 44, 53, 87, 132; *DN*, 19 November 1977, p. 24.

56. *DN*, 24 August 1977, p. 11; 13 December 1979, p. 16; Ortzi 1979, 77.

57. Larrainzar 1979, 23; *Punto y Hora*, no. 55 (29 September–5 October 1977): 45; no. 63 (24–30 November 1977): 6.

58. "Foral bird" from Mina 1981, 171.

59. Billig 1995.

60. *El Mundo* (Edición del País Vasco) [hereafter *El Mundo*] 24 September 1998, p. 9.

61. *El Mundo,* 25 February 1998, p. 11; 26 February 1998, p. 12.

62. *El Mundo,* 3 March 1998, p. 8.

63. *El Mundo,* 25 May 1999, p. 26.

64. *El Mundo,* 22 May 1998, p. 10; 7 September 1998, p. 13; 14 September 1998, p. 11.

65. *El Mundo,* 1 April 1998, p. 8; 14 April 1998, p. 12; 12 February 1998, p. 11.

66. *El Mundo,* 28 May 1998, p. 19; 31 May 1999, p. 14. See also the comments on this made by the leaders of the main Navarran parties in *El Mundo,* 29 May 1999, pp. 18–19.

67. *El Mundo,* 22 March 1998, p. 12.

68. *El Mundo,* 13 May 1998, p. 9.

69. *El Mundo,* 22 June 1998, p. 7.

70. *El Mundo,* 28 July 1998, p. 7.

71. *El Mundo,* 9 March 1999, p. 10; 16 May 1999, p. 24.

72. On this EC investigation and its consequences, see *El Mundo*, 8 March 1999, p. 3; 5 May 1999, pp. 2–3; 6 May 1999, p. 3.

73. *El Mundo*, 6 September 1998, p. 13; 12 May 1999, p. 18.

74. *El Mundo*, 16 July 1998, p. 14; 6 April 1999, p. 24; 3 June 1999, p. 16.

Bibliography

Azcona, Jesús. 1984. *Etnia y nacionalismo vasco*. Barcelona: Antropos.

Billig, Michael. 1995. *Banal Nationalism*. London: Sage.

Collins, Roger. 1986. *The Basques*. Oxford: Blackwell.

Del Burgo, Jaime Ignacio. 1976. *Los fueros del futuro. Ideas para la reforma foral*. Pamplona: Gomez.

————. 1979. *Navarra es Navarra. Tres años de lucha en defensa de nuestra identidad*. Pamplona: Gráficas Irujo.

Fusi, Juan Pablo. 1984. *El País Vasco. Pluralismo y nacionalidad*. Madrid: Alianza.

Jimeno Jurio, José María. 1975. *Historia de Pamplona*. Pamplona: Ediciones y Libros, S. A.

Larrainzar, Francisco Javier. 1979. *Navarra sola o con leche*. Pamplona: n.p.

Lo que debe conocer todo navarro. 1978. Pamphlet. Pamplona: n.p.

MacClancy, Jeremy. 1993. "At Play with Identity in the Basque Arena." In *Inside European Identities*, edited by Sharon Macdonald, 84–97. Oxford: Berg.

————. 1996. "Biological Basques, Sociologically Speaking." In *Biological and Social Aspects of Ethnicity*, edited by M. Chapman, 80–116. Oxford: Clarendon Press.

Mina Apat, María Cruz. 1981. *Fueros y revolución liberal en Navarra*. Madrid: Alianza.

Nafarrako Biltzarrea. n.d. *Sobre la realidad histórica de Navarra*. Pamphlet. Pamplona: n.p.

Ortzi [Francisco Letamendia]. 1979. *El no vasco a la reforma*. Vol. 1, *La consolidación de la reforma*. San Sebastián: Txertoa.

Sánchez-Albornoz, Claudio. 1984 (1974). "Trayectoria histórica de la nueva Vasconia (El País Vasco o la España sin romanizar)." In *Orígenes y destino de Navarra. Trayectoria histórica de Vasconia. Otros escritos*. Barcelona: Planeta.

James E. Jacob

The Future of Basque Nationalism in France

The more things change, the more they remain the same.

—French adage

The opportunity is dear and time is a sword.

—Afghan proverb

The coming of the new millennium is at best an artificial benchmark in the history of Basque nationalism in France. Viewed from this fin de siècle, many of the issues affecting the nationalist cause are much the same as they have been for the past twenty years or more. Elsewhere, I have described in more detail the historical trajectory of Basque nationalism in France from the French Revolution to the 1990s.[1] It is my intention in this paper to discuss the state of Basque nationalism at century's end, and examine what continue to be the most important issues and obstacles facing the *abertzale* cause in Iparralde.

The State of Basque Language and Culture

The poet John Donne reminds us that no man is an island, alone to himself. Since the early French Third Republic, French history has recorded the steady intrusion of the French state and its agents into the most isolated regions of the country.[2] By the second half of the twentieth century the process of cultural assimilation had become a relentless process confronting rural and ethnic France. The process of assimilation has many causes, some of them now long-standing. Some are the deliberate result of French government policy. Others reveal the impact of the "syndrome of modernization"—a set of broader socioeconomic and demographic changes at work here as elsewhere.

One of the greatest indicators of the process of assimilation has been the decline in Basque language use in France. The decline is most serious in the case of Basque youth between the ages of 16 and 25. Forty years ago fully *47 percent* of Basques of this age spoke Basque.[3] By the end of the twentieth century, the number of that age speaking Basque had fallen to only *17 percent*. Today, only *6 percent* of Basque children under the age of 16 speak Basque as their mother tongue. According to Erramun Bachoc, President of the Institut Culturel et Sociolinguiste de Formation, the use of the Basque language by families and adults is now in virtual "free fall."[4] This decline comes despite *forty years* of efforts by Basque cultural groups (IKAS, Ikastola, Gau Eskola, and Ikastaldi) to preserve Basque as a living language in France.[5] IKAS and Seaska in particular have provided more than thirty years of faithful and devoted service to safeguarding the Basque language. It has been a commendable effort, carried out in a climate of indifference or hostility in most public agencies.

Most recently, the defense of the Basque language appeared prominently in the still unrealized "Schéma d'aménagement et de developpement du Pays Basque" first issued in 1996.[6] Efforts to create a Conseil de la langue basque continued to be held hostage to conflicts between competing Basque cultural groups. The greatest victim of these tactical quarrels may well be the survivability of the Basque language in France. The twentieth century has chronicled the steady decline of minority language use in France. This trend in the Pays Basque, as elsewhere, is long-standing and deeply troublesome. Without corrective action, the decline in the language will reach a point of irreversibility in this new century. This state of affairs is all the more unfortunate because the squabbling among Basque cultural associations has prevented them from focusing their full efforts on safeguarding the language.

To be sure, the challenge facing the preservation of the Basque language in France is more critical than in Spain. Representing approximately 10 percent of the total Basque population, the three Basque provinces of France include a total linguistic population estimated optimistically at less than 70,000 Basque speakers. The quasi-totality of these Basque speakers is bilingual. Those for whom Basque is the primary language are aging and changing the demographic composition of Basque language use in France. The family and church that were transmission belts of the language and Basque culture at the turn of the twentieth century have less influence at century's end. This process of deculturation and assimilation can be seen directly in the decline in Basque language use among young Basques. Part of the explanation is clearly socioeconomic in nature. If the rural and agricultural interior has been the cradle of Basque language use in France, then the strength of the agricultural economy is crucial to keeping people on the land. Unfortunately, there has been a pattern of rural depopulation that began in some communes in the middle of the nineteenth century. The lack of opportunity in the village led to numerous outlets. For example, the Basques had traditionally had one of the highest rates of ordination into clerical orders in France. Furthermore, emigration to either North or South America was another avenue of upward mobility for young nonheirs seeking their fortunes. For young Basques on the threshold of adulthood, language choice affected economic prospects. Many young Basques chose to migrate to bilingual cities along the Basque coast, or elsewhere in France. As Albert Dauzat put it early in the twentieth century, "Le français rapporte. Le patois ne rapporte rien" ("French earns money. Patois earns nothing."). Without extensive agricultural subsidies by both France and the European Union, the rural population of France would decrease even further.

The Passive Aggressive State

As I was going up the stair, I met a man who wasn't there.
He wasn't there again today, I wish, I wish he'd stay away.
—Hughes Mearns

Given the socioeconomic pressure for assimilation into French culture in the twentieth century, the French government has been able to adopt a passive policy stance toward the unfolding of seemingly inevitable historical trends working against the survival of minority languages. The government's reaction to the issue of minority language and cultural rights seems to define the nature of the "passive aggressive" state and its policy. One characteristic of this policy stance is to delay as long as possible, and then engage even apolitical cultural associations in long and inconclusive discussions that have no end, or that provide only token levels of financial support. Whether the result of genuine policy uncertainty or psychological warfare, the effect of state behavior was to dispirit Basque militants seeking to negotiate in good faith for the preservation of the language. In matters of national education, the state controls the agenda; Basque cultural associations can only appeal to good will and decency in asking for government subsidies. The lack of a broader public support for the language gives these cultural associations little leverage on one of the most Jacobin of French ministries. Not even thirty years of public appeals and demonstrations by the abertzale camp has swayed government policy. Each day increases the forces acting against the Basque language in a climate of apparent state indifference.

Opposition to minority demands continues to be a polar star of French administrations across the political spectrum. This steadfast French policy is reminiscent of Daniel Patrick Moynihan's 1960's concept of "benign neglect." The apparent goal of French language policy is to make as few concessions as are necessary, and wait for the inevitable tide of economic and social forces to dilute minority language use to the point where it no longer poses a political threat to France.[7] The state believes the Basque movement is too weak and fragmented to reverse these broader social trends; can't afford to fully fund a Basque language school system without state support; and lacks the public support necessary to force government action. Ironically, it was the conflict over Seaska and efforts to save the language that gave rise, in part, to Iparretarrak (Those of ETA of the North). It was frustration over France's seemingly cavalier indifference to Basque culture that led to the appearance of indigenous Basque violence in France for the first time. Iparretarrak sought to use violence as a lever to force the state to make concessions to end the conflict that it otherwise would not have made. The effect, of course, was just the opposite; separatist violence tapped directly into the "limbic system" of Jacobin values. The integrity of French territory and culture has been central to the French civic religion since the time of the Revolution, and made Basque nationalism all the more threatening as a result.

Despite the lofty ideals of the revolution, the strength of Basque in the rural interior remained largely unchallenged until the Crisis of Church and State in 1905–1906.[8] The clergy played an important cultural and political role by using the Basque language as a barrier against assimilation by the anticlerical French Third Republic. At the turn of the twentieth century, *inspecteurs d'académie* reported to Paris that they had found mayors in Basque villages who were unable to speak French. Yet, French policy in the twentieth century has been to deny the undeniable: the existence of minority language groups that predated the unification of France itself.[9] At the Versailles Peace Conference following World War I, French representative Henri de Jouvenal explained France's refusal to vote on the minorities treaty dealing with central Europe by claiming that France, itself, *"had no minorities."*[10] This is part of what Charles de Gaulle meant when he spoke of a "certain idea of France." In their foreign policy, both France and Spain have been loath to create any precedent that might stimulate support for self-determination within their restive minority regions. For that reason, in 1991, both France and Spain were greatly troubled by Germany's insistence on independence for Croatia and Slovenia, fearing the precedent it would create for their own restive minorities. The same is true regarding the future of Kosovo, another potential precedent for other peoples like the Basques or Kurds making similar demands for independence.[11] In this regard, it is interesting to note the controversy sparked by the Spanish Basque offer to host a meeting of the Kurdish National Parliament.[12] The Spanish government vowed to take "all necessary steps" to prevent the meeting, and the threat that this move might well derail any prospects of peace talks with Spain led the Basques to look for a face-saving alternative site for the Kurdish Parliament to meet.[13]

The broader political issue posed by a united Europe is this: once the international community has embarked on the dismemberment of sovereign states and the recognition of minority demands for autonomy, if not self-determination, where does that process stop? Which state whose foreign and economic policies are so intertwined with Europe can long resist the next stage of incursions into domestic policy as well? If Europe has spoken of the plight of the Slovenians, Croatians, Kurds, and now Kosovar Albanians, then what of analogous indigenous groups within the European Union itself?

Today, the inexorable logic of European integration poses clear political and economic advantages for France, as well as potential challenges to domestic policy and tradition. Some of these issues appear fanciful, but cut to the core of tradition and the homogenizing fear that European integration has always elicited. These are the stuff of low politics, and the fears that a united Europe have provoked. For the French, one of the European Union's greatest threats was in attempting to prevent the manufacture of cheese with unpasteurized milk—a ruling that would have rendered Brie and Camembert and a host of other French cheeses extinct. Other examples include the suggestion that Spain abandon use of the tilde accent in order to make word processing easier elsewhere in the EU; a challenge to Germany's centuries-old beer purity law, the *Reinheitsgebot;* and the question of whether chickens sold in the supermarkets in the EU will have their innards intact (France) or in paper packages (Germany). These questions are not about politics, but about the profound influence government can have on the smallest and most meaningful details of people's lives.

One of the first areas in which the broader politics of a united Europe risk colliding with domestic policy is the area of human rights. Turkey has already been severely criticized by the EU for its treatment of the Kurds, as well as political dissidents and journalists. Most recently, the EU has criticized a proposed new language law in Latvia that discriminates against its ethnic minority Russian speakers.[14] As the EU focuses on issues of minority rights in other countries, it will inevitably see the application of a set of language rights as part of its general commitment to human rights.

The issue of language policy is one area that may ultimately bring France into conflict with others in the EU. The dilemma of the French government is that it is being pressured to make concessions in language policy by both its linguistic minority groups and the EU. The adoption of the long debated and amended European Charter on Regional and Minority Languages was at best a symbolic gesture at recognizing the existence of Europe's linguistic minorities. Yet, the charter did seem to be a step toward the federalism or "Europe of ethnic peoples" that Enbata had supported beginning in 1963.[15] The reality is that the charter was *only* symbolic in nature and in no way forced changes in French policy. While France finally signed the amended charter, it did not formally ratify it.[16] Then, in 1999, France's highest court ruled that the charter posed a threat to French unity and violated Article 2 of the French Constitution, which states that, "The language of the republic is French."[17] Symbolic or not, the charter raised the specter of the EU imposing political decisions in the area of language use in ways similar to those that were already occurring in foreign or economic policy.

Today, much of French language policy is defined by the growing threat to the French language itself. This threat is marked by the decline in the study of French, and by the preference for English by both the United Nations and even the European Union.[18] One of France's responses has been to nourish an international group of Francophone-speaking states or regions. This has been a pillar of French cultural policy overseas. However, with the majority of these states in Africa, the movement has done little to boost the prospects of French in Europe or the West. Today, the French language is more threatened by English than ever before in its history.[19] Nowhere is this clearer than in the rise of the Internet that will be the medium of exchange of the twenty-first century. While more than *82 percent* of all Internet messages today are in English, barely *4 percent* are in French. In this perilous climate of threat to the French language, it is understandable why the French would be reluctant to further undercut their own language by encouraging the spread of minority language use in France.

The result is that today only 350,000 students are studying one of seven minority languages in France, and these schools exist for the most part as poorly funded "charter schools" without full official status or funding from the French Ministry of Education. The government has also been unwilling to create a full university in Bayonne. For two years, Seaska, the association running the Basque language ikastolas in France, has joined with other minority groups in trying to negotiate with a largely indifferent French Ministry of Education.[20] In the current "Schéma d'aménagement et de développement du Pays Basque," a prominent place is given to efforts to reverse the decline of the Basque language.[21] The creation of a Conseil de la Langue

Basque grew out of the Schéma and the Pays Basque 2010 report that raised the specter of Basque becoming a *foreign language* in the daily life of the Pays Basque.[22] While overall progress has been disappointing in implementing the Schéma, ongoing squabbling among Basque cultural groups have complicated efforts to put in place an effective Basque language policy in the Pays Basque.

The irony of the French government position is that while it has encouraged the weakening of minority language use through active policy or passive neglect, it now celebrates its regional cultures as indicators of the cultural richness of *France* itself. With the decline in language use and the elimination of political threats to French unity, France has celebrated the transformation of minority cultures into folklore. In this way, culture becomes *performance art*, and a faltering motor for seasonal tourist-based economies, particularly in the Pays Basque, French Catalonia, Brittany, and Occitanie. Thus, government refusal to accord meaningful linguistic and educational rights is accompanied by a commodification of culture much like that on Indian reservations in the United States.

Transcending Political Fragmentation and the "Basque Tradition of Tribal Struggle"

It would be wrong to attribute the threats to Basque culture and politics in France to French institutions and policies alone. To be sure, France's policy toward the Basques and other minorities has been relatively constant, if not always principled, for more than two centuries. However, the second greatest obstacle to Basque political mobilization in France reflects an internal Basque dynamic. For three generations, internal politics and interpersonal conflicts have too often marked abertzale politics. By focusing abertzale attention inward, these tendencies have prevented the nationalist camp from winning broader public support. The early radicalism of the nationalist camp turned some electors off to politics of any stripe. Indeed, it is interesting to note the appearance in recent elections of a new "apolitical" grouping, "Hunters," which became the third largest vote winner in some communes.

The late historian and Basque nationalist Eugen Goyheneche spoke often of the "curious tradition of tribal struggle" among the Basques. In his view, the potential of Basque nationalism was too often squandered by internecine feuds that often turned more on personality than on points of politics or strategy. Personality conflicts of this kind have marked the last three generations of Basque militants, stretching back to the 1940s. The presence of these conflicts has unnecessarily sapped the energy of the nationalist cause and prevented it from winning broader public support. As each new generation of militants arose, there was the temptation to engage in symbolic political patricide—the need to "kill the fathers" in order to legitimate a new ideological trajectory. This was further exacerbated by the tendency of French Basque nationalist movements since the 1960s to adopt both the ideologies and the conflicts afflicting kindred movements in Spain. The history of Basque nationalism in France has been marked by interpersonal conflicts, ideological disagreements, and schisms. They are followed by the rise of new generations to political awareness and their optimistic creation of still new structures. Such is the endless dance of Basque politics.

Since the rise of Pierre Lafitte's clerical regionalism in the 1930s, each successive generation of Basque nationalists has faced the indifference or hostility of the Basque electorate. One of the greatest obstacles to the growth of Basque nationalism in France is that successive movements have been unable to attract sufficient support to make them more than a symbolic force in local politics. This was particularly true when the movement's goals threatened the traditions of conservative Basque society or their elected elites. The rise of secular nationalism became a struggle over who was going to legitimately control Basque culture symbols and language.

Yet, as the Basque nationalist movement has shifted its goals away from independence to the bread-and-butter issues of regional economic development, the teaching of the Basque language, and the administrative and economic advantages of a Basque department, it has been able to galvanize public support as never before. When viewed over the past third of a century, there has been an undeniable increase in public support for abertzale candidates and issues. The pro-abertzale vote has more than *doubled* in size from 1967 to 1999. In the French elections of 1998, the vote for abertzale candidates globally in the Pays Basque was 9.35 percent in the cantonal elections and 8.40 percent in the regionals.[23] This reflects a growing willingness, especially in the rural interior, to look at new ways of ensuring economic survival in an expanding European Union. It also reflects the growing maturity of Basque movements, which have come to understand that politics is the art of the *possible.*

This realization has led to ongoing efforts to unite the abertzale movement and overcome their tradition of internal strife. Much hope was placed on the Lizarra-Garazi Accord of 1998 that laid out—along with ETA's cease-fire—a still unrealized framework for unity, peace, and dialogue with France and Spain.[24] In February 1999, Abertzaleen Batasuna (Patriotic Unity) called for the creation of a public coalition uniting all parties in issues ranging from a Basque department to the condition of Basque prisoners in France and Spain.[25] Today, out of 560 Basque prisoners in the two states, 74 are incarcerated in French prisons. The majority of prisoners in both countries are far from their family homes. Their plight continues to be a potent cause for political mobilization in both Spain and France.

This willingness to embrace a "big tent" approach to abertzale political action represents the greatest opportunity to escape the sectarian conflict of the past third of a century. In recent years, the celebration of the Aberri Eguna (Basque national day) in France has been sponsored jointly by all political parties. In 1999, Abertzaleen Batasuna proposed that the four abertzale political parties in Iparralde agree to create a common list for the European elections. As Richard Irazusta noted in *Enbata,* the proposal was based on a rational "strategic and mathematical analysis."[26] In February 1999, French Basque elected officials joined a far greater number of their counterparts in Spain in the first Assembly of the Cities of the Basque Country. *Enbata* called this the first national institution uniting Basques across the border.[27] Some press observers saw it as a clear step toward Basque unification and independence.[28]

The Idea of a Separate Basque Department in France

One of the greatest truisms in politics is that ideas once considered revolutionary may become commonsensical in another age. Indeed, the "tincture of time" has served to legitimize many of *Enbata's* goals that today have passed into the broader political vocabulary of the region. The most successful of Enbata's early demands, for which there has been growing support, is the creation of a separate department for the Basques, now subsumed in the *département* of the Pyrenées-Atlantiques.

By March 1999, 70 municipal councils out of 158 had voted in favor of a Basque department compared to 11 voting against.[29] Even as long-standing an opponent of Basque nationalism as Deputy Michel Inchauspe sponsored legislation to permit the creation of new departments.[30] One of the greatest arguments for a separate department for the Basques is their claim that the existing department is biased toward Bearn, and only with a department of their own can they implement meaningful economic development. In January 1999, the regional newspaper, *Sud Ouest,* published a list of the ten richest and ten poorest communes in the department of the Pyrenees-Atlantiques. It revealed that all the ten *richest* communes were in Bearn and that all the ten *poorest* were in the Pays Basque.[31] This has led to a growing public consensus that only a Basque department can ensure the future economic and cultural survival of the Pays Basque.

French reaction has been mixed. François Mitterrand in his 1981 presidential platform had called for the creation of a Basque department in order to undercut more radical Basque goals. Once in power, however, the Socialists proved no more willing to risk provoking separatism in this region than were the Gaullists before them. Yet, the creation of new departments *does have* historical precedents in France. In 1964, five new departments were created in order to improve the administration of the growing region around Paris. Then, in 1975, Corsica was divided into two departments for clearly political reasons in order to demonstrate the state's commitment to the island and to try to undercut criticism from the Corsican nationalist camp.[32] Given the continued violence in Corsica, and the potential for separatism there as well as in the Pays Basque, the French government is clearly reluctant to create a Basque department in France that might encourage further demands leading to independence and unification with Spain. In 1998, the government called the idea "premature" and tied it to the evolving process of peace between ETA and Spain. Yet, by 1999, Interior Minister Jean-Pierre Chevenement, speaking

for French Premier Lionel Jospin, announced that the creation of a
Basque department had been rejected by the premier in "a very clear
and thus definitive fashion."[33] Most significantly, Chevenement justified the government's position by stating that breaking up existing
states along ethnic lines risked "Balkanizing" all of Europe. What is
clear is that the French government is still deeply concerned about
the potential downside of the creation of a Basque department, and
sees no need to make concessions to even modern Basque goals despite their growing public support.

Basque Nationalism in France and the Impact of ETA and Spanish Basque Politics

The Basque nationalist cause in France has not faltered for want of
ideas. For much of the nineteenth and twentieth century, the Basque
clergy served as the primary cultural elite. Beginning with the Chanoine Lafitte's Aintzina in the 1930s, the French Basque movements
have looked also to other groups for their ideological inspiration.
Lafitte and Goyheneche were in clear contact with other minority
groups in France in the 1930s. While ETA has been one of the greatest
ideological inspirations in the north, it was not the only one. Following the crises of French decolonization, the Basque movement embraced the language of ethnic federalism and internal colonialism
to describe their structural relationship to the French state. Several
movements, beginning with Enbata in the 1960s, chose to define
themselves in terms of the ideological and political positions surrounding ETA and other parties in Hegoalde. More recently, sections
were created in the French Pays Basque of Spanish Basque parties,
including the Parti Nationaliste Basque and Eusko Alkartasuna, to
name but two. Too often, however, the effect of this has been to import
the ideological quarrels of the south into the north and further com-
plicate the issue of attracting public support.

The impact of the Spanish Basque case has been critical to French
Basque culture and politics since the arrival of refugees in the north
from the Spanish Civil War. This refugee community provided much
of the source for Basque cultural and linguistic revival in France as

well as an associated awareness of Basque nationalism. The impact of ETA, however, also served to contaminate the fledgling French Basque movement, and make it suspect in the eyes of rural Basques who were among the most conservative and Catholic populations in France. Ironically, then, the force (i.e., ETA) that served to inspire the rise of secular Basque nationalism in France was also the factor that until recently prevented the movement from winning significant public support among those in the agrarian interior most culturally Basque.

One of the greatest beliefs in the history of French ideas has been France's commitment to providing asylum for those suffering from political persecution. For many years, this deeply held belief in asylum led the French state to turn a blind eye to the reality that ETA was using its sanctuary in the Pays Basque to mount continuing attacks on the Spanish state. France's refusal to deal with the ETA problem led Spain, in turn, to mount one of the greatest examples of state-sponsored terror in postwar Europe, with the creation of the GAL to assassinate ETA militants residing in France. France called this violence the greatest it had experienced since the time of the German occupation in World War II. Despite the political risks to Spain, this campaign succeeded in changing French policy on ETA, and led to the arrest and incarceration or expulsion of ETA militants to Spain or abroad. As the full story of the creation of the GAL became known, the subsequent scandal in Spain led all the way to the office of then-Premier Felipe González. It was clear that the French police were working closely with their Spanish counterparts, and until the level of violence got out of hand, were turning a blind eye—if not actively cooperating—with Spanish agents acting on French soil.

Today, France is solidly supportive of Spanish policy regarding the Basques, and has observed with interest the efforts to bring about peace talks between ETA and the Spanish state. But over the last decade France has solidified its diplomatic relationship with Spain and has acted accordingly toward ETA. Large arms caches are still being found in the French Pays Basque.[34]

France also seized the opportunity to make a clear public statement of its support for Spain in its struggle against ETA. In March 1999, French authorities in Paris arrested the head of ETA's military wing on the *same day* that Spanish Premier José María Aznar began an official visit there. The arrest came despite the fact that ETA had been observing a unilateral cease-fire against Spanish targets that began six months before.[35] Some feared that these arrests would derail the peace process and squander an opportunity to end thirty years of conflict.[36] During his visit to Paris, Aznar said he was willing to hold peace talks with ETA, but would not consider their demand for secession from Spain. He noted, "But it would be very naïve to think that after 30 years of terrorism everything can be resolved in a few weeks. But I hope it will be solved over the next 10 years."[37]

The Struggle to Save Basque Agriculture and Rural Life

Today, the agricultural economy in rural Labourd, Basse-Navarre, and Soule is characterized by marginal, small holdings. Agricultural unions like ELB are still seeking a viable means of family farming. Until then, Basque farmers are like others across Europe in being dependent on subsidies from France and from the European Union. One interesting cultural consequence of the marginality of rural agriculture has been a change in the tradition of Basque inheritance. Where in centuries past the farm would pass undivided to the *eldest* son or daughter, today it is often the *youngest* child who is identified as the heir by older siblings who themselves have already decided to leave the land and pursue their fortunes in more lucrative occupations on the urban coast or beyond.

In the absence of any other economic engine, it was hoped that tourism would be a motor for economic development in the scenic rural interior. Yet, despite hopes to the contrary, the much-vaunted tourist economy functions *at most* three months a year. For many in the nationalist camp, tourism has made Basque culture a commodity to be sold, where French tourists come to see colorful costumes, and enjoy the spectacles of village festivals, competitions of Basque strength, and *pelote*. The rise of *gîtes ruraux* (essentially rural bed-and-breakfast rentals) throughout France demonstrates the competition for tourist dollars as one of the only economic strategies available in rural France.

Sociologically, the rural Pays Basque has been threatened by economic decline and the out-migration of young Basques on the one hand, and by the immigration of francophone French on the other. The sale of homes to outsiders only extends a process that has existed on the coast (namely, the English colony in Biarritz) for more than a century. For more than thirty years, French have bought marginal farms as vacation residences, and real estate speculation has been one of the strongest elements in the regional economy. More threatening in the long run to Basque culture is the fact that new housing developments are spreading inland from the coast and defining the Pays Basque as a prime location for retirement. When combined with the self-conscious decision of many Basques to live "French" lives, this in-migration is another threat to the continued viability of Basque culture and language in its own territory.

Economic development is a two-edged sword. Nowhere is that more clear than in the proposal to create a new "interstate highway" that would follow one of three paths cut through the center of the rural Pays Basque, passing closest to either St. Etienne de Baigorry or St. Jean Pied de Port.[38] For several years this project has been held up for ecological reasons, as it threatens the last redoubts of the Pyrenean bear and other wildlife species. The building of a highway linking Spain with southern France would undoubtedly improve trade and the transit of goods to market. For the Basques, however, its greatest impact would be to create service jobs in rest stops along the way, or provide low-paying jobs in budget motel chains owned by outside capital. The economic gains to the Pays Basque seem unlikely to outweigh the harm. This isn't being done for the economic development of the Pays Basque; it is being done for the economies of France, Spain, and the European Union. For in cutting through the heart of the most scenic regions of Basse-Navarre, this project would deal a fatal cultural blow to the rural Basque interior. The threat to Basque culture is apparently a less persuasive argument than the traditional calls for defense of Pyrenean wildlife and the environment.

Conclusions

The advent of the twenty-first century finds the French Basque nationalist movement struggling with many of the same issues and obstacles that have marked its existence since the 1960s. Today, the most important issues facing the abertzale camp in the north are the defense of the Basque language, the creation of a Basque department, and the implementation of a new economic development policy for the region. In a larger political sense, the French Basque movement has been greatly influenced by unfolding political events in Spain, and its focus today is on the possibility of peace talks leading to a lasting peace between ETA and Spain.

One of the greatest strengths of Basque nationalism in France—of whatever political tendency—has been the fidelity and devotion of its militants. The transmission of abertzale political values across generations has ensured the optimistic birth of new political movements as new generations are socialized to the nationalist cause. In the past thirty years, electoral support for abertzale candidates has more than doubled. Much of that can be attributed to public reaction to the failure of either the French left or right to make good on its promises to the Basques. What successive governments have done has been minimal if not illusory.

However, this period has also witnessed the maturation of the Basque movement in France. The last decade of the century has been marked by a clear desire to unite abertzales across the spectrum. It appears that the nationalist camp now recognizes that through unity they may be more successful in pursuing goals that are critical to the future of the Pays Basque. Having put aside their own personal and political differences for a time, the nationalist camp has been able to focus on putting a more coherent and unified platform before the Basque population. As a result, the espousal of moderate political demands has brought a level of support from the Basque electorate and Basque elected officials that exceeds that at any other time in the history of Basque nationalism in France.

To that extent, the coming of the millennium holds the promise of continued support for moderate and attainable political goals. The end of one millennium and the beginning of another also reminds us that time hastens onward. As the Afghans put it, "The opportunity is dear and time is a sword." Without concerted action, and government support, there will come a time when the Basque-speaking population of France will decline to a point below sustainability. In that case, in the twenty-first century the Pays Basque will become a region not of Basques but of the grandchildren of Basques. Every indication points to the conclusion that this is the preferred solution the French government seeks. Any French willingness to consider concessions in the areas of language and culture has been trumped by fears of stimulating more radical political demands, including independence. The idea of the creation of a Basque department is held hostage in this drama, and not even a peace between ETA and Spain may sway the French government in their Jacobin opposition.

However, the European Union and the logic of its markets may trump French policy by making the existing borders between member states as fictional in the Pays Basque as they have been for many years between France and Belgium, or Belgium and the Netherlands, for example. Moreover, the common economic policy of the EU may encourage the development of the natural regional economic market that stretches from Bayonne to Bilbao, a richer potential tie than to Bordeaux to the north. In that case, the agrarian north may join the industrial south in creating an economic and social zone where the Basque language can function as the primary medium of exchange. The survival of the Basque language in France will need the cultural boost of the vital cultural productivity of Spanish Basque authors and media.

One of the most common challenges facing minority cultural groups is being seen as quaint and retrograde vestiges of a simpler time. For them to survive into the twenty-first century, these languages and cultures must embrace change. Those that survive will maintain their identities by adapting their cultural traditions to the needs of the modern age. In the end, that may be the greatest symbolic contribution of Frank Gehry's Guggenheim Museum in Bilbao. It stands as proof that Basque culture and society need not be retrograde, a museum of a dusty past. It stands as an example of the way that Basque culture and the modern world can coexist.

Basque nationalism has been the product of the hard work, dedication, and dreams of generations of militants since the time of Sabino de Arana y Goiri, and of Chanoine Pierre Lafitte in the 1930s in France. The historical evolution of nationalist goals in France has swung like a pendulum. Today, the steady evolution in electoral support demonstrates the rise of a moderate Basque center whose goals have broader appeal than the contentious and dubious earlier goal of independence. The past has demonstrated that by uniting in common and cooperative political action, the Basque movement can more effectively address issues of political, economic, and cultural importance. Indeed, the survival of Basque culture in France would have not been possible during the course of the twentieth century without the devotion of abertzale militants over four generations whose beliefs spanned the political spectrum.

At the dawn of this new millennium, the survival of the Basque language will depend on it becoming a vehicle of the modern age, and not simply a nostalgic repository for the historical memory of an ancient people. This new millennium bears witness to one of the longest cultural trajectories in the history of mankind, and that is the history of the Basque people. The Basques have the unique ability to represent an unbroken chain of human experience stretching back to the Stone Age. The fact that a people who descended directly from the Cro-Magnon may now enter cyberspace suggests that this millennium is really a small and artificial threshold in the history of the Basques. The challenge of Basque nationalism is to turn its eyes to the future and away from the past. It is to define a meaningful role for Basque language and culture in the century to come. One of the greatest indications that that moment has come will be the day when Basque militants join Basques of all walks of life in defining their future together at www.Euskadi.com. Fittingly, if you visit that Web site today, it says simply, "under construction."

Notes

1. See my *Hills of Conflict: Basque Nationalism in France, 1789–1992* (Reno: University of Nevada Press, 1994).

2. See the magisterial account by Eugen Weber, *Peasants into Frenchmen: The Modernization of Rural France, 1870–1914* (Stanford, CA: Stanford University Press, 1976).

3. Enbata, *Hebdomadaire Politique Basque,* no. 1571 (1 April 1999): 5.

4. Ibid.

5. Ibid.

6. "Gestation difficile du Conseil de la langue Basque, " *Enbata,* no. 1571 (1 April 1999): 4–5.

7. See James E. Jacob and David C. Gordon, "Language Policy in France," in *Language and National Unity,* ed. William R. Beer and James E. Jacob (Totowa, NJ: Rowman and Allanheld, 1985), 106–133.

8. See my "Ethnic Identity and the Crisis of Separation of Church and State: The Case of the Basques of France, 1870–1914," *Journal of Church and State* 24, 2 (1982): 303–320.

9. See my earlier "Ethnic Conflict in Contemporary France," *Contemporary French Civilization* 5, 1 (fall 1980): 23–42.

10. Cited in the Minutes of the Sixth Committee (Political Questions) (Fourth Meeting), Records of the Sixth Assembly, Special Supplement #39, *Official Journal* (Geneva: League of Nations, 1925), 17.

11. Noel Malcolm, "Independence for Kosovo," *New York Times,* 9 June 1999, p. A31.

12. "Basques to Host Meeting of Kurdish Parliament," AP wire story, Nando Media, 10 February 1999.

13. "Spain: A Move to Halt Kurds," *New York Times,* 17 June 1999, p. A8.

14. See "Latvia: Language Law Sent Back," *New York Times,* 16 July 1999, p. A6; and Anatol Lieven, "No Russian Spoken Here," *New York Times,* 16 July 1999, p. A21.

15. "Federalisme Basque-europeen," *Enbata,* no. 1570 (25 March 1999): 2.

16. "La France signe la Charte européenne," *Enbata,* no. 1576 (6 May 1999): 3.

17. Jon Henley, "France Makes Sure French Is Nation's Only Language," *San Francisco Examiner,* 4 July 1999, p. A22.

18. "Bad News for Francophiles: United Nations, European Union Prefer English," Agence France Press Dispatch, Nando News Online, 22 January 1999.

19. *Le Figaro,* for example, opposed the European Charter because it would threaten French when, "it is being bastardized by Anglo-Saxon words." Ibid.

20. "L'Education nationale negocie avec Seaska," *Enbata,* no. 1578 (20 May 1999): 4.

21. "Pour Abertzaleen Batasuna, le Schéma n'est toujours pas realisé," *Enbata,* no. 1560 (14 January 1999): 4–5.

22. Ibid., 5.

23. *Enbata,* no. 1559 (7 January 1999): 3.

24. "Consolider l'Accord de Lizarra-Garazi," *Enbata,* no. 1572 (8 April 1999): 4–5. The parties or groups involved included the PNV, EB, EA, IU, AB, Batzarre, the syndical movements, LAB, Elkarri, Senideak, and Autodeterminazio aldeko bazordea. See Richard Irazusta, "Un accord, des projets . . . ," *Enbata,* no. 1567 (4 March 1999): 8.

25. "Emergence d'une force politique," *Enbata,* no. 1563 (4 February 1999): 2.

26. "Batasuna Europan," *Enbata,* no. 1571 (1 April 1999): 8.

27. "La premiere institution nationale Basque est en marche," *Enbata,* no. 1564 (11 February 1999): 4–5.

28. See "Basques Form 'National Assembly'," Agence France Presse dispatch, Yahoo News Online, 11 February 1999; and "Basque Nationalists Take 'Step to Independence'," Agence France Presse dispatch, Yahoo News Online, 11 February 1999.

29. "Un sondage grandeur nature," *Enbata,* no. 1568 (11 March 1999): 5.

30. "L'amendement Michel Inchauspé," *Enbata,* no. 1562 (28 January 1999): 4.

31. "Le fracture Bearn/Pays Basque," *Enbata,* no. 1562 (28 January 1999): 4.

32. "Rendre spectaculaire la revendication majoritaire," *Enbata,* no. 1562 (28 January 1999): 2.

33. "Chevenement est le Milosevic français de l'An 2000," *Enbata,* no. 1568 (11 March 1999): 4–5.

34. See, for example, "France: Basque Arms Seized," *New York Times,* 7 April 1999, p. A9; Al Goodman, "Peace Efforts Threatened by Arrest of Basque Leader," *San Francisco Examiner,* 14 March 1999, p. A22; and "ETA Weapons Cache Found in France," *Newsday.com,* 3 May 1999.

35. See "Police Arrest Senior Basque Leader," *Newsday.com,* 9 March 1999; "ETA Arrests in Paris," *BBC News Online,* 9 March 1999; and "French Police Arrest Basque Leader in Paris," *San Francisco Chronicle,* 10 March 1999, p. A14.

36. "Peace Efforts Threatened by Arrest of Basque Leader."

37. "Police Arrest Senior Basque Leader."

38. See "Ces projets autoroutiers qui balafrent la Basse-Navarre," *Enbata,* no. 1579 (27 May 1999): 4–5.

Ane Muñoz Varela

Redefining Euskadi as an Autonomous Community and Participant in the Construction of Europe

The Regional Phenomenon in Global Context

When we consider international relations in the contemporary world we confront a complex universe of transactions, communications, and influences that provide a model diametrically opposed to the one of nation-states that we have previously known. Since the end of World War II the changes have been vertiginous. One of them has been the huge increase of transnational integration throughout the world, and particularly in Europe.

At the same time certain forces have challenged the traditional system of nation-states in their search for a redefinition of political organization. The challenge to the nation-state from above by the supranational organization is complemented by one from below—from the growing participation of substate entities or regions. The latter are becoming increasingly important within the global international context. But it is within the European framework in particular that we can observe the rapid evolution of the political participation of substate entities since at least the 1960s and 1970s.

One possible explanation is a growing world interdependence that penetrates the social base of every nation-state and, like two sides of the same coin, encompasses both fragmentation and integration, diversity and uniformity. The specific shape of any national identity is somewhat nebulous, while the opportunities for its self-affirmation are numerous. It is within this dichotomy that the state operates and seeks to configure its future. It is also important to consider a functional factor: namely, that subnational units are sometimes in a better

position than states or suprastates to confront the economic challenges of their territories because of their better understanding of local problems and potentialities.

The European Union, presently embroiled in complex processes of
definition and construction, should work toward a political model
that includes the individual and his or her most intimate political surroundings, those with which he or she most identifies. The model
should encompass *recognition* of the various actors and their role in
international life, *flexibility* and *agility* in relating particular actors
with others, and the *transparency* obtainable through working with
the smallest and most independent entities, those which defend the
rights of the individual, in part through electronic communications.
Such a model fits best within the framework of an integral federalism
that guarantees personal liberty while making it compatible with
communitarian integration. This is the federalist paradox: uniting in
order to protect diversity.[1]

During the construction of a European supranational entity, endowed with ever-increasing political weight (not only with respect to
its member states, but before the world as a whole), tension ensues as
subnational entities demand consideration within not only the supranational communitarian institutions but also with respect to their
own member nation-states. Initially, all of the decisions regarding the
execution of the European Union during its formative phase and its
subsequent operation were reserved for the representatives of the
constituting nation-states. Since 1992 this power arrangement has
come under increasing challenge by subnational regional entities.

In 1986 Spain entered the European Community and initiated a
complete reformulation of Euskadi's primary premises, at both the
political and the socioeconomic levels, including a reevaluation of
generational assumptions and even of Basque identity itself. For Euskadi, defined for present purposes as the autonomous community
formed by Bizkaia, Gipuzkoa, and Araba, pertaining to a united
Europe would suppose a necessary (and painful) reconversion of
an economy in crisis. It would demand improved efficiency of the
Basque business establishment to ensure greater competitiveness. It
would change the educational system at all levels, given the new emphasis upon cultural exchange and competency in foreign languages.
Above all, it would modify political strategy from bilateral negotia-

tions between Vitoria and Madrid to a multilateral situation encompassing Brussels, Bordeaux, etc.

It is premature to pass judgment on the political consequences for Euskadi of its participation in Europe, whether with respect to the "contentiousness" that has traditionally characterized the relations with the Spanish central authority, to Euskadi's contributions within the framework of the complex of European regions and distinctive peoples with whom it maintains contacts, to the new external European influences upon Euskadi's own culture and traditions, or to the very nature of Basque people and their *savoir faire*. However, in what follows I shall delineate the multiple ways in which Basques now interact within the new supranational European reality.

Euskadi's Europeanist Vocation

There is a strong tradition of commercial ties between the European community and Euskadi, and it should not be forgotten that this small territory manifested an undeniable European aspiration or "vocation" from the very beginning of the attempts at European integration. The challenge was to combine the necessity of realizing a European Union with that of guaranteeing an atmosphere of peace and conviviality among Europeans while still respecting the unique identities of the constituent peoples. Indeed, even during the epoch of Sabino de Arana we find references to an Euskadi within the context of the European nationalities, although in this case the aim is to constitute a state for Euskadi modeled after Europe's others.[2]

The relationship between Basque nationalism and Europeanism as regards creation of a supranational European entity dates from the 1920s (despite contentions otherwise) as a consequence of a nationalist reading of the works of the pan-Europeanist Coudenhove-Kalergi and such propositions as the Briand Memorandum.

Basque Europeanism is evident in the attendance of a Basque delegation at the Third Congress of the Union of Nationalities (Lausanne, 1916), in the membership of the Basque Nationalist Party in the Congress of European Nationalities throughout the 1930s, and in its participation over the years in several of the CEN's annual meetings held in Geneva and other European cities.

In 1932 *Aberri Eguna* (Day of the Country) was held in San Se-
bastián/Donosti with the slogan "Euzkadi-Europa," and that same
year the Basque nationalist workers' movement ELA-STV joined the
Confederation of Christian Syndicates—later the World Workers'
Confederation.

Nevertheless, it was with the constitution of the first Basque government, under President José Antonio Aguirre, that the notion of
integrating Euskadi within Europe gained force. Since 1936 international relations have been an essential part of Basque political
strategy.

During the Spanish Civil War, the Basque case attracted much at-
tention. In France the International League of Friends of the Basques
was created in 1938, and was later characterized by José María de
Leizaola as "the embryo of European Christian democracy." Manuel
de Irujo and José Ignacio Lizaso, as representatives of the Basque
General Council (of the Basque-government-in-exile) participated, in
September 1942, in the foundation of the Cultural Union of Western
European Countries.

After World War II the exiled Basque nationalist leaders, through
the Christian Democratic Movement, contributed to the reconstruction of Europe. From the outset, Aguirre sought to involve the various
factions within the exiled Basque government and advisory council
in the major decisions on the wider European scene that would also
impact the Basque Country. In April 1946 a conference was held in
San Francisco to constitute the United Nations. Aguirre attended to
press for international recognition of the peculiarities of the Basque
cause and of other national minorities.

Between October 14 and 16, 1946, the First European Federalist
Congress was held in Luxembourg, and was attended by Basque
representatives as observers. In 1947, in the Paris headquarters of
the Basque government, representatives of different European Christian Democratic groups (including the Basque nationalists) met and
agreed to create an international organization—the New International Teams (NIT), first called the Christian Democratic International, that embraced all of the post-war European groups of this political bent. José Antonio Aguirre was a member of the presidency.
Such Christian Democrats as Adenauer, De Gaspari, and Schuman
would emerge as the true architects of European reconstruction, as

well as the prime advocates of European suprastatist integration. The only Christian democratic parties within the Spanish State to be recognized internationally for many years were the Basque Nationalist Party and the Democratic Union of Catalunya.

In November 1948, a Basque delegation attended the Congress of the Federalist Union in Rome. Basque representative Landaburu was named to the central committee. It is out of this meeting that the federalist initiative known as the European Movement emerged. Its fundamental goal was to preserve democracy in Europe. Basques would remain active members of the European Movement, advocating restoration of democratic government as a condition for Spain to receive foreign aid or recognition. The Basque representative also advocated respect for the smaller peoples and nationalities by the nascent united Europe.

With the outbreak of the cold war and its maximal expression in Korea in 1950, Basque nationalist political aspirations and illusions were effectively blocked, given the international community's more pressing political priorities at that time. Further weakening their collective efforts was the fact that Basques were scattered throughout the world. Consequently, in September 1956 a World Basque Congress was held in Paris with the goal of uniting the representatives of Basque workers' movements, political parties, the Advisory Council, and the various Basque centers and associations of the Americas, as well as Basques of the homeland, in a common effort. It was attended by 363 persons.

In his Gabon message of 1956 President Aguirre insisted on the need to reorganize a united Europe and an Atlantic alliance. In June 1957, Leizaola and Landaburu attended the Congress of the European Movement at which there emerged a continental political structure pointing toward a Europe of Peoples. Six months later, on January 1, 1958, the Treaty of Rome (signed on May 25, 1957) went into effect, putting into motion European political restructuring.

On March 22, 1960, President Aguirre died in Paris. This removed the main spokesman of the Basque cause within the international arena, as well as a prime advocate of Basque integration within a Europe of Peoples. After Aguirre's death there was further significant movement in the direction of a united Europe and continued European ostracism of the Franco regime, but with less of a Basque presence and specific content. For example, at the 1962 Congress of the European Movement in Munich, anti-Franco political forces were heavily represented (by both those from within Spain and those exiled from it)—the Spanish Socialist Party, the Basque Nationalist Party, Gil Robles of the Christian Democrats, and others. A resolution was passed stipulating the conditions that the Spanish State, or any other, would have to meet in order to associate with, or belong to, the European Economic Community. Each state was required to have representative and democratic institutions that ensured human rights. Each was to be free of official governmental censorship and be willing to recognize and respect the uniqueness of different communities and the natural rights of peoples. Even though the Spanish Federal Committee was headed by Manuel de Irujo, it was decided not to pass specific resolutions regarding Basques and Catalans merely to satisfy their representatives. Indeed, this was so much the case that ELA subsequently accused the Basque Nationalist Party of having severely compromised certain fundamental aspects of the Basque Country's cause through its inaction.

It was not until approval of the post-Franco Spanish Constitution in 1978, guaranteeing the autonomy of Spain's regions and nationalities, that democratically elected Basque institutions could implement a dynamic foreign initiative. In the case that we are considering, official Basque initiatives within the wider European context would have to wait until January 1, 1986, the date when Spain entered the European Community. It is only since approval of the Treaty of European Union in 1992 that such Basque involvement has become truly significant.

The Impact of Membership in the European Community Upon the Basque Economy

Prior to the integration of Spain into the European Community, or in the early 1980s, the Basque economy was precarious. This was particularly true with regard to its traditional driving force, heavy industry, due to its aged infrastructure. Consequently, integration of the Spanish (and hence Basque) economy into the wider European one posed serious challenges. Within Spain the Basque area had one of the highest standards of living, but within the European context it was one of the lowest. Standard of living is obviously related to the level of both industrial and agricultural development, in terms of which the Basque Country was behind the European norm (although it is interesting to note that by 1979–1980 the Basque economy was approaching acceptable European levels before suffering a severe downturn). Indeed, despite its extensive heavy-industry sector, in terms of per capita income the Basque economy trailed Denmark and even the Aquitaine, both of which have greater dependence than does the Basque Country upon agricultural production.

In the period between 1969 and 1975 the European Community's market share of (Spanish) Basque exports increased from 31% to 40%. Indeed, the integration of Basque commerce within the European Community is superior to that of Spain's, since the Basque Country is industrialized and possesses infrastructural advantages, a specialized labor force, ancillary industries, and so on. A significant portion of foreign investment in Spain is in the Basque Country (it is in third place behind Madrid and Barcelona). There is significant European Community investment in the Basque economy, noticeably in the rubber, chemical, plastics, and electronics sectors, France being the leading investor. Regarding licenses, patents, and intellectual property, the relationship between the Basque economy and the European Community is asymmetrical, with most of the Basque payments going to French and German firms.

The actual process of integration was effected against the backdrop of an economic crisis in both the Basque and the European economies. When the European Commission required an annual economic growth rate of 4–5% for candidates seeking admission to the EEC, the Basque economy was expanding at only about 1–2%. Inflation within it was greater than that of the member countries and unemployment in the Basque Country in 1979 was about 10%.

There was the additional challenge that those sectors of the European Community's economy that were in crisis—namely, the steel and shipbuilding industries—were the cornerstones of Basque heavy industry. Nor had the sorely needed modernization of Basque heavy industry transpired. Consequently, integration into the European Community, with the resulting reduction in protectionism, posed a serious threat to Basque heavy industry in particular.

The Spanish incorporation into the EEC would fundamentally change the playing field for Basque industry. One effect was that the potential internal market expanded by a factor of twenty and the number of consumers by a factor of twelve. The tradeoff, of course, was that the Basque domestic market became totally accessible to external competition and was without tariff protections, the primary instrument by which nation-states control the pricing and volume of their international commerce.

The generally inferior condition of Basque industry compared with that of the member states of the EEC meant that, after Spanish membership, it was essential for Basque industrialists to modernize their facilities, while possibly changing their scale and diversity. In fact, it led to a proliferation of smaller scale plants producing a wider variety of products. Above all, to compete within the European Community it was essential to increase productivity. Basque industry was challenged to lower costs, to effect economies of scale, to intensify use of new technologies, to attract new investment, to effect better procurement, and to streamline administration and management. That is, Basque industry had to be revamped entirely if it was to survive the transition to free-market involvement in the European economy.

Nor did the effects of EEC membership fall equally upon all sectors of Basque industry. Processing industries actually benefited from access to raw materials at cheaper prices, whereas basic industries found themselves in direct competition with more efficient providers of their products. It was also necessary to redefine a business mentality which had previously privileged the domestic market over export ones and viewed competitiveness in terms of wage scales alone. In the new arena, competitiveness was more a function of efficiency derived from specialization and economies of scale in producing goods for an expanded market. It also turned upon the ability to effect research and development of new product lines. In short, Basque industry required both serious restructuring and modification of its corporate culture.

Basque agriculture, by the 1980s, was in profound structural crisis, in terms of both its economic and its demographic significance. The production of milk, meat, and other basic products was declining. With Spain's entry into the Common Market, Basque agriculture was subjected to the agricultural policy of the European Community. In those sectors where there is excess production, such as dairy products, there would be no subsidies or incentives; on the other hand, membership would open up new avenues for funding of restructuring and rationalization of Basque agriculture. However, given the anemic status of agriculture within the Basque economy overall, there would not be significant funding of it from the EC.

Within a few years after integration into the Common Market, the Basque economy had undergone profound transformations. Particularly in the industrial sector there was a notable aperture to the outside world, with respect to both sales and purchases. The Basque economy, by 1990, was clearly integrated into a European transnational market structure.

On the other hand, despite the fact that the Basque government of Euskadi defined its economy as primarily a service one, in this respect it lagged behind the European norm. In fact, heavy industry and manufacturing, with 46% of production and 43% of employment, clearly predominated within the Basque economy. This should not be regarded, however, as a peculiarity of the Basque Country so much as a sign of its relative backwardness. The steelmaking sector is particularly sensitive to international economic cycles. It is characterized by weak demand in the world economy (with an annual growth rate of less than 2% in recent years).

In terms of scale, Basque industry has become atomized. Almost 90% of the firms have fewer than 50 employees. After a period of plant closures in the early 1980s, since 1985 the Basque government has helped to stimulate a gradual increase in the number of plants based almost exclusively upon small-scale industry. This fragmentation poses its own problems in that Basque firms have shown little propensity for collective action. There is a real scarcity of manufacturing and business organizations. As the Basque economy finds itself competing increasingly within an international marketplace, such individualism is its own weakness in the face of better-organized competition.

Entry into the European Community has produced greater emphasis upon commercial ties and exchanges with other member countries, as well as a certain gradual transformative process throughout the Basque economy. These transformations are in large part derived from the EEC's common policies (Agrarian Policy, Fishing Policy, Regional Policy, Commercial Policy, Environmental Policy, for example) and from the furthering of the four fundamental liberties (the free flow of goods, services, persons, and capital) in anticipation of the 1993 European Common Market.

The first impact upon the Basque economy in its external dealings was the reciprocal suppression of restrictions on commerce in the form of a dismantling of tariffs on trade among member states (1986–1992). At the same time, the implementation of a value-added tax, as a substitute for former ones, rationalized the EEC tax system while favoring investment. By 1992 there was also liberalization in the flow of capital that modified fundamentally the cost and structure of short-term debt.

The major challenge that the Basque economy faced was the EEC limitation upon public subsidy and incentives for private enterprise. Given the need to modernize the antiquated Basque industrial infrastructure, the EEC's laws regarding free competition hindered development of Basque public-private partnerships. Another problem was the economic impact of EEC environmental policies. To be in compliance, the Basque economy had to spend 1.2 billion pesetas on this aspect alone.

Finally, there were other preparations that had to be made for entry into the Common Market. These included a greater emphasis upon research and development, development of a global export strategy, creation of business associations, strengthening of commercial ties, price stabilization, restructuring of government finances along the lines of those of other member states, improvement in professional training, education reform, establishment of business services by government (practically lacking in the Basque Country) and improvement of a deficient transportations and telecommunications infrastructure in the Basque Country.

European Community Assistance
to the Basque Country (1989–1993)

The relative high level of development of the Basque economy ruled out its subsidization within the Objective One Structural Funds (rural development) available to qualifying underdeveloped European regions. However, the Basque Country has benefited from all of the other funds and different initiatives of the European Community within recent years. Such assistance is designed to carry out the necessary reforms to permit the Basque Country to confront the consequences of pertaining to the Community. Accordingly, between 1989 and 1993, the Structural Funds earmarked 392.97 million ecus (or nearly 136,600 million pesetas) for the Basque area. Of this funding, 75.56% came from the ERDF (European Regional Development Fund). The European Social Fund (ESF) and the European Agricultural Guidance and Guarantee Fund (EAGGF) contributed, respectively, 18.86% and 1.58% of the overall total.

TABLE 1. *EU Funds for the Basque Country (1990–1993)*

Funds	1990	1991	1992	1993
ERDF	4.9	7.6	11.6	19.2
ESF	0.2	3.4	2.1	2.8
EAGGF	1.0	3.0	1.2	4.7
Infrastructural	6.1	14.0	14.9	26.7
EAGGF (guarantees)	—	—	—	0.1
Cohesion	—	—	—	0.3

(In thousand millions of pesetas)

Under Objectives 3 and 4, the European Union also furnished a total of 20,567 million pesetas for retraining and other measures during 1993 and 1994 to combat Basque unemployment. Recipients of such aid during the two-year period numbered 241,000 persons.

The reclamation of urban blight, the effort against contamination, support for Centers of Technological Research, assistance to business firms, and, in general, improvement to the transportations and communications infrastructure are all additional areas of collaboration between the European Union and the Basque government. For example, the EU loaned 2,000 million pesetas for the first phase of the co-financing of the Technological Park in Zamudio (Bizkaia). Through its RESIDER and RENAVAL programs, the EU funded reconversion of the steel and shipbuilding sectors of the Basque economy. It also supported other projects, such as construction of the Bilbao metro and improvement of the water treatment and delivery system in San Sebastián.

The Maastricht Treaty (1992) and the Validation of Regional Aspirations

Each new expansion of the European Community[3] supposes an obvious increase in its regional heterogeneity. Furthermore, more recent entries are countries with economically depressed regions of their own, requiring enhanced communitarian sensitivity to the need for subnational regional economic development programs. Consequently, creation in 1975 of the European Regional Development Fund (ERDF) signaled the beginning of the so-called Community Regional Policy. It should be noted, however, that at first this was not direct assumption by the community of the problems (and their solutions) of individual member states, but rather an adjustment of the quotas paid by each into the budgets of the various EC programs according the impact of the applications of community policies upon each contributor.

In effect, with the One Europe Act of 1986, which conferred membership upon Spain and Portugal, the regional diversity and their necessities increased dramatically. Given the ideal that economic differences among regions ought to be reduced if not abolished, in 1988 there was important reform of EEC regional policy. Since 1993 regional economy parity is one of the major priorities of the European Union. Of the EU's various funds, the principal ones devoted to achieving this objective are: the European Regional Development Fund (ERDF), which assists the poorest regions by stimulating investment, improving infrastructure, and stimulating small business; the European Agricultural Guidance and Guarantee Fund (EAGGF), which, within the Common Agricultural Policy, underwrites the transition of traditional farmers to modern modes of agricultural production as well as the development of alternative economic activities in rural areas; and the European Social Fund (ESF), which concentrates upon professional training and employment. All three funds engage in a common coordinated effort in distributing their support and resources.

At the same time the European Parliament is increasingly aware of regional issues. As early as the projected European Union Treaty (1984), the need to permit participation of local and regional authorities in the construction of a united Europe was noted. That same year, the First Regional Conference was held as clear recognition of the importance of involving the regions (in addition to the states) in the European Community's decision-making processes.

Paralleling this institutionalization of the regional awareness at the suprastate level, during the 1960s and 1970s a number of organizations at the regional level coalesced throughout Europe, with representational political aspirations that amounted to more than simply technical and economic concerns. Their first forum, and one of the most important, is the Council of European Local and Regional Powers, a cooperative context directly dependent upon the Council of Europe and the first international organization to give explicit recognition to the participation of local substate entities as such in the emerging united Europe.

The second regional associational forum is the Assembly of European Regions (AER), which is the major exponent of the interregional associative process initiated in the 1960s. It aspires to be the political vehicle for all sectorial regional initiatives. Born in Strasbourg, France, on January 18, 1985, among its several objectives are:

- To organize and foment dialogue; to formulate and realize the common action of the European regions.
- To reinforce regional representation within the European institutions and facilitate regional participation in the construction of a suprastate Europe.
- To cooperate with all European associations representative of local powers.
- To support the actions of "Regional Associations" and those of associations that are likely candidates for future membership in the AER.

Its purposes are to cooperate and coordinate efforts with the Committee of the Regions, the Chamber of the Regions of the Council of Regional and Local Powers and to elaborate regionalist doctrine.

The Maastricht treaty of February 7, 1992 is a watershed for region-alist concerns within a united Europe. Before this treaty the empha-sis was upon the economic revival of the poor regions. Afterward, the driving force became the political and economic concerns of the richest ones (particularly the German Länder). Regionalism was not the overriding issue, but it did pose the paradox of how to reconcile the internal structuring of profoundly decentralized member coun-tries (particularly Germany) with a communitarian structure that could only accommodate partial regional participation in the political process. It seemed likely that the treaty would resolve the issue, given that the moment seemed propitious.

We may now consider the ways in which a post-Maastricht Europe has dealt with regional issues as reflected in the Basque case. Eus-kadi's involvement in the process operates at the following levels:

Basque Participation in European Institutions

a. *European Council*—The reform of Article 146 of the Treaty on European Union reads: "The European Council will be com-prised by a *minister level* representative of each member state, au-thorized to commit the government of each member state." This has been interpreted to mean (as in the case of Germany) that the minister in question need not represent a member nation-state but rather could be appointed by an autonomous community within it, insofar as the matters under consideration regarded the domains transferred to it by the central state authority. Given that the communitarian context is one in which a multitude of such previously internally regional competencies come into play, there transferred is the delicate issue of how such matters can be dealt with without "external intervention" that might erode the very regional autonomy that had been negotiated at the nation-state level. For its part, the European Union does not block the participation and input of the regions in the political structuring and elaboration of rules for Europe, nor does it intervene in how communitarian decisions are to be implemented subsequently. It is the member state that decides on such procedural matters.

In the Spanish case, the central government was quite reticent to allow representation of the autonomous communities on the Council until the spring of 1998, at which time it was resolved by the European Congress of Deputies to open negotiations with the Spanish government regarding the possible representation of the country's autonomous regions in the Congress. Nor was it until January 1998 that they were represented in the European Council's committees, at which time the rules were changed in this regard—a development that the Basque government deemed to be "very positive."

b. *The European Commission*—This Commission formulates the legislative initiatives of the European Union and is the context that lacks participation by the autonomous communities, including Euskadi. It is paradoxical that regional participation is limited, since this body seeks to commit Europe's various autonomies to the EU's process and goals. We have the case, for example, that when Basque authorities wish to direct themselves in writing to the Commission regarding Basque fulfillment of communitarian obligations the documentation must be signed by an official of the Spanish State. There is, however, a positive development, one that has improved the situation, in that a Basque, Sr. D. Eneko Landaburu, is the present head of the Commission's General Directorate 16, that which is responsible for Regional Policy.

c. *Committee of the Regions*—Article 4.2 of the Treaty states that the Council and Commission are to be assisted by an Economic and Social Committee and by a Committee of the Regions, both of which are advisory. Representatives of the seventeen autonomous communities of Spain, along with four representatives of Spanish municipalities, sit on the Committee of the Regions. Its purview includes education, professional formation, youth matters, culture, public health, transEuropean networks, and funding of governmental structure. It can also take the initiative in convening without being asked. Its conclusions are forwarded to the Council and the Commission, along with the record of its debate and deliberations.

Euskadi has one representative on this committee: the Basque president (or his substitute). Despite its solely advisory capacity, the Committee has issued several influential dictums across a wide range of issues.

d. *The European Parliament*—Both Basque regionalist political parties as well as Spanish ones active in the Basque Country are represented in the European Parliament. After the 1995 European elections Euskadi had six parliamentarians: three representatives of the Socialist Party of Euskadi (PSOE), one of the Basque Nationalist Party (PNV), and two of the Popular Party (PP). Within the context of the European Parliament, representatives are organized into Parliamentary Groups, without concern for their geographical origin, nor is there a coalition of representatives from different countries that reflects regional concerns. In anticipation of the 1999 European parliamentary elections there have been several meetings of the nationalist parties of Euskadi, Catalunya, and Galicia to study the possibility of presenting a common slate of candidates.

e. *Regional Policy*—Between 1994 and 1999, policy for economic development of the Basque Country has envisioned a series of measures to be applied by local and regional officials. Partial funding for them was to derive from the Structural Funds and other sources available within the European Union. The main purpose was to identify and address the key problems arising from the integration of the Basque economy into a united Europe.

Between 1994 and 1996 Euskadi, as a region of industrial decline, received 179,193 million ecus. The funds were used to support employment, improve the competitiveness of Basque firms, sponsor research and development, and protect the natural environment. They also included incentives for local development and urban renewal, as well as various forms of technical assistance.

Communitarian support provided under Objective 5b (rural concerns) is of great importance. It is estimated that between 1994 and 1999, 81.2 million ecus have been invested in this sector, 26.5% of which came from the European Union. The priorities of EU assistance include improvement of agrarian infrastructure, promotion of rural economic diversification, protection of agrarian resources and the natural environment, improvement of rural habitat, and professional upgrading of agricultural skills. There is also emphasis upon agrarian research and development, ecotourism, and upgrading of services and the quality of leisure time.

All of the foregoing EU assistance complements that provided under Basque Government economic and social policy. We now consider the details of some programs carried out in the Basque Country for the period 1994–1999 under such arrangement.

THE RESIDER II PROGRAM

Given the excellent results of the first RESIDER program in the Basque setting, a second phase of it has been approved in which the EU, under Objectives 2 and 5b of the European Regional Development Fund, will provide 50% of the funding to facilitate the reconversion of the steelmaking sector of the Basque economy. It is intended that such measures will complement and reinforce both the initiatives of local authorities and those of other communitarian agencies and programs in a common effort to improve the standard of living of those in the Basque region. This common effort is conceived as a stimulus designed to strengthen the ties between the European Union and its regions by convincing the citizenries of the latter of the advantages of belonging to the former. It is anticipated that the variety and magnitude of such cooperative efforts will increase over time.

THE INTERREG PROGRAM

The Basque Country's INTERREG Program, 1994–1999, with total funding of 15,299 million ecus to finance economic development of the Basque borderland, is subdivided into three initiatives:

1. A program designed to stimulate economic diversification and development in the transborder region, with 3 million ecus of funding.

2. A program which fortifies territorial identity through the development of regional cooperation, mobilization of human resources, and cultural formation, with a budget of 9,923 million ecus.

3. A program that stimulates transpyrenean cooperation, minimizing the obstacles posed by the international frontier while fostering a better exchange of information and ideas through transborder projects and structures, funded by 2,140 million ecus.

THE AUKERA PROJECT

Headed by the Municipal Agency for Women of the city government of Bilbao, this initiative receives EU funding under its Program of Communitarian Action (1996–2000), which promotes the development and exchange of information and experience aimed at promoting gender equity within the European Union. Project Aukera's budget totals 20 million pesetas. It is coordinated by the women's association Emakunde, with the participation of the municipal governments of Bilbao, Ermua, Arrasate, Eskoriatza, Elgeta, Antzuola, and Oñati, as well as the Association of Basque Municipalities (EUDEL), the women's association "Bagabiltza," and the Sociology Department of the University of the Basque Country. There are also two transnational municipal members: Bristol (United Kingdom) and Brussels (Belgium). Their presence facilitates a transnational understanding of the issues as well as their European projection.

NOW-EKIMEN

This is an EU-sponsored program under the auspices of the Communitarian Employment Initiative. The participants are the municipalities of San Sebastián, Lezo, Oiartzun, Pasaia, and Rentería. Also involved are Camargo (Cantabria), Sabrosa (Portugal), and Toulouse (France). There is a constant exchange of information among the players. The total budget of NOW-EKIMEN is 42.5 million pesetas, of which the EU provides 20 million. The main objective is to design a strategy that provides self-employment opportunities for 200 women.

RECITE II

The European Commission has approved a project to revitalize the mining district of Bizkaia, as well as to create a "mining park" as a tourist attraction. The initiative for this effort came from the Department of Commerce, Consumption and Tourism of the Basque Government, as well as from the municipalities of Abanto, Trápaga, Ortuella, and Muskíz. It was one of 55 projects (out of 301 proposals) selected for funding under the EU's RECITE II program. Its total cost is 140 million pesetas, of which the EU is providing half. Implementation began in 1998 and will take three years to complete.

Basque cofunding of the foregoing projects is largely within the purview of the so-called *Plan Euskadi XXI*. This is a common effort by the various levels of government in the Basque Country with, at times, participation from the private sectors as well. It was approved on December 19, 1995, and designed primarily for the period 1996–1998, although it is anticipated that a number of the Plan's initiatives will continue into the next century. Its eleven programs address the two concerns of the improvement and modernization of infrastructure and the revitalization of depressed areas and sectors of the economy. In 1996 and 1997, 25,510 million pesetas of an anticipated total of 47,936 million were expended on these projects. Seventy-five percent of the plan's funding is from public sources, of which more than half comes from the Basque Government, a third from the Foral Deputations, and the remainder from local entities and other sources (some from Europe and others from income generated by public enterprises). The remaining 25% is provided by the private sector.

f. Through the Subsidization Principle—understood by some states as their defense against the ever greater and more intrusive power of the European Union, participation of the substate regional entities in the communitarian agenda is the counterweight that meets the spirit of Article A, which prescribes that "the decisions will be made in the fashion most proximate to the citizenry." It may be noted that, in this regard, during the framing of the Treaty the swords were drawn. Both the central states and the substate entities on one side argued for this principle in order to retain their several powers vis-à-vis the wider communitarian ones. On the other side were those advocating ever greater concession of power to a central European authority. In the reform carried out in the Treaty of Amsterdam (1997), Germany, Austria, and Belgium ratified an annexed Declaration that expressly recognizes that this principle applies at the substate level. The Spanish authorities refused to sign the document, arguing that it was not an integral part of the Treaty's text. Basque and Catalan nationalists criticized this Spanish reticence.

Basque Participation in Europe

UNILATERAL BASQUE PARTICIPATION IN EUROPE

This would include foreign visits made by Basque officials and business people to gain contacts, enhance awareness, and establish economic ties, though it should be noted that, in this regard, the efforts of the Basque government have been directed more toward the Americas than Europe. Nevertheless, in recent years the frequency of European visits has increased as Basque officials have sought to improve the image of the Basque people, promote tourism, and attract foreign investment for Euskadi.

The Basque government clearly supports the creation of a united Europe as being in its own best interests. Consequently, it has sponsored numerous meetings and conferences on the communitarian theme, while constantly informing the local mass media of the importance of Basque involvement in the wider European framework. The Basque government has also made an effort to project a positive Basque image to the entire world through the Internet.

The Basque government has opened an office in Brussels, where it maintains its Delegation of Euskadi. This, in turn, is the transformation of the former Basque Commercial Office in the Belgian city. The purpose of both is to have Basque representation at the seat of European decision-making, while at the same time serving as an information service and facilitator for Basque business firms. This is one of the Basques' most important vehicles for operating within the wider European framework, an approach that the Basque government has developed and emphasized to a greater degree than have Spain's other autonomous communities. The Basque government has also opened a tourism office in Paris to promote a positive image of the Basque Country, while attracting visitors to it in keeping with the slogan "Ven y Cuéntalo" (Come and Talk About It).

The Basque government publishes considerable information about the European Union. In 1996, for example, it published *Euskadi ante la reforma de la Unión Europea.* It outlines the process of European construction, underscoring those aspects deemed by the Basque government to be deficient, such as the need to enhance the input of autonomous communities into the decision-making process directly rather than through their respective nation-states.

BILATERAL BASQUE PARTICIPATION IN EUROPE

The majority of bilateral agreements of the Basque government are within the confines of the European Union (possibly involving three or four different regions). These agreements, which have different names (though never "treaties"), operate within the broad framework of "mutual understanding, cooperation, funding of a particular bilateral relation, contribution to European peace and security," and so on.

The bilateral agreements are generally supported by the institutional structure of the European regional movement—for example, the Communitarian Regionalization Charter of the European Parliament, concrete programs of the Regional Policy (like INTERREG and LINGUA), the Council of Europe, the Assembly of European Regions, and the Peripheral Maritime Regions of Europe. These agreements are usually simple and straightforward, often employing existing arrangements or structures to carry out a particular project. Usually they deal with practical matters, such as business promotion of both contracting regions and exchange of technology between them. There are also a few bilateral agreements beyond Europe, such as those with the University of Nevada, Reno and Boise State University (1988) and with the Chilean Government (1998), both reflecting in part ties facilitated by the presence of Basque emigrants in those respective areas.

There is even an eastern European initiative reflected in the agreement signed in 1991 with a visiting Russian delegation.

Then there is the trilateral agreement (Protocol of Cooperation) among Euskadi, Navarra, and the Aquitaine. It began as a bilateral arrangement between Euskadi and the Aquitaine, signed on October 3, 1989, in Bordeaux. In September 1990, an annex protocol was signed in Irún which financed the Fund for Aquitaine-Euskadi Cooperation. In this fashion, bilateral transborder projects could be funded. On February 13, 1992, Navarra joined the effort.

There is now active cooperation among the three regions, which has attracted other public and private entities as well. The quantity and quality of transborder projects have grown incrementally, as has their funding: from 40 million pesetas in 1990 to 270 million in 1994. In 1997, the Basque government alone earmarked approximately 110 million pesetas for such projects.

Euskadi has also entered into a bilateral agreement with Bavaria, the scope of which is limited to technological exchange and the sharing of information regarding regional political strategy. This is a key tie, since Bavaria is one of the so-called four engines within the European Union. This specific bilateral arrangement may well be extended to other regions, notably Flanders and Lombardy.

MULTILATERAL BASQUE PARTICIPATION IN EUROPE

Interregional cooperation "has shown itself to be an adequate instrument for the development of peaceful relations among the different European peoples and as an ideal means of constructing a Europe that is more proximate to its citizenry."[4] Thus Euskadi, as its institutional presence within the Spanish state matures, is developing parallel ties within the different European regional associations. At times Euskadi assumes a leadership role, such as is the case, along with the Aquitaine region of southern France, in the development of the so-called Atlantic Front region of shared interests.

There is a common denominator in such organizations—namely, the geographic location of their members on the periphery of the European Union's center of gravity (the continent's central regions). Recently, such regional initiatives have been shifting eastward, particularly with regard to regional economic development. The geographical considerations obviously inform Euskadi's interest in peripheral Atlantic associational initiatives, particularly with the Aquitaine, as a means of creating a more powerful lobby capable of influencing (or ameliorating the consequences of) future communitarian policy.

On the other hand, it should be noted that the Basque government expends greater efforts on some of its associative initiatives than it does on others. Often this reflects the degree of political interest of a particular association in regional autonomism. Of particular interest is the Association of European Regions, since it is a pioneering and doctrinal body dedicated to the cause of European regionalism but recognized by the international community. Then there is the Atlantic Arc Commission, which includes the United Kingdom, Ireland, France, Spain, and Portugal, united to lobby for certain economic considerations within the deliberations of the European Union.

Finally, of considerable interest is the Pyrenees Working Committee, created on November 4, 1983, in Pau (France). Participating regions include Catalunya, Aragón, Navarra, and Euskadi in Spain and the Aquitaine, Midi-Pyrénées, and Languedoc-Rousillon in France, as well as the Principality of Andorra. This association has a wide range of activity, including transportation and communications, energy, agriculture, forestry, resource conservation and protection of the natural environment, and preservation of cultural patrimony.

Euskadi's participation in multilateral organizations is also important for its collateral benefits, particularly the opportunity to foster contacts that transcend or bypass the established Vitoria-Madrid bilateral avenue of communication. In this fashion, it becomes possible to negotiate at least a part of Euskadi's destiny through multilateral channels articulated through Brussels. Thus, the Basque Country has entered directly into the negotiations that will determine the route of the extension of the rapid train between Paris and Madrid. There is also the possibility of independent participation of Euskadi in the creation of a "Cantabrian Corridor" of interested regions. Among other activities, Euskadi also conducts independent negotiations regarding maritime and fishing matters and facilitates contacts between business firms in several European regions. Nor should the value of access to the collective lobbying power of each of the regional associations to which Euskadi now belongs be underestimated.

It may be anticipated that, in the future, Euskadi will be an active force in shaping the political doctrine of the Association of European Regions and in the Pyrenees Working Committee, the latter because it is a forum that includes Navarra and the Aquitaine and because of the relevance of the representative from Rousillon (who was president of the EU's Committee of Regions).

Relations within the Spanish State

Despite the recent notable decentralization of Spain, since its entry into the EEC there has been a degree of recentralization. That is to say, the central administration has exhibited a degree of reticence regarding the direct participation of representatives of the several autonomous communities in the European Communitarian decision-making process. There is, however, some involvement articulated through an advisory "conference" that considers European matters affecting Spain and its regions. In this manner the regions do have some input in the formulation of Spanish policy. This arrangement is spelled out in Article 4 of the EU's Law of Autonomous Process. The conference has three functions:

1. That of informing the autonomous communities of the deliberations of the European Council, particularly those regarding the process of constructing a united Europe.
2. That of dealing with communitarian matters that lack their own specific sectorial conference or other mechanism facilitating their review.
3. That of approving the procedures and formulas whereby the autonomous communities participate in matters affecting them as they relate to the European Union.

It should be noted that, to date, the results of this conference arrangement have not been as encouraging as might have been expected. However, the future is more hopeful, since there is recent agreement, within the Sectorial Conference for European Affairs, to negotiate the terms of participation of the autonomous communities in the Council of Ministers.

Euskadi and the European Challenge

The construction of a European Union has posed, and continues to raise, two major challenges for Euskadi. One is political, the other socioeconomic (but with clear political implications). Immediate reference is to the Reform of the Treaty of Union, signed under the Treaty of Amsterdam on October 2, 1997 and to the impending reform of the Structural Policy that will determine the EU funding that Euskadi can anticipate receiving beginning in the year 2000.

REFORM OF THE TREATY OF UNION

Euskadi has always confronted its future energetically, and still does, now with its gaze fixed northward toward Europe (the source of decisions that will affect the Basque Country and configure the contexts in which it may wish to participate). For this reason, the Basque government works diligently to clarify and improve its political mandate. This is clearly reflected in the declaration made by Basque officials with regard to the Intergovernmental Summit, begun in 1996, which culminated in the signing of the Treaty of Amsterdam. The Basque government's declaration was directed not only at the EU but also at Spain's other autonomous communities, as well as at Spanish central authorities.

The declaration, which was written prior to and for the meeting of the representatives of Spain's seventeen autonomous communities charged with formulating their priorities for the European Intergovernmental Summit, reiterated the demands presented by the Committee of the Regions. The agreement that emerged from the meeting of Spain's seventeen autonomous regions maintained that there should be gradual reform that would enhance regional political input in European decision-making and improve the complementarity of all levels of government in the interest of diversity, while creating a more effective "citizen's Europe" more responsive to the aspirations of its different peoples.

The text of the Treaty of Amsterdam incorporates some of the regionalist concerns. For example, because it modifies Protocol 16 of the Maastricht Treaty, which provided the same administrative

structure for the Economic and Social Committee and the Committee
of the Regions, these committees will have different administrative
structures in the future. Also, the Treaty of Amsterdam did not require that measures of the newly unified Committee be approved by
the Council, as was the case with rulings of the two former committees. The possibility that the Committee might be consulted directly
by the European Parliament (in addition to the Commission and
Council) was also addressed. It was mandated that the Committee
be consulted regarding social and environmental issues, as well
as those concerning the European Social Fund, transportation, employment, and public health. Under duress, it was also agreed that,
in an advisory capacity only, the Committee would be involved
in questions regarding transnational cooperation. But the two major
objectives of the Basque government (in accord with the sentiments
of the Committee of the Regions) were rejected. Those objectives
were that the said committee should be given formal institutionalized recognition and that it should be authorized to seek recourse
in the European Union's Tribunal of Justice should either the EU or
one of its member states infringe upon accorded regional powers and
competencies.

Efficacious decision-making within the European Union rests upon
the horizontal relations among the member states. Regarding the protagonism of the "citizen" and the need to convince him/her of the
value of the united Europe project, there is more lip service than reality. A truly federalist European Union remains elusive, although
there have been positive strides in the areas of public relations and
involvement of civil society in the process on the one hand, and a
growing openness to the greater citizens' social and political involvement that is envisioned by reform of the Treaty on the other. Such
populist gains are evident despite the opposition of some of the EU's
core countries. The reforms were designed to prepare Europe for four
great challenges: creation of the monetary union in 1999; enlargement
of the EU to twenty-six member states by 2003; the financial challenges posed by the new millennium; and pan-European security
issues.

It should be noted that there has been a notable shift in the Spanish
government's response to the demands of Spain's autonomous com-

munities for direct European participation. Thus, while formerly there was disagreement between the central power and the regions, which was resolved only by rulings of the Constitutional Tribunal, the situation has improved. In April 1997, the Spanish government supported the regionalists' position that the EU's Committee of the Regions should be independent of the Economic and Social Committee. Spain further favored the election of Committee members, a broadening of its consultative purview, the right of the European Parliament to consult with it directly regarding regional matters, and the right of the Committee to take matters before the EU's Tribunal of Justice. Nevertheless, the Spanish government refused to sign the tripartite declaration proposed by the German Länder (and signed by Germany, Belgium, and Austria) at the final stage of the Treaty reform negotiation that would have broadened the EU's Subsidization Principle to the substate level.

At the same time, it should be noted that the greatest success to date, particularly of the Basque political representatives within the precincts of the EU's Congress of Deputies, is the right of the autonomous communities to representation on the Council of European Ministers (the context in which questions regarding the structure of political power and competencies are deliberated). This was a hotly debated issue, since the Popular Party (PP) wanted to limit such regionalist participation to membership on the advisory committees alone, which was done in January 1998. When the Basque representatives of the two moderate nationalist parties (PNV and EA) demanded that the Congress apply Article 146 of the Treaty of European Union, which permitted participation of regional representatives at the autonomous ministerial level (as Germany, Austria, and Belgium were allowing), the PP asked the PSOE for its support in rejection of the measure. When the latter sided with the regionalists, the PP changed its position and supported the motion proposed by Eusko Alkartasuna whereby Spain's central government and its seventeen autonomous communities would, beginning in June 1998, and within the framework of the Sectorial Conference for European Affairs, study the formula whereby the autonomies could be represented within the EU's Council of Ministers.

B) FUTURE REFORM OF REGIONAL POLICY

On June 16, 1997, the president of the European Commission, Jacques Santer, presented Agenda 2000 to the European Parliament. Agenda 2000 is designed to update the Union's political structure while expanding its borders and to strengthen the EU in the twenty-first century by stimulating economic growth, competitiveness, and employment. Its specific challenges include:

- How to reform and strengthen the Union's political structure to prepare it for enlargement while sustaining economic growth, fuller employment, and improvements in the standard of living.
- How to negotiate the specifics of the expansion of the EU and preparation of the candidates for membership.
- How to finance the expansion, including the necessary preparations and internal adjustments within the EU, to receive the new member states.

In Edinburgh (1992), the European Council based the EU's operational financial stability upon receipt of 0.46% of the Gross Domestic Product (1994–1999) of its members. Nevertheless, in 1999 there is a shortfall due to member-state budgetary constraints. This is not an insuperable problem either for the fifteen present members or for future ones, given anticipated greater efficiencies in the use of available resources. Consequently, structural interventions (subsidies) will continue to play a primordial role within the EU's budget.

In the period 2000–2006 the Structural Funds and Cohesion Fund will receive 275,000 million ecus, or 75,000 million ecus more than budgeted during 1993–1999. The total transfers from both funds should not surpass 4% of the Gross Domestic Product of any present or future member state. Forty-five-thousand million ecus are reserved for the new candidates, of which 7,000 million ecus will be made available to them prior to their incorporation. The future increase in transfers to new member states will be phased in according to their capacity for absorption.

Greater flexibility, decentralization, and streamlining of administration of the structural funds are indispensable if the greater efficiency is to be achieved. It is also necessary for the EU authorities to work more efficaciously with those of the member states. Finally, it will be important to improve upon the evaluation, follow-up, and accountability of EU-sponsored initiatives.

From a Basque perspective, we may make the following observations of the likely direct consequences of the future reforms in European Commission Regional Policy:

- To date the member states have successfully limited the scope of the European Commission in matters regarding transnational, transborder, and interregional cooperation, as well as rural development and equal opportunity, in part by reducing the amount of the EC's budget devoted to such matters from 9% to 4%.
- The states have maintained control over the Commission, the regions, and interregional cooperation through the RECITE programs, given that such initiatives remain under communitarian authority rather than becoming pilot projects beyond the control of the individual member states.
- There has also been reform in the definition of the areas qualifying for EU regional aid. In the case of Euskadi, this means that a smaller proportion of the populace will be benefited under the new Objective 2.[5] Regions undergoing economic and social reconversion, whether industrial or agricultural, maritime (fishing) or urban, are encompassed under the guidelines of this Objective. The assistance programs afforded to the Spanish regions within this category, including the Basque Country, Catalunya, the Balearic Islands, Madrid, Navarra, and La Rioja, are those experiencing the greatest cutbacks. Euskadi may lose as much as a third of what it has been receiving, or 100,000 million pesetas. This will be a serious setback in its capacity for reinvestment. Given that each member state has considerable latitude in identifying areas qualified for Objective 2 assistance, it is imperative that careful attention be given to unemployment statistics for particularly sensitive districts such as the Left Bank of the Nervión and the industrial belt around San Sebastián. It may be that they will qualify for greater EU assistance even if the remainder of Euskadi does not. These districts still have a per capita income below 75% of the EU norm, a necessary criterion to qualify for the subventions, but they are left out of consideration given that the figure for Euskadi as a whole is about 90% of the European norm.

- The proposals of the European Commission to create a new "Objective 3" designed to subsidize the adaptation and modernization of national policies regarding employment, education, and professional formation. Under this category the Basque Country has received 54,000 million pesetas over six years. But under the new rule, only those regions not included in the number-one and -two categories can qualify for such aid. Which is to say, should the Basque Country manage to retain its Objective 2 status, it will forfeit access to these funds. In short, the central government should try to change this situation, or seek offsets from other sources, with an eye toward retaining the present levels of EU funding in Euskadi.

- There is also confusion at present created by the richest members, led by Germany and Holland, who advocate a plan whereby countries qualifying for membership in the Monetary Union (adoption of the euro) would cease to receive Cohesion Funds. Such savings would be used to meet the costs of expanding the European Union. In June 1998, at German insistence, the European Parliament adopted the same policy. Spain's response[6] was that such limitations on access to the Cohesion Fund should not be approved, given that such aid is provided for under the treaties. However, it seems likely that this argument will prove insufficient and that there will be future challenges to such continued assistance to Monetary Union countries.

In sum, the EU is currently embroiled in intense negotiations between the various interested parties regarding the restructuring of social and economic programs and subsidies against the backdrop of the impending expansion of the European Union. In the case of Euskadi, it is necessary to influence and control the negotiations conducted by the Spanish central authorities in these matters, if the level of development realized until now is to be sustained.

Conclusion

The construction of a united Europe has evolved considerably, while, at the same time, Euskadi has consolidated its own level of self-government. The maturing of these two parallel processes points toward a convergence in the not-too-distant future in which Euskadi will play a truly active part in the decision-making of the European Union. Until now such participation has been largely subsumed within that of the Spanish State, given that the EU respects the institutional autonomy and procedures of its individual member states. However, membership in the European Union does not justify undermining the substance of the competencies ceded to Euskadi under the Statute of Gernika. It is to be anticipated that the internal Spanish debate over the scope of such competencies, as they relate to European matters, will become increasingly favorable to the Basque Autonomous Community.

The ever-increasing involvement of Euskadi in European construction has multiple political, economic, cultural, and social connotations and repercussions. It has become the prime vehicle for the modernization of Basque socioeconomic reality. Thanks in part to European financial support, there is now dynamic involvement of both public and private entities in the formulation and implementation of creative projects designed to confront the principal challenges to the Basque economy and contemporary society. At the same time, there is now greater awareness throughout the EU of Basque cultural reality, of the language and traditions, and of its creative capacities. This flows from Basque involvement in EU institutional contexts, as well as from cultural exchanges and visits by individuals. Conversely, Basque society is now more sensitized through outside contacts with other cultural and linguistic realities. Basques are now more aware of how others confront common problems and formulate solutions. Such sensitivity is particularly evident in the youth, and is primarily the result of the many exchange programs.

Nevertheless, it should be remembered that this is a political process whereby the parameters of the relations between the representatives of Euskadi and the Spanish State are broadened to new contexts. This "Europeanization" of formerly bilateral issues is played out against a history of internal conflict within Spain sometimes referred to as "the Basque problem." In the words of Basque President Ardanza:

Articulating Basque nationality within a Spanish and European citizenship might suppose the occasion, in the new political framework, for losing a large part of the emotional load that has been the ballast until now. . . . I would venture to prognosticate four fundamental parameters which, if they come about, would be decisive in the future of Euskadi: in the first place, within the future European Union there will be progressively more Europe, which is to say, more communitarian administration over what today are part of sovereign state powers. Consequently, secondly, there will be increasingly less State, which is to say the domains of strictly state sovereignty will be reduced due to the pressure that the European Union will exert over the States from above, as well as those that emanate from infrastate sources from below. Thirdly, there will be increasingly more nation, which is to say the political entities capable of integrating cohesive groups of citizens linked together by common membership will be empowered. Finally, there will be much more society, that is to say a much larger citizenry with Europe as the referent in its sense of belonging. If this were the proximate European framework, Euskadi would find within it a much more favorable context in which to overcome, definitively, the present problem of its political and institutional fit.[7]

Notes

1. J. L. Castro, "El fundamento teórico y doctrinal: El federalismo integral superador del Estado-nación." In J. L. Castro, ed., *La emergente participación de las regiones en la construcción europea,* 134–150 (Oñati: Instituto Vasco de Administración Pública).

2. Alexander Ugalde Zubiri, *La acción exterior del nacionalismo vasco (1890–1939): Historia, pensamiento y relaciones internacionales* (Bilbao: Instituto Vasco de Administración Pública, 1996).

3. Founder countries (1957) were Germany, Belgium, France, Italy, Holland, and Luxembourg. Subsequently, in 1973, the United Kingdom, Ireland, and Denmark joined, followed by Greece (1981), Portugal and Spain (1986), and Sweden, Finland, and Austria (1995).

4. Gobierno Vasco, *Informe sobre la participación institucional de Euskadi en la construcción europea* (Vitoria-Gasteiz: Servicio de Publicaciones, 1993), 13.

5. Until now, all of the territory of the Basque Country qualified under either Objective 2 (regions of industrial decline) or Objective 5 (rural development). Between 1994 and 1999 Euskadi received EU aid of 231,743 million pesetas, of which 118,000 million were for industrial incentives, 54,600 million were for Objectives 3 and 4 (to combat unemployment and foster professional formation), 20,500 million were agricultural subsidies and rural development funds, and 14,700 million were for improved infrastructure. Of the total amount, 23,000 million came directly from the Spanish government, by way of Cohesion Funds. The above disbursements represent 3.3% of the total EU funding received by Spain during this same period.

6. In absolute terms Spain receives the most EU funding of any member state (an annualized 1.1 billion pesetas in the period 1995–1996), although the proportions change if Gross National Product and/or population size are taken into account. On a per capita basis, Spain received 28,195 pesetas a year. In Portugal the figure was 46,461, in Greece it was 60,000, and in Ireland it was 96,567 pesetas. At the same time some richer nations receive aid—Denmark receives 17,000 pesetas per inhabitant. Germany, however, pays 17,400 pesetas into the EC for each of its citizens.

7. "El País Vasco: Apuntes para una reflexión política." Speech by José Antonio Ardanza, President of the Basque Country, given to the Foreign Affairs Commissions of the Senate and House of Representatives of the Republic of Uruguay. Montevideo, October 30, 1997.

William A. Douglass

Creating the New Basque Diaspora

Currently there is much fascination in the humanities and social sciences with borders—ranging from the effects upon borderland peoples of international frontiers to the transnational and global networks that transcend them and the "hybridity" of individuals whose life experiences incorporate more than a single cultural reality—often of both a First- and Third-World/colonizer and colonized nature. Within transnational studies a major concern is with what has been called "postmodern hyper-space" (Rouse 1991: 8) or "diaspora space" (Brah 1996: 16).[1] Reference is to a world inhabited by persons who are born into one cultural context, migrate across an international boundary to another, and then live a reality that encompasses both but without being defined fully by either. A prime example is afforded by the Mexican migrants studied by Roger Rouse (1991, 1995) and Michael Kearney (1996), both in their natal Mexican community and as labor migrants in California who move with regularity between the two contexts, who utilize modern electronic means of communication to maintain vital contacts in both, and who serve as conduits for the transfer of people, technology, capital, and ideas between the sending and receiving areas. In their case, as well as in that of most of the planet's modern migrants, the creation of diasporic space is a grassroots phenomenon, resulting from an individualized organic process rather than from a programatic collective one.[2]

Such was the case as well in the last century and in the earliest decades of the present one when European emigrants, the "huddled masses" of transatlantic migration fame, contributed to the creation of what the historian Denoon (1983) has labeled the world's Euro-settler societies—such countries as Australia, New Zealand, South Africa, Canada, the United States, and the southern cone nations of South America. However, for the most part the era of massive European emigration had ended midway through the present century, its progressive interdiction effected by the two world wars, the Great Depression, and increasingly restrictive immigration policies within several of the former receiving countries. Relocation of Europe's war refugees during the late 1940s and early 1950s represented the last paroxysm of significant overseas European emigration. Since then the movement of Europeans has been largely intracontinental—the migration from south to north of guest workers and, more recently, from east to west of former Soviet-bloc peoples in search of economic opportunity.

Consequently, Europe's overseas emigrant diasporas have aged for at least the last half-century with little infusion of new blood in the form of Old-World-born immigrants. My concern herein is with how this aging of the Basque emigrant diasporas or collectivities around the globe relates to the conscious recent attempts to create a new Basque diaspora. These aging and creative processes must be understood against the backdrop of certain historical realities.

First and foremost there is the demonstrated ethnic staying power of Basques both in their European homeland and in the Basque emigrant diasporas. While Basques have never had their own nation-state and, for the past several centuries, political hegemony over the Basque Country has been divided between Spain and France, many Basques retain a sense of their ethnic uniqueness vis-à-vis other Spaniards and French people. In the case of Spanish Basques such sentiments have actually increased during the present century, and have produced one of western Europe's most active ethnonationalist political movements. Furthermore, over the last five centuries, wherever Basques have emigrated in sufficient numbers to create a critical mass they have exhibited a tendency to configure at least a part of their behavior in terms of Basque ethnic affiliations and networks, including, in different periods and places, the formation of voluntary associations that reinforce and maintain a formal hyphenated Basque presence within host societies (Douglass and Bilbao 1975). The "hostlands" include several Latin American countries (notably Chile, Argentina, Uruguay, Peru, Colombia, Venezuela, Cuba, and Mexico), as well as the United States, Canada, Australia, the Philippines, Great Britain, Belgium, and the former Soviet Union. Basques also migrate in considerable numbers to metropolitan areas within Spain and France, and now constitute noteworthy "colonies" in such cities as Madrid, Barcelona, and Paris.

Second, since Franco's death in 1975 Basques have been prime architects of Spain's present "federalist" reality, successfully pressing their claim for considerable political autonomy which, for all but the Navarrese, is currently articulated through Eusko Jaurlaritza, or the Basque Government of the Autonomous Community of Euskadi overarching the traditional provinces of Bizkaia, Gipuzkoa, and Araba. Eusko Jaurlaritza has its own president, parliament, and capital (Vitoria-Gasteiz) and enjoys broad and expanding powers. At the same time it is poised somewhat precariously at the juncture where moderate Basque nationalism meets Spanish federalism, an accommodation criticized vehemently by both irredentist Spanish nationalists (centrists) and radical Basque ones (separatists). This article examines the conscious attempts of Eusko Jaurlaritza to "energize" Basque collectivities around the world for specific purposes.

First, there is the attempt to maintain "Basqueness" in the diasporic population—but a Basqueness defined from and by Euskadi rather than in more parochial "Argentine-Basque" or "Australian-Basque" terms. Indeed, at times it is consciously pedagogical in that it seeks to educate hyphenated Basques (and interested non-Basques) regarding modern Old-World Basque reality, rather than reinforcing the fragmentary and stale stereotypes of it as transported abroad in the minds of emigrants leaving Europe one or more generations ago. With respect to the American West, for example, it is not the purpose, or at least the main one, to reinforce the imagery of Old-World farming and fishing ways of life and a folkloric culture, on the one hand, and a New-World sheepherding tradition, on the other—imagery that even today pretty much sums up most of the intended audience's preconceptions of Basqueness.

The second goal is to create a bond between hyphenated Basques and the Basque Country to secure the support of the former for the latter's economic and political agendas (both Old World and New).

In what follows I am limiting my analysis to the diasporic activities of Eusko Jaurlaritza. Excluded from consideration are the less developed, though not entirely absent, efforts of Navarra and various governmental agencies in Iparralde (the French Basque area).

Basque nationalists, and particularly the Basque Nationalist Party (PNV), controlled Eusko Jaurlaritza from its creation in 1979–1980 until a schism within the party's ranks in 1986. Since that year a coalition of both Spanish and Basque nationalist forces governs, with neither able to muster an absolute majority. Consequently, the past decade of Basque political history has been characterized by compromise and post-electoral pacting among the political parties contesting elections. To date the Basque nationalists have been able to retain the presidency and, from their viewpoint, the key ministry of culture— key in that it is instrumental in the campaign to both save and revitalize Euskara (the Basque language), while influencing, as well, the evolution of arts and letters within Basque society.

Practically from the outset nationalist forces within Eusko Jaurlaritza recognized the potential value of the world's Basque collectivities. In part this reflected a debt of gratitude, since, from a Basque nationalist viewpoint, the Basque government was created during the 1930s, in the heat of civil war, with José Antonio Aguirre serving as its first president. When that initiative was defeated and driven into exile, Basque resistance became in large measure a diasporic phenomenon.

President Aguirre and his immediate entourage opted to reside in New York City, whence during World War II they collaborated closely with Allied officials to defeat the Axis powers, in particular by organizing a Basque diasporic spy network to monitor Axis activities in Latin America. After the end of the conflict the Aguirre contingent remained in New York for several years to both lobby Washington in the continuing effort to topple the Franco regime and to argue the Basque case in the forum of a nascent United Nations.

In retrospect, the Basques suffered a second defeat in their attempts to internationalize their cause. As the Western world settled into a cold war with the Soviet bloc it accommodated Franco's Spain. The pleas and agendas of western Europe's ethnonationalist minorities, including the Basques, were largely ignored.

However, from a Basque political viewpoint the exercise had been far from futile. In various parts of the world diasporic Basques had intervened in their own countries to facilitate resettlement of Basque refugees from the Spanish Civil War. For example, in Mexico President Cárdenas was prevailed upon to accept refugee children, whom he housed in an orphanage in Morelia (Legarreta 1984: 183–197). The Basques of Argentina convinced President Ortiz to allow a considerable number of Basque refugees into his country, and they then formed a committee to facilitate the newcomers' adaptation (Azcona Pastor et al. 1992: 249–270). There was a similar effort in Venezuela (San Sebastián and Ajuria 1992).

Indeed, with few exceptions, the refugees had either resettled in Iparralde or emigrated to an established Basque diasporic community. In this regard Mexico, Colombia, Chile, Argentina, Uruguay, and Venezuela all received Basque exiles, many of whom have influenced configuration of Basqueness within these host societies over the past half century. In 1956 the Basque government-in-exile organized a World Basque Congress in Paris, funded by Basque businesses in the diaspora. Its purpose was to "bring together political leaders, scholars, intellectuals, artists, and other Basque figures from around the world in a celebration of Basque culture and a renewal of the Basque struggle for survival" (Clark 1991: 13). The political relationship between the Motherland and its exiled offspring was further complicated by a return to the Basque Country by some refugees (and even by their descendents) upon the death of Franco. While they were not the prime architects of post-Franco Basque political reality, neither were they excluded entirely from the process.

In short, during the early 1980s, or in the infancy of Eusko Jaurlaritza, both precedent and personnel were available to remind policymakers of the potential value of the emigrant diaspora—at least regarding the agenda of the Basque nationalist forces within the new government.

In 1982 Minister of Culture Labayen invited delegates from the world's Basque collectivities to a congress to discuss the future of the diaspora. There was no real agenda and the discussions proved openended. But the seeds of communication and dialogue were sown. Shortly thereafter Labayen established a Servicio de Relaciones con los Centros Vascos (Service for Relations with the Basque Centers) under the direction of Jokin Intxausti. Intxausti made several trips to Basque collectivities in North and South America to explore ways in which Eusko Jaurlaritza might assist them. However, his efforts were cut short by his untimely death in 1986. Within forty-eight hours

President Ardanza had appointed Josu Legarreta to the post, underscoring his government's commitment to its relations with the diaspora.

In May 1989 the first issue of the magazine *Euskal Etxeak* ("Basque Houses," a euphemism for the world's Basque centers) appeared. Except for the opening statements by President Ardanza and Minister of Culture Arregi, given in both Basque and Spanish, the entire publication was in the latter language. The intention was to publish monthly, a plan that was quickly modified. At present *Euskal Etxeak* appears five times a year. A second major shift is evident in the second issue (no. 2–3), by which time the publication had bifurcated into separate Spanish and English editions in recognition that a Spanish one alone failed to reach the entire Basque diaspora.

The purpose of the magazine was stated succinctly in the formal greetings of the first issue. President Ardanza noted:

> . . . Some of you left this country with sadness, others of you were born in the land that your parents went to. But none of you have forgotten your place of origin, Euskadi. For this reason . . . *Euskal Etxeak* was born, and through it we will present contemporary Basque reality in its many aspects, its principal achievements and its future aspirations . . . (*Euskal Etxeak* 1 [1989]: 2)

Minister Arregi invited the readership to submit for publication consideration items regarding Basque activities abroad. Thus, the various Basque collectivities around the world were, for the first time, to be provided with a systematic means of communicating with each other.

It is far from coincidental that the first article in the first issue is entitled "Euskadi camina hacia la paz para afrontar el reto europeo" (Euskadi moves toward peace in order to face the European challenge), an article which captures neatly the two major political preoccupations of the Basque government over the last decade. Reference is, on the one hand, to the relentless campaign to counter the world's perception that the Basque Country is a nest of terrorism, while on the other, it is to the desire for the Basque Country to play a meaningful role within a united Europe, thereby circumventing the political tug-of-war inherent in the framework of a federal Spain.

There follows a "Declaración conjunta de los partidos democráticos vascos" (Joint declaration of Basque democratic political parties) denouncing ETA's continuing campaign of violence.[3] The first issue also contains news of the efforts to create sister-city relationships between three Basque and three Argentine towns, a report on the visit of a Basque-Argentine choir to Euskadi, details of the trip to Euskadi by two Basque-Argentine youths "in search of their roots," and a smattering of news items from several Basque centers around the world.

The most important substantive announcement was by Josu Legarreta, that Eusko Jaurlaritza planned to expend 105 million pesetas in 1989 to strengthen ties between Euskadi and the "the Basque community" throughout the world, also referred to as "la diáspora." That year's budget was a more than twenty-fold quantum increase over the token five million pesetas dedicated to relations with the diaspora but two years earlier.

The funds were to support an ambitious agenda. Educational materials would be sent to all of the world's seventy-five Basque centers.[4] In addition to the *Euskal Etxeak* publication, they would receive books, videos, and radio programs. "Basque national weeks," consisting of a series of activities, were to be funded in the countries that had Basque festivals (note the emphasis upon "national" versus the largely "cultural" nature of the existing diasporic celebrations). Grants were to be made available to investigate the Basque presence in countries that had received significant Basque immigration. Financial aid was made available to subsidize trips to Euskadi by needy elderly hyphenated Basque "aitonas" (grandparents) and curious young Basques. A Congress of Basque Centers was planned for year's end, with delegations from throughout the Basque diaspora. It would explore the "problematics" of the world's Basque centers and their future prospects. Meanwhile, Legarreta was pledged to lobby the Basque Parliament to gain recognition for the Basque centers as Euskadi's official cultural delegations abroad (*Euskal Etxeak* 1 [1989]: 10).

The entire effort was fraught with both internal and external political risks. Internally, the Spanish nationalist political parties within the Basque political process were ambivalent about an agenda seemingly designed by Basque nationalists and for their purposes. Some questioned the expenditure of scarce resources on what they regarded as either irrelevancies or utopian dreams, arguing that if Basque culture and language were on shaky ground in Euskadi itself, how could they possibly be maintained in Buenos Aires and Boise? Consequently, over the past decade, funding for diasporic relations has been challenged regularly within the Basque Parliament.

There were two main external risks in implementing the diasporic agenda. First and foremost there was the delicate matter of the interest within the targeted population itself. Each of the several diasporas had their own histories. Hyphenated Basques in much of Latin America could trace their particular national version of New-World Basque history over several centuries, with the details varying considerably by country. What most had in common was an elitist legacy during the colonial period of Basque church prelates, crown officials, military figures, and financial magnates. Some, though not all, had a postcolonial overlay of both ordinary emigrants from modest backgrounds in search of economic opportunity and, as we have seen, refugees from nineteenth- and twentieth-century conflicts in both Spain and France.

By contrast, Basque immigrants in the Anglo contexts of the United States and Australia were relatively recent arrivals, attracted in the main by the need for sheepherders (Douglass and Bilbao 1975) in the former and sugarcane cutters (Douglass 1996) in the latter.

While Eusko Jaurlaritza represented certain gains for a late-twentieth-century Basque nationalist agenda, it speaks only for three of the Spanish Basque provinces. Navarra constituted its own autonomous community within Spain, with its own (and less anti-Madrid) agenda. Iparralde is a part of France. French Basques have generally exhibited scant support for Basque nationalism. Yet in many of the diasporas the hyphenated Basque population contained a Navarrese and/or French Basque component.

In short, each of the diasporas, as well as segments within them, manifested differing postures toward the Basque Country in general and Basque nationalism in particular. Some held a politicized orientation toward Old-World-Basque issues, while others were indifferent or even hostile on this score. Furthermore, for many hyphenated Basques throughout the world, continued orientation to their heritage was more sentimental than systematic and incorporated elements of local rather than European Basque culture and history. To the extent that they were organized, it was through their own efforts and leadership.

Therefore, when Eusko Jaurlaritza reached out to the already established collectivities of the Basque diaspora there was a sense in which it was inviting itself to the party by offering to bring the gifts. At times, Old-World-Basque officialdom has been sensitive in this regard, at others, less so. In fact, a history of both successes and failures, of bonding and miscommunication, of expectations met and missed underscores the delicate nature of the enterprise.

The second external risk regards the very nature of the exercise from the Spanish State's viewpoint. Eventually, the Servicio de Relaciones con los Centros Vascos would pass from the Ministry of Culture and Tourism to the Office of the Basque Presidency, where, after a name change, it continues as the most modest of three initiatives of a Secretaría General de Acción Exterior (Secretariat of Foreign Action) headed by Andoni Ortuzar. By far the most elaborate of the three functions is the Dirección de Cooperación al Desarrollo, or the Office of Economic Development Cooperation, headed by Josu Legarreta, former head of the Servicio. The effort was launched in 1988 with a commitment of 2.5 million dollars. In 1998 Legarreta oversaw a budget of 4.5 billion pesetas, or nearly 30 million dollars. The Dirección de Asuntos Europeos, or Office of European Affairs, under Juan Diego, will expend slightly more than 500 million pesetas, or about 3 million dollars. Finally, the Dirección de Relaciones con las Colectividades Vascas, or Office of Relations with the Basque Collectivities, under the direction of Iñaki Aguirre, had a 1998 budget of approximately 250 million pesetas, or about 1.5 million dollars.

As we can appreciate, through the Secretariat, Eusko Jaurlaritza currently has three external (to Spain) initiatives. The primary function of the Office of European Affairs is to represent Basque interests within the European Union. The Office of Economic Development Cooperation is the Basque government's commitment to aid the underdeveloped world in compliance with the United Nations' standard that each developed country should dedicate 0.7 of one percent of its GNP to international humanitarian purposes.

Since under the letter and spirit of the Spanish Constitution and Statute of Autonomy that mandates Eusko Jaurlaritza Madrid retains the exclusive prerogative to conduct Spanish foreign affairs, all such initiatives by the Basque autonomous government risk "pushing the envelope." In point of fact, the Office of European Affairs must proceed cautiously within the legacy of the Spanish State's legal challenge in 1986 to the formal establishment of a Basque delegation in Brussels. During eight years of litigation, Basque interests in Brussels were furthered by Interbask, a corporation established by the Basque government. When, in 1994, the right of Spain's autonomous communities to maintain their own delegations in Brussels was affirmed by the court, the Interbask facility was renamed the "Delegation of the Basque Government in Brussels," and was inaugurated with considerable fanfare (*Euskal Etxeak* 29 [1996]: 25). Similarly, Eusko Jaurlaritza's humanitarian aid to the underdeveloped world in strict accord with the UN's expectations of nation-states might be interpreted as a thinly disguised Basque claim to national sovereignty. Finally, the Dirección de Relaciones con las Colectividades Vascas had its own difficulties with Spain's minister of foreign affairs when it established "institutes" for developing economic ties in Argentina, Venezuela, Mexico, and the United States.

In the decade since the launching of *Euskal Etxeak* in 1989, there has been considerable continuity in the Basque government's policy regarding the diaspora. Throughout the period the publication has continued to inform hyphenated Basques of newsworthy developments in the Basque Country—including election results, economic statistics, social programs, pacification of Euskadi, and relations with Europe. At the same time, the pages of *Euskal Etxeak* have also provided a common forum in which the various Basque collectivities throughout the world have been able to enhance their awareness and knowledge of one another's activities. In addition, the publication is the primary source of information regarding Eusko Jaurlaritza's ongoing initiatives with respect to the diaspora. In this regard, highlights worthy of special mention include the following:

1. In November 1989 the World Conference of Basque Centers that was announced in the first issue was indeed held in Bahia Blanca, Argentina (*Euskal Etxeak,* 8 [1990]: 6–12).

2. In 1990 the Basque government dispersed subsidies to more than forty Basque centers and three federations of Basque cen-

ters—the FEVA in Argentina, NABO in the United States, and Euskal Herria in the Spanish State—averaging $10,000 for each center and $45,000 for each federation. By this time, the annual budget for diasporic affairs was about $1.2 million, an amount that, as we have seen, has since grown only slightly (*Euskal Etxeak* 12 [1990]: 30–31).

3. In November 1991 a Basque week was held in Necochea, Argentina, which included the First National Congress of Argentine Basque Centers, attended by representatives from thirty centers. The congress designated FEVA as the representative of Argentine-Basques for their relations with the Basque government, while formally affirming Eusko Jaurlaritza as the only legitimate government of all Basques, including the Navarrese and the French Basques. The Argentine-Basques further ratified an Old-World-Basque right to self-determination through democratic means and issued an invitation to the world's remaining Basque centers to join them in an international Basque brotherhood (*Euskal Etxeak* 14 [1991]: 20–21).

4. By the end of 1991 there was a clear policy of using the Basque centers in three ways. First, they were being asked to facilitate meetings between Basque government officials and those at the highest levels of New-World governments, thereby underscoring the quasi sovereignty of the Basque Country. In 1991, for example, a Basque delegation was received by Chile's President Aylwin. Second, there was an initiative to place a part of Eusko Jaurlaritza's humanitarian aid in countries with significant Basque diasporas, while involving local Basques in the efforts. The primary targets were Mexico, the Philippines, and several South American countries. (As it turned out, the hyphenated Basques were largely indifferent to these initiatives.) Third, there were the first serious attempts to create economic ties between the Basque Country and countries of its diaspora when the Association of Electronic Industries of the Basque Country sent a government-approved commission to Chile, Argentina, and Uruguay with an itinerary prepared by the Basque centers in the respective countries (*Euskal Etxeak* 16–17 [1991]: 3, 30–33, 42–44).

5. In 1992, during its Basque Week, President Ardanza visited

Mexico where, through the mediation of local Basques, he was received by President Salinas de Gortari. On his way back to Europe Ardanza stopped in New York to sign the agreement for the now-world-famed Guggenheim Museum project in Bilbao. Later that same year Ardanza visited Chile, where he met with President Aylwin. Throughout his travels the Basque president emphasized the importance of creating economic ties between Euskadi and the host countries (*Euskal Etxeak* 20 [1992]).

6. In 1993 the Basque government announced the creation of the Instituto Vasco-Argentino de Cooperación y Desarrollo, the Fundación Vasco-Chilena para la Cooperación y el Desarrollo, the Fundación Instituto Vasco-Venezolano de Cooperación Eguzki, and the Instituto Vasco-Mexicano de Desarrollo. This was the culmination of efforts initiated in 1982 to create economic ties between the Basque Country and several New-World nations utilizing the local contacts facilitated by the Basque diaspora (*Euskal Etxeak* 24–25 [1993]: 33).

These were the initiatives denounced by the Spanish Government as Basque trade missions. Josu Legarreta admitted as much when he declared in the next issue of *Euskal Etxeak*, "In this number . . . you will discover more about the foreign policy of the Basque Government. The jurisdiction in this field is somewhat controversial, for the State Government claims it as its arm. However, the Basque Government spares no effort to contribute to the defense of the interests of Euskadi."

Legarreta partly based his defense of the initiative upon the historical relationship between the Basque Country and America (*Euskal Etxeak* 26 [1994]: 3). It was scarcely coincidental that the foundations had been established in those countries with the greatest Basque presence.[5]

7. In 1994 President Ardanza traveled to the United States, where he visited with Vice President Gore and Speaker of the House Foley. Ardanza announced the formation of an American-Basque Foundation (modeled after the Latin American Institutes), based in Washington, D.C. He also negotiated placement of part of the Basque Country's public debt in the U.S. financial markets (*Euskal Etxeak* 26 [1994]).

8. In 1994 the Basque Parliament debated and passed a comprehensive "Law of Relations with the Basque Collectivities and Centers Abroad." In the future, formal relations between Eusko Jaurlaritza and the diaspora, as well as financial assistance to the latter, were to be articulated through the Basque centers. To qualify, a Basque center had to be democratically constituted and be inscribed in Eusko Jaurlaritza's formal Registry of Basque Centers. Qualified centers were to be provided with libraries of Basque materials, assistance in meeting their operating costs, and assistance in organizing Basque language instruction.[6] There was also to be educational exchange of students and faculty, particularly under the auspices of the University of the Basque Country. Basques of the diaspora and their descendants were accorded full citizenship in Euskadi should they wish to reside there. Indeed, needy ones were to be given public assistance. A Council to Assess Relations with the Basque Collectivities was established, consisting of representatives from Basque governmental ministries, the Basque Parliament, the three provinces, the university, and the cultural organization Euskaltzaindia. It also included three representatives of the Basque collectivities appointed by delegates to attend a Basque World Congress to be held every four years. The Council was to be presided over by the Basque president.

In short, the legislation mobilized the highest spheres of Basque governmental, educational, and cultural institutions in the effort to enhance ties with the diaspora. It even foresaw intervention with Spanish State policy whenever treaties or other arrangements were being negotiated with countries around the world containing a significant Basque collectivity (Ley de Relaciones con las Colectividades y Centros Vascos en el Exterior de la Comunidad Autónoma del País Vasco, 1994).

9. In 1995 the Basque Parliament formalized the relationship between Eusko Jaurlaritza and the Basque centers abroad. The following year more than fifty delegates were brought to the Basque Country for a World Congress of Basque Communities. Represented were Argentina, Australia, Belgium, Canada, Chile, Spain, France, Mexico, Peru, Puerto Rico, El Salvador, Uruguay, the United States, and Venezuela. The two main is-

sues dealt with during the week of deliberations were the future viability of the Basque collectivities around the world and the ways in which the Basque government could facilitate better relations between them and Euskadi. The major announcement was the pending initiative by Euskal Telebista (Basque Television) to broadcast programming via satellite to the Americas (*Euskaldunak Munduan*, 1996). Indeed, today it may be seen in parts of Latin America and the southern United States.

10. In 1996 Iñaki Aguirre stated that the four-year plan for aid to the centers abroad was proceeding, but it was necessary to be patient as the details were still being worked out. He also noted that of the 129 Basque Centers in sixteen countries only 85 had filed for inclusion in Eusko Jaurlaritza's Basque Center Registry. It was necessary to do so in order to qualify for assistance under the 1994 legislation (*Euskal Etxeak* 30 [1996]: 3). The Basque Parliament had approved 206 million pesetas, or about 1.5 million dollars, for the centers, all of which were to be provided with technology for interconnection through the Internet (ibid.: 11). In 1998 Eusko Jaurlaritza also intended to make 500 million pesetas available in loan guarantees to allow Basques in countries with exorbitant interest rates to borrow funds at 4 percent to purchase or refurbish center facilities (interview with Iñaki Aguirre, March 1998).

On balance, if during its first decade of existence Eusko Jaurlaritza was aware of the several Basque collectivities around the world and intrigued with the possibility of harnessing their potential, it was creation of the publication *Euskal Etxeak* and sponsorship of the Bahia Blanca congress in 1989 that marked the watershed between a passive and an active policy. The two most recent directors of the Office of Relations with the Basque Collectivities, when asked to assess their efforts, concurred that there have been neither great successes nor failures, nor could there have been, given the relatively limited funding at their disposal.[7]

Nevertheless, after the probably inevitable fits and false starts, the Basque government now provides interested Basque centers and federations of centers with welcome subsidies that facilitate, but without dictating, Basque cultural initiatives throughout the world. The effort

has also provided a somewhat efficacious vehicle, the *Euskal Etxeak*
journal, for educating hyphenated Basques around the globe regarding the contemporary political, economic, and social realities of the
Basque Country. It also described significant international cultural
initiatives, such as creation of a Basque pavilion at the Seville World
Expo of 1992 (*Euskal Etxeak* 16–17 [1991]: 22), the visit of the Dalai
Lama to what was touted as "Euskadi Capital of Peace" (*Euskal Etxeak*
34 [1997]: 1), completion of the famed Guggenheim Museum in Bilbao (*Euskal Etxeak* 35 [1997]: 1), and signing of a mutual cooperation
agreement with UNESCO (*Euskal Etxeak* 35 [1997]: 25–26). At the
same time, this bridge between Eusko Jaurlaritza and the Basque diasporas has facilitated raising international consciousness regarding
the Basque cause, particularly through the quasi-state visits of President Ardanza and other Basque officials to countries such as Argentina, Uruguay, Chile, Mexico, Venezuela, and the United States. Finally, the various institutes and foundations that we have considered
might alone justify Eusko Jaurlaritza's expenditure to date on diasporic relations. During the last two years some thirty-five Basque
firms have invested in Latin American economies through their mediation, although, as yet, they have failed to attract New-World investment capital for the Basque economy.

However, it is also well to consider the initiative in a comparative
perspective, since the Basques are scarcely unique in maintaining relations between homeland and hostland(s). Neither are they unique
in packaging a political and economic agenda in the more benign
guise of cultural maintenance of "folkloric" forms.

In fact, it is apparent that the nation-state building process is, at
times, the result of interaction between an ethnic homeland and its
emigrant diaspora. The classic case is, of course, Israel, a successful
example of a "new" (if beleaguered) nation-state that would have
been impossible without the support and intervention of the world's
diasporic Jews. This is so much the case that Israelis and the diasporans regularly contest the claim to the "center" of Judaism (Elazar,
1986; Boyarin 1996). There are numerous other examples. It is said
that Greece was the nineteenth-century creation of the Greek diaspora (and western European intellectual fellow travelers) (Jusdanis
1991: 209; Banks 1996: 152) and that "Khalistan" was the dream of
Canadian Sikhs (Israel 1991: 384).

Conversely, there are examples of established and staid diasporas becoming energized and even radicalized by the rather unanticipated emergence of a nation-state in the ethnic homeland. Recent examples include the world's hyphenated Croatians and Armenians in the aftermath of the creation of the nation-states of Croatia (Winland 1995) and Armenia (Pattie 1994).

Indeed, it would seem that the opportunity and temptation to maintain and manipulate diasporic relations is greatest when dealing with relatively small populations of subnational peoples holding nation-state aspirations and with extensive histories of emigration. The Basques are a prime example. It seems equally evident that, at least within the European experience,[8] older and larger established nation-states (and even those with extensive historical emigration) remain largely insensitive to diasporic potential (if we exempt ubiquitous "heritage" tourism). Thus, Spain, Portugal, France, England, Germany, and Italy have all been indifferent to the kinds of diasporic "projects" described herein.

Thus far the attempts by Eusko Jaurlaritza have not resulted in serious political confrontations; however, it should be noted that there is always the possibility. The visits to heads of state by Ardanza and other Basque officials have, to date, been fairly low key and cautious. Nevertheless, as we have noted, Basque "foreign" initiatives, whether in Brussels, Buenos Aires, or Boise, are not particularly lauded by officials in Madrid. Armenian, Jewish, Irish, Greek, and Palestinian history all bespeak the potential of subnational peoples to lobby world opinion for recognition of their political sovereignty.

Sheffer, in fact, sees diasporas, and particularly their intelligentsias, as potentially powerful political forces within their host societies—advocates of mobilizing hostland support for the particular ethnic group's homeland agendas (1996: 9–10). A prime example is the capacity of Irish-Americans to influence United States' policy regarding Ulster, even to the point of angering Great Britain—America's strongest ally (Arthur 1991). In short, diasporic space is fraught with minefields as well as meadows.

Will conditions favoring ongoing ties between the Basque Country and its diasporas persist indefinitely into the future? Possibly. However, there are also reasons for pessimism. First, arguably the driving force for maintaining ties between the Basque homeland and its diaspora is Eusko Jaurlaritza, yet its Old-World mandate does not include either the Navarrese or the French Basques, which limits its ability to appeal to all Basques of the diaspora.

Second, Eusko Jaurlaritza is modeled upon the nation-state at a time when the very structure and concept of nation-states are being challenged (Jauregui Bereciartu 1986; Castells 1997). Part of Eusko Jaurlaritza's political strategy is to situate the Basque Country as an autonomous player within a united Europe rather than a regionalized Spain. It is unclear how success of the European strategy might affect relations between the Basque Country and its diaspora, and it is possible that a new Euro-configuration of Basque politics might actually inhibit or eclipse meaningful ties between the Basques of the homeland and those of the several hostlands.

Furthermore, the staying power of the various collectivities as unique ethnic groups within their host societies is a serious concern. While some investigators underscore the capacity of hyphenated ethnics to maintain at least a hybrid version of their Old-World traditions, others argue that over time, and lacking renewed immigration of Old-World-culture bearers, ethnicity in such contexts becomes merely symbolic before disappearing altogether (Alba and Nee 1997; Gans 1997). The question, then, is, in the future which, if any, Basque Country will be reaching out to which, if any, emigrant Basque collectivity around the world?

Finally, we should note that from a technological viewpoint, of course, the prospects of maintaining diasporic relations have never been greater and are only getting better. Each new advance in transportation, telecommunications, and the realm of the Internet reduces the physical and conceptual distance between Bilbao, Buenos Aires, and Boise. To the extent that the viability equates to ease of contact, there is room for considerable optimism. We have all heard how globalization threatens the planet with cultural homogeneity. However, in the Basque case that we have been considering, it has the clear potential of reinforcing cultural particularism in the diaspora,[9] as well as of creating a kind of interstitial Basque reality that is situated neither in Euskadi nor in the diaspora, but rather somewhere in cyberspace.

Nor would I anticipate that the cyberspatial encounter between the several varieties of Basqueness (that of the homeland and those of the several diasporas) will necessarily be passive and benign. Rather, we might anticipate the emergence and exacerbation of a dialectical debate regarding such issues as Basque essentialism (the importance of language and descent) and the necessity of a Basque nation-state versus Basque incorporation in other transnational political configurations. Indeed, it is not impossible that the very locus of the "Basque center," as in the Jewish case, might itself be contested by homeland Basques and diasporans—particularly since (subject to definitional consideration) [10] the latter may actually outnumber the former within the world's population.

Notes

1. See Clifford (1997: 245), who tells us, "an unruly crowd of descriptive/interpretive terms now jostle and converse in an effort to characterize the contact zones of nations, cultures, and regions: terms such as 'border,' 'travel,' 'creolization,' 'transculturalism,' 'hybridity,' and 'diaspora' (as well as the looser 'diasporic')."

2. I would argue that the institutionalized attempt that we shall consider in detail is also paralleled by the participation as individuals of the world's hyphenated Basques in the kinds of transnational opportunities and realities afforded to all immigrants (and their descendants) by the technological advances in transportation and communication of our postmodern, globalized world. Indeed, I believe that the consumption and maintenance of their Basque identity by the world's hyphenated descendants of immigrant ancestors may well become a largely individualized (more personal than group) experience, transpiring mainly in cyberspace (Douglass 1996).

3. In the makeup of its signatories there were several metamessages underscoring serious political divisions within the Basque Autonomous Community. Absent was HB (Herri Batasuna), the party closest to ETA if not its direct political voice. Present, however, was EE (Euskadiko Eskerra), a radical left nationalist party descended from ETA-PM, or that segment within ETA which had opted to pursue a political solution to the "Basque Problem" by participating in the parliamentary process. Also absent was EA (Eusko Alkartasuna), a more middle-of-the-road nationalist party that resulted in 1986 from a schism within the ranks of the EAJ/PNV (the Basque Nationalist Party). EA adherents, as schismatics, were the objects of ostracism.

4. There were also missing cases. For example, neither the Basques of

the Philippines nor those of Quebec appeared on Eusko Jaurlaritza's radar screen. Both were remote historical realities, the latter was exclusively an extension of Iparralde, and neither had Basque centers. Conversely, the diasporic project incorporated an internal migrant dimension as well, which embraced the Basque centers of Madrid, Barcelona, and Paris.

5. Legarreta engaged the Spanish Minister of Foreign Affairs in a semantic debate by distinguishing between "international relations" and a Basque right to engage in "relevant acts abroad" (interview with Josu Legarreta, March 1998).

6. In fact Eusko Jaurlaritza has been careful in its support of Basque language instruction in the diaspora. On occasion it has sent an instructor from its own language-instruction division (HABE) to such places as Boise, Santiago de Chile, and several Argentine towns. However, when Argentine-Basques requested a more massive effort, Legarreta was skeptical. He decided to put them to the test, arguing that the instructors should be Argentinian and that their dedication be demonstrable. He organized a three-month summer course in Macachín, a quiet provincial town in tropical Argentina. Thirty-six aspiring Basque instructors were required to spend several hours in class daily. The second year the same group spent three months in Tandil studying eight hours daily. The experiment was such a success that Legarreta brought the students to Euskadi the third summer. Today they constitute the core of an ongoing successful program in Argentina. Whenever Basques of other collectivities of the diaspora have requested language-instruction aid, they are asked to meet the rigorous Argentine standard. To date none have. Actually, in terms of numbers of students the most successful program is that of the Basque Center in Madrid. There, some 280 people attended a free class in Euskara last year.

7. Interview in Vitoria-Gasteiz, March 1998.

8. Recently China has successfully attracted vast economic investment from its diaspora (Bolt 1996). The same is not true of India, however, although the Indian economy, like others—that of the Philippines, for example—receives considerable cash infusions in the form of emigrant worker remittances.

9. Such is indeed the case for other diasporic groups as well. See Rai (1995) for a discussion of the role of Web sites in the creation of a transnational Hindu identity.

10. Who qualifies as Basque is an issue in both the homeland and the diaspora. Regarding the Basque Country, internal migration, particularly in Spain, has created a situation in which nearly half of the residents of Euskadi were born elsewhere or are descended from such internal mi-

granto. We have already noted the generational "genealogical erosion" in all of the Basque collectivities around the world through exogamy over time. The results are particularly evident once significant immigration from the Basque homeland ceases.

Bibliography

Alba, Richard, and Victor Nee. 1997. Rethinking Assimilation Theory for a New Era of Immigration. *International Migration Review* 23(4): 826–874.

Arthur, Paul. 1991. Diasporan Invervention in International Affairs: Irish America as a Case Study. *Diaspora* 1(2): 143–162.

Azcona Pastor, José Manuel, Inés García-Albi Gil de Biedma, and Fernando Muru Ronda. 1992. *Historia de la emigración vasca a Argentina en el s. XX.* Vitoria-Gasteiz: Servicio Central de Publicaciones. Gobierno Vasco.

Banks, Marcus. 1996. *Ethnicity: Anthropological Constructions.* London and New York: Routledge.

Bolt, Paul J. 1996. Looking to the Diaspora: The Overseas Chinese and China's Economic Development. *Diaspora* 5(3): 467–496.

Boyarin, Jonathan. 1996. *Thinking in Jewish.* Chicago: University of Chicago Press.

Brah, Avtar. 1996. *Cartographies of Diaspora. Contesting Identities.* London and New York: Routledge.

Castells, Manuel. 1997. *The Power of Identity: The Information Age— Economy, Society and Culture.* Oxford: Blackwell Publishing, 1997.

Clark, Robert P. 1991. José Antonio de Aguirre: His Life and His Legacy. Introduction to José Antonio de Aguirre, *Escape via Berlin. Eluding Franco in Hitler's Europe.* Reno, University of Nevada Press.

Clifford, James. 1997. *Routes: Travel and Translation in the Late Twentieth Century.* Cambridge, Mass. and London: Harvard University Press.

Denoon, Donald. 1983. *Settler Capitalism: The Dynamics of Dependent Development in the Southern Hemisphere.* Oxford: Clarendon Press.

Douglass, William A. 1996. *Azúcar amargo: Vida y fortuna de los cortadores de caña italianos y vascos en la Australia tropical.* Lejona: Servicio Editorial de la Universidad del País Vasco.

Douglass, William A. 1996. Basque-American Identity: Past Perspectives and Future Prospects. In Stephen Tchudi (ed.), *Change in the American West: Exploring the Human Dimension.* Reno: Nevada Humanities Committee and University of Nevada Press.

Douglass, William A., and Jon Bilbao. 1975. *Amerikanuak: Basques in the New World*. Reno: University of Nevada Press.

Elazar, Daniel J. 1986. The Jewish People as the Classical Diaspora. In Gabriel Sheffer (ed.), *Modern Diasporas in International Politics*, 212–257. New York: St. Martin's Press.

Euskaldunak Munduan. 1996. *Building the Future*. Vitoria-Gasteiz: Central Publishing Service of the Basque Government.

Gans, Herbert J. 1997. Toward a Reconciliation of "Assimilation" and "Pluralism": The Interplay of Acculturation and Ethnic Retention. *International Migration Review* 31(4): 875–892.

Israel, Milton. 1991. Transformations of the Sikh Diaspora. *Diaspora* 1(3): 373–384.

Jáuregui Bereciartu, Gurutz. 1986. *Contra el estado-nación. En torno al hecho y la cuestión nacional*. Madrid: Siglo XXI.

Jusdanis, Gregory. 1991. Greek Americans and the Diaspora. *Diaspora* 1(2): 209–221.

Kearney, Michael. 1996. *Reconceptualizing the Peasantry. Anthropology in Global Perspective*. Boulder, Colorado: Westview Press.

Legarreta, Dorothy. 1984. *The Guernica Generation. Basque Refugee Children of the Spanish Civil War*. Reno: University of Nevada Press.

Ley de Relaciones con las colectividades y Centros Vascos en el exterior de la Comunidad Autónoma del País Vasco. 1994. Vitoria-Gasteiz: Servicio Central de Publicaciones del Gobierno Vasco.

Pattie, Susan. 1994. At Home in Diaspora: Armenians in America. *Diaspora* 3(2): 185–198.

Rai, Amit S. 1995. India On-Line: Electronic Bulletin Boards and the Construction of a Diasporic Hindu Identity. *Diaspora* 4(1): 31–57.

Rouse, Roger. 1991. Mexican Migration and the Social Space of Postmodernism. *Diaspora* 1(1): 8–23.

Rouse, Roger. 1995. Questions of Identity, Personhood and Collectivity in Transnational Migration to the United States. *Critique of Anthropology* 15(4): 351–380.

San Sebastian, Koldo, and Peru Ajuria. 1992. *El exilio vasco en Venezuela*. Vitoria-Gasteiz: Servicio Central de Publicaciones. Gobierno Vasco.

Sheffer, Gabriel. 1986. A New Field of Study: Modern Diasporas in International Politics. In Gabriel Sheffer (ed.), *Modern Diasporas in International Politics*, 1–15. New York: St. Martin's Press.

Winland, Daphne N. 1995. "We Are Now an Actual Nation": The Impact of National Independence on the Croatian Diaspora in Canada. *Diaspora* 4(1): 3–29.

List of Contributors

Begoña Aretxaga was born and raised in San Sebastián. She is the John L. Loeb Associate Professor of Anthropology at Harvard University and has written extensively about nationalism, gender, and political violence in Northern Ireland and the Basque Country. Her publications include *Shattering Silence: Women, Nationalism and Political Subjectivity in Northern Ireland* (Princeton University Press, 1997) and *Los Funerales en el Nacionalismo Radical Vasco* (Baroja, 1987).

Manuel Castells is a professor in the Department of City and Regional Planning at the University of California, Berkeley, where he is also Chair of the Center for Western European Studies. His research interests include sociology of information technology and urban sociology. Recent publications include *The Information Age: Economy, Society, and Culture, Volume 1: The Rise of the Network Society; Volume 2: The Power of Identity; Volume 3: End of Millennium* (Blackwell, 1996–1998), an analysis of the economic and social impacts of the information technology revolution.

William A. Douglass is a social anthropologist and is Director of the Basque Studies Program of the University of Nevada, Reno. His numerous books on Basque topics include *Death in Murelaga: Social Significance of Funerary Ritual in a Spanish Basque Village* (University of Washington Press, 1969), *Echalar and Murelaga: Opportunity and Rural Exodus in Two Spanish Basque Villages* (Christopher Hurst and St. Martin's Press, 1975), *Amerikanuak: Basques in the New World* (University of Nevada Press, 1975) (co-authored with Jon Bilbao), and *Azúcar amargo. Vida y fortuna de los cortadores de caña italianos y vascos en la Australia tropical* (Servicio Editorial de la Universidad del País Vasco, 1996).

James E. Jacob is Professor of Political Science and former Dean of the College of Behavioral and Social Sciences at California State University, Chico. His research interests lie in the fields of French Basque politics, French language policy, cross-cultural communications, and terrorism. He is the author of numerous works on the French Basques, including *The*

Hills of Conflict; Basque Nationalism in France (University of Nevada Press, 1994).

Gurutz Jáuregui Bereciartu is Professor of Constitutional Law. He has been head of the Department of Constitutional and Administrative Law, and Dean of the Faculty of Law at the University of the Basque Country in San Sebastián. He has published nine books and more than sixty articles on ethnic violence, ethnic nationalism, political decentralization, and the theory of democracy. In English, he has published *Decline of the Nation-State* (University of Nevada Press, 1994).

Jeremy MacClancy, Senior Lecturer in Social Anthropology, Oxford Brookes University, has been carrying out fieldwork in the Basque area since the mid-1980s. His latest book is *The Decline of Carlism, 1939–1999* (University of Nevada Press, forthcoming). He is at present completing a book on the modern cultures of Basque nationalism.

Ane Muñoz Varela is a European Studies specialist and doctoral candidate in political science and sociology at the University of the Basque Country. Her publications include *Política y sociedad: la España de las autonomías* (Fundación Antonio de Nebrija, 1994).

Alfonso Pérez-Agote is Professor of Sociology at the University of the Basque Country. He is head of the research committee "Identity, Space and Politics" in the AISLF (International Association of French Speaking Sociologists). He has published several books on sociological theory, collective identity and nationalism, and Basque nationalism including *La reproducción del nacionalismo: el caso vasco* (CIS/Siglo XXI de España, 1984) and *Mantener la identidad: los vascos del Río Carabelas* (Universidad del País Vasco, 1997).

Xavier Rubert de Ventós is Professor of Aesthetics at the University of Barcelona. He has also taught at the University of California, Berkeley, Harvard University, and New York University, where he founded the Professorship Barcelona–New York and the Institute for the Humanities. He has been a member of the Spanish Parliament and of the European Parliament. His publications on philosophy and aesthetics include *La estética y sus herejías* (Editorial Anagrama, 1974) and *Por qué filosofía* (Península, 1990); his publications on politics include *El laberinto de la hispanidad* (Planeta, 1987) and *Nacionalismos: El laberinto de la identidad* (Espasa Calpe, 1994).

Cameron Watson was Assistant Professor of History at the University of Nevada, Reno from 1996 to 1999. He is now an Adjunct Professor with the Basque Studies Program at the University of Nevada, Reno with re-search interests in Basque nationalism, ethnic conflict, political violence, and cultural studies. His publications include "Ethnic Conflict and the League of Nations: The Case of Transylvania, 1918–1940" in *Hungarian Studies* (1994), "Folklore and Basque Nationalism: Language, Myth, Re-ality," in *Nations and Nationalism* (1996), and "Gernika, Guernica, *Guernica?* Contested Meanings of a Basque Place," (co-written with Pauliina Raento, forthcoming). He is currently writing a book on the cultural ori-gins of Basque political violence.

Iñaki Zabaleta is Professor of Journalism and Media at the University of the Basque Country (Bilbao). His publications include "Private Commer-cial Television versus Political Diversity: The Case of Spain's 1993 Gen-eral Elections," in *Refiguring Spain: Cinema, Media, Representation* (Duke University Press, 1997), *Komunikazioaren Ikerkuntzarako Metodologia* (Edi-torial Udako Euskal Unibertsitatea, 1997), and "La televisión de acceso público por cable y el euskara: un futuro compartido" in *Zer: Revista de Estudios de Comunicación* (1998).

Titles in the Basque Studies Program Occasional Papers Series

1: *The Long Journey: Social Integration and Ethnic Maintenance among Urban Basques in the San Francisco Bay Region,* by Jean Francis Decroos (1983) (out of print)

2: *Basque Politics: A Case Study in Ethnic Nationalism,* edited by William A. Douglass (1985) (out of print)

3: *Arriaga, the Forgotten Genius: The Short Life of a Basque Composer,* by Barbara Rosen (1989)

4: *Essays in Basque Social Anthropology and History,* edited by William A. Douglass (1989)

5: *Basque Cultural Studies,* by William A. Douglass, Carmelo Urza, Linda White, and Joseba Zulaika (1999)

6: *Basque Politics and Nationalism on the Eve of the Millennium,* edited by William A. Douglass, Carmelo Urza, Linda White, and Joseba Zulaika (1999)

7: *The Basque Diaspora/La Diáspora Vasca,* edited by William A. Douglass, Carmelo Urza, Linda White, and Joseba Zulaika (1999)

Available from:
The Basque Studies Program/322
University of Nevada
Reno, NV 89557